Cracking the New European Markets

Timothy Harper

John Wiley & Sons, Inc.
New York • Chichester • Brisbane • Toronto • Singapore

Recognizing the importance of preserving what has been written, it is a policy of John Wiley & Sons, Inc. to have books of enduring value published in the United States printed on acid-free paper, and we exert our best efforts to that end.

Copyright © 1992 by Timothy Harper

Published by John Wiley & Sons, Inc.

Library of Congress Cataloging-in-Publication Data

Harper, Timothy
        Cracking the new european markets / by Timothy Harper
              p.   cm.
        Includes index.

        ISBN 0471-54769-7

Printed in the United States of America.
10 9 8 7 6 5 4 3 2 1
Printed and bound by Courier Companies, Inc.

For Bud and Eleanor

Preface

Much of the American business community's new interest in Europe grows out of the many recent changes on the other side of the Atlantic, notably the European Community's drive toward a single market and the political and economic upheaval in Eastern Europe. Perhaps even more significant, however, are the changes now reshaping American business. We Americans are realizing that business in the 21st century will be increasingly global, and those who ignore global marketing and investment opportunities are going to be left behind. Already in the 1990s, American industry is relying on exports, and particularly exports to Europe, as never before. Similarly, it has become routine for investment portfolios large and small to include significant holdings in foreign stocks, bonds, and real property.

This book seeks to act as an informal guide for the American who is considering or committed to doing business in Europe: corporate executives making decisions about plants and personnel in Europe; entrepreneurs and traders buying and selling products back and forth across the Atlantic; private or institutional investors scouring the world for the best risk-versus-reward opportunities, and professional-management employees posted by their U.S. headquarters to European offices.

As an American journalist and lawyer who has run my own entrepreneurial freelance business from London since 1984, I have based this book on dozens of company case studies and hundreds of interviews with Americans doing business in Europe, both successfully and unsuccessfully. The experiences and observations of these Americans, and sometimes of the Europeans they dealt with, look beyond the cold facts of what happened to the personal motives and human emotions behind their actions. Their stories tell us what they did right, what they did wrong, and why.

Some of the anecdotes and comments in this book first appeared in my stories for U.S. and European newspapers and magazines, but any errors of fact or interpretation are strictly my own. Besides the cooperation of the many friends and associates who generously shared their information and insight, and the unstinting patience and support of my family during this project, I must recognize the invaluable assistance of Sean Kelly, my longtime associate and friend.

Tim Harper, London

Contents

CHAPTER 8
Media and Marketing   **150**

The myth of the Euroconsumer. The single market has
underscored local, regional, and national differences in
consumer tastes and preferences. As the single market
brings down barriers in Europe in particular and as
business becomes more global in general, production and
distribution for many companies are likely to become
more centralized. But marketing and sales will become
more localized.

CHAPTER 9
After the Deal Is Done   **171**

Problems are inevitable in any business venture, but are
particularly prevalent in cross-border deals with their
inherent cultural and communications obstacles. Here's
how to deal with a broad range of issues from contract
disputes to employee relations.

CHAPTER 10
Eastern Europe   **189**

Real changes are happening in Eastern Europe, but
they are happening slowly. Even more than in
Western Europe, North Americans need to be careful
in approaching business opportunities and deals in
Eastern Europe. Here's what to look for and look
out for.

CHAPTER 11
Money Matters   **210**

Trading foreign currency is like sex. You don't
appreciate the pleasures and frustrations unless you've
done it. Nobody who does business in Europe remains a
foreign-exchange virgin for very long. A basic manual on
what you need to know.

CHAPTER 12
Social Sensibilities

North Americans doing business in Europe cannot avoid
or ignore the social aspects of everyday life, the
confounding and confusing cultural quirks from country
to country. Here are some of the cultural peculiarities
most common to Europe in general and certain
European countries in particular.

CHAPTER 1

◆ ◆ ◆

The Myth of European Unity

After Iraqi forces invaded Kuwait in early August 1990, hundreds of Europeans who had been working in Iraq and Kuwait were rounded up and placed under house arrest in Baghdad hotels. Before they were finally released and allowed to go home several long weeks later, these "guests" of Saddam Hussein had various ways of keeping busy. The British played parlor games and swapped memories of pleasant summer days in the English countryside. The Italians noisily concocted nightly feasts based on pasta dishes they delighted in inventing from the dwindling food supplies. The Swedes organized themselves into classes to learn the Arabic language and study the history of the Middle East.

Yes, Europeans are different, not only from Americans but from each other. One of the biggest misconceptions promoted throughout the world in recent years is that Britain, France, Germany, Spain, Scandinavia, and their neighbors are becoming part of a new United States of Europe. For Americans considering working, living, or doing any sort of business on the other side of the Atlantic, this is important to remember: European unity is a much-hyped myth.

1

The people, the language, the culture, the traditions, the lifestyles, and the ways and means of doing business are different from country to country. And while the European countries do share many concerns and goals, they remain and will remain separate nations. They may all be Europeans, but a Greek regards a Norwegian as just as foreign, probably more so, than an American. To the English, the French are still "frogs" and a condom is still a "French letter." To French, the English are still "roast beefs" and a condom is still an "English overcoat." And a French magazine not long ago advised Parisian mothers to hire English girls as nannies because their husbands would be much less likely to be tempted into affairs. The British like to joke about the French reeking of garlic; the French counter that Britons know how to behave at the dinner table but have no idea what to serve on it.

Some Europeans believe the cheese course comes after dessert, others before. Different nationalities believe men meeting each other should say hello, shake hands, and kiss once on the cheek or have full-blown hugs with smooches on both cheeks. The French think the Dutch are heathens because they come to France carrying packed lunches, while the Dutch (and everyone else) believe the Belgians are dull. In 1990, England marked the 50th anniversary of the Battle of Britain, when London was decimated by waves of Hitler's bombs, with a blessedly short-lived television sitcom, "Heil Honey, I'm Home," that portrayed Germans as equally aggressive and stupid. Swedes think Finns are backward, and the British believe Spaniards are lazy. Germans think Italians are too nonchalant, and Italians think Germans are too authoritarian. Italians love to hunt and see nothing wrong with blasting birds sitting on their nests—which would be extremely unsporting to Scandinavian hunters.

Studies show that northern Europeans like big, sturdy, dull-colored cars; southern Europeans prefer smaller, lighter, brightly colored cars, often with vivid plaid upholstery. Northern couples are more likely to prefer twin beds, southern couples double beds. One study found that the best place in Europe to work is Luxembourg for the high pay, the best place to pay taxes is Spain, the best place to live is Portugal for the climate, and the best place to die is France, which has the highest life expectancy. Great regional disparities also exist within countries; in Britain, for example, a Scot is offended if mistaken for English, and in the Netherlands the southern Hollanders joke about the slowness of northern Frisians. They all believe the grass is greener on their side of the fence.

Beyond the superficial stereotypes, late 20th-century Europe is plagued by serious inequities. Even amidst the wealth of the European Community, life in much of Portugal and Greece is quite different, markedly closer to the Third World, from life in most of Denmark and France. The two most significant ongoing developments addressing those inequities – politically, economically, and socially – are the EC's drive to create an internal "single market" and the emergence of Eastern European countries such as East Germany, Poland, Hungary, and Czechoslovakia from the stranglehold of Soviet communism.

It's too early to tell what's going to happen in Eastern Europe and how successfully those countries can reshape themselves as fledgling free-market democracies. It is already clear, however, that the efforts of Eastern Europeans to join the capitalist world are not enhancing the cause of peace and harmony among the people of Europe. Everyone wants to see the Eastern European countries succeed, but no nation, even their closest neighbors, is eager to sacrifice its own standard of living or quality of life. That's why Italy sends back fleeing Albanians and Germans beat up Poles who come across the border seeking jobs. Even in Germany, the initial euphoria of reunification rubbed off when the *Wessis* ("Westies") realized that absorbing the *Ossis* ("Easties") and their creaking postcommunist economy brought the prospect of higher inflation, interest rates, and unemployment. Democracy for all is fine, but not if it means scaling down this year's vacation or waiting until next year for that new BMW.

3

It's not too early to see some of the effects of the European Community's single market, however. Many strides have been made toward the goal of unrestricted movement of people, products, services, and money among the 12 EC nations. But there are still many problems in meeting the full goals of the single market – what euphemistically used to be called "1992" – among the EC member states. And even if those goals were somehow all realized on paper overnight, there would still be vast gaps between perception and reality, largely because something on paper may be interpreted and implemented much differently in countries as naturally diverse as, say, Ireland, Portugal, and Denmark. How can Britain, where 1 in 50 people works on a farm and the constitutional monarchy has been in place for centuries, understand or appreciate the concerns of Spain, where 1 in 6 works on a farm and democracy did not come until after Generalissimo Francisco Franco, the fascist dictator, died in 1975?

Some background might be helpful. The concept of European unity always offered an elusive goal, weighing the promise of economic advancement against the preservation of national sovereignty. Through the decades, many of the positive steps toward cooperation have come from economic weakness – when the need for economic improvement outbalanced national political interests. A single Europe is hardly a new idea; it's what Napoleon and Hitler had in mind. A movement for a "United States of Europe" grew out of World War I, and a "European Union" was proposed under the League of Nations. However, it wasn't until World War II left Europe's once-powerful national economies in tatters that the first real steps toward unity were taken. Cooperation became a way of rebuilding.

The Organization for European Economic Cooperation was formed in 1948 to help administer Marshall Plan aid from the United States. The North Atlantic Treaty Organization was created a year later for transatlantic military support. Although ostensibly as much European as American, NATO's importance to the U.S. military meant that America provided more missiles, money, and men for Europe's joint defense than the Europeans did themselves during the long Cold War faceoff with the Warsaw Pact, NATO's now-defunct counterpart of Soviet-sphere nations. Various other pan-European groups were formed as Europe recovered from World War II—the Organization for Economic Cooperation and Development, the Western European Union, and the Council of Europe, for example—but the roots of the modern European Community lie in French Foreign Minister Robert Schuman's 1950 plan for pooling steel and coal production.

Six countries (France, West Germany, Belgium, Italy, the Netherlands, and Luxembourg) signed the 1951 Paris Treaty creating the European Steel and Coal Community (ECSC), which went into effect in 1952 after ratification in each country. In 1957 "the Six," as they were by then called, signed the Treaty of Rome, which established the European Economic Community (EEC) and the European Atomic Energy Community (EAEC). In 1958 those two, together with the earlier ECSC, formed what is collectively known today as the European Community (EC). The primary goals of the Brussels-based EC remain the same three-plus decades later: a "common market" allowing the free movement of goods, services, people, and capital between member nations. The goals also included common policies for agriculture, transportation, competition, fisheries, the environment, and social welfare.

Many landmarks have pointed to the growth of the EC's economic and political influence over the past 30 years as trade within the community has grown from barely one-third to more than one-half the members' exports. Perhaps most significantly, the Six became the Twelve. The United Kingdom, Denmark, and Ireland joined the EC in 1973, at a time when their economies were suffering from what has become known as the first oil shock. Greece joined in 1981, followed by Spain and Portugal in 1986. (Incidentally, the EC flag has always had 12 stars, even when there were only 6 members. It's a mere coincidence that there have been 12 members in recent years. Presumably the flag will stay at 12 stars if and when new members are added.)

A number of other countries, notably Sweden, Austria, Switzerland, Finland, and Norway, have either formally applied or are preparing to apply for EC membership. The post-communist countries of Eastern Europe, notably Czechoslovakia, Poland, and Hungary, see cooperation with the EC and ultimately full EC membership as critical to their emerging democracies and free-market economies. Cyprus and Malta are interested and even Turkey, a predominantly Muslim country with only about 5 percent of its land mass actually located in Europe, wants to join. It's no wonder that Euro-enthusiasts predict the EC will have 20 member nations by 2010, with a single-market population of 700 million.

New pan-European laws and policies, some of them dating back to the 1960s and 1970s, formed the early framework for the single market. Foremost were the European Monetary System to restrain exchange-rate fluctuations among European currencies and cooperative financing programs for everything from farming to scientific research. Nearly all the EC's steps forward in its first quarter-century, however, came one at a time, in piecemeal fashion. This painstaking advancement, especially in the face of the need to compete economically with North America and the Far East, led to calls for a comprehensive approach. The result was the European Commission's 1985 White Paper. Endorsed by the EC's Heads of State or Government, the plan spawned hundreds of specific legislative proposals aimed at sweeping away the last of the border barriers by 1992 and, finally, realizing the original Treaty of Rome goals of a Europe without frontiers.

In the late 1980s, the date "1992" became the business world's shorthand reference to the single market, even though no one seemed sure of the exact deadline. At first, the EC's

Eurocrats, the paper pushers based in Brussels, vowed that the entire structure would be in place and the single market would be a reality by January 1, 1992. As the date approached, however, they began fudging and making reference to "the end of 1992." Today they say there is no exact date, or that an exact date is not important because achievement of a single market is an ongoing, evolving movement rather than an event fixed at one moment in time. There is some truth in that, but the Eurocrats are sometimes forced to admit the larger truth: The single market has proved more difficult to achieve than its architects imagined. Countries have been slow to approve the legislation needed to make it happen, and many major obstacles still block the single market's goals of the free movement of people, money, products, and services among the 12 countries.

One of the biggest obstacles is the structure of the EC itself and its unwieldy decision-making process. The EC is run from its headquarters in Brussels, where 15,000 employes, including 3,500 policy-making civil servants–the Eurocrats–carry out broad directives passed by the 17-member European Commission. Each of the 12 countries has a seat on the Commission, with the five largest holding two seats, though there are plans to reduce the number to 12, one for each country. Unofficially, the most influential country is Germany, more because it accounts for nearly one-third of the EC's gross domestic product (the pan-European equivalent of the U.S. GNP) than because its unified population of 80 million is the largest. Others with two votes include France (55 million people, 20 percent of the GDP), the United Kingdom (56 million, 12 percent), Italy (57 million, 12 percent), and Spain (40 million, 7 percent).

The European Commission debates everything from television advertising standards to branch banking procedures, but its directives are hardly carved in stone. Its policies can be summarily dismissed by the Council of Ministers, made up of the 12 countries' foreign ministers (or agriculture ministers, or trade ministers, or whomever each country chooses to send to a particular meeting, depending on the topic). The Council of Ministers, which becomes the Council of Europe during the twice-annual meetings attended by the heads of each country's government, can also initiate policies that set the agenda for the Commission's directives.

The 518-member European Parliament, largely made up of Eurorepresentatives elected after frustrated political careers in their own countries, has some limited ability to initiate EC policy and to review directives handed down by the European Council. But for the most part, the Parliament has been little more than a rubber stamp for the council in recent years. One of the glaring inefficiencies of the Parliament, and one of the reasons it has deserved so much of the scorn heaped on it, has been its inability to find one place to work. Some Euroreps have their offices in Luxembourg and some in Brussels, and once a month everyone packs up and jets or supertrains to Strasbourg, at EC taxpayer expense, for a five-day session. Afterward, they pack up and go back to their offices until the next monthly session.

Of somewhat more significance than the Parliament, but less probably than the Commission, is the European Court of Justice, 13 judges based in Luxembourg. They decide disputes, mostly commercial but sometimes political, among the 12 nations in much the same manner as the U.S. Supreme Court decides federal issues and disputes between states or residents of different states. In Europe, however, the court's guiding light is the Treaty of Rome rather than the U.S. Constitution. But just as U.S. judges sometimes interpret the Constitution broadly in order to decide cases the "right" way, the Eurojudges often read between the Treaty's specific lines, particularly in cases involving open competition and restraint of trade, to come up with decisions promoting their own view of the future shape of the single market. The overriding goal of the single market, *la Grande Marche* to the French and *Europaische Binnenmarkt* to the Germans, is to increase the quality of life in Europe. That, of course, requires higher living standards, which in turn can come only from improved economic conditions. To its credit, the EC has tried for the most part to build the single market on the framework of economic growth through true open markets and free competition – which means the end of many national monopolies, trade restraints, and other practices that traditionally protected "home" markets.

For example, EC single-market rules mean that the French government can no longer require that a certain percentage of its contracts let in any particular industry or service must go to French companies. When the British government announced the sale of the Rover car group to British Aerospace, the EC decided British taxpayers were paying too much for a government aid package and ruled that the deal could go through only if the aid was reduced. The package was trimmed down and the sale went through. When Pearson, the London-based publisher of the *Financial Times,* bid to take over *Les Echos,* a leading Paris business newspaper, the EC cited its pro-competition rules in warning the French government to drop plans to block the deal.

The EC has also chopped away one of Germany's major economic bulwarks, the program that pours state subsidies into private industry. The Eurocrats have ruled that this state aid, allowing German companies to grow more quickly and operate more cheaply than their competitors in other EC countries, is an unfair trade advantage that violates the spirit of 1992. Meanwhile, some of the countries trying to catch up, notably Spain, have held the single-market movement hostage in the European Commission by demanding increased aid levels from the richer countries in exchange for favorable votes on monetary union and other pillars of the new Europe. Naturally, this blackmail has not gone well in Germany, France, and Britain; their support of the single market was based on the idea that everyone would get richer, and especially them; equality was never part of the attraction. Some unity.

The basic principles of the single marketplace remain

straightforward and offer this basic benefit for any non-EC company: Products made or marketed legally in one EC country—even by parent companies based in America, Japan, or anywhere else—are allowed to circulate freely throughout the community. An American company that legally exports its products to Greece cannot be barred from selling those products throughout the other 11 EC countries, too. The lifting of duties and tariffs means that instead of up to 70 different forms, exporters moving goods between EC countries have to fill out only one, the so-called Single Administrative Document. Border delays that previously added an estimated 7 percent to the cost of consumer goods are being sharply cut.

The EC believes the single market means more competition, fairer prices, reduced inflation, lower interest rates, and $300 million worth of annual economic growth that will create 5 million jobs and bolster member countries' GNPs. "The progressive impact of EC market integration could, in the space of a few years, put 4 to 7 percentage points on the European Community's gross domestic product. This vista is not a tantalizing chimera. On the contrary, it is a firm prospect," according to Paolo Cecchini, author of an EC report that surveyed 11,000 European companies. Initially, many European business leaders were enthusiastic about the concept of the single market. They reckoned only on the benefits: fewer forms to fill out, the removal of duties and tariffs in selling to neighboring European countries, and the lifting of local protectionist manufacturing requirements. Instead of designing and producing 12 different computers for the 12 different markets, an electronics company could look forward to producing one all-purpose European model and selling it throughout the EC.

On paper, the single market sounded great to everybody. But it is turning out to be great only for the best companies, both European-based and foreign-based firms doing business in Europe. These are the companies with management and marketing flexibility to adapt to a whole new set of rules. The playing fields, as the British say, are being leveled. Many companies, after years of operating comfortably in their cozy little protected home markets, found that the single market meant competition from leaner, meaner rivals from across the border. In the face of this tougher competition, some European companies have been forced out of business. Many, both large and small, have been swallowed up by larger companies seeking the economies of scale needed to become pan-European and operate throughout the EC. Larger companies have decided that they need to go beyond pan-European; they need to be global to compete with the American, Japanese, and other non-EC invaders that see the EC's vast and wealthy consumer market as rich pickings. This is the main reason there have been so many mergers, joint ventures, research or marketing alliances, and other forms of corporate cooperation among European companies in recent years. As a result, the effects of the single market have been in many ways a self-fulfilling prophecy. Anticipating the changes that could come from the single market, many companies have restructured and realigned, thereby making the changes happen just as predicted.

Take the example of a British computer services company, CAP Group. As president of the company, Michael Smith could see his company being drawn into a grow-or-die dilemma in the late 1980s. Smith reckoned that by 1992 his CAP Group could no longer rely solely on its share of the British market. With restrictions lifted on the movement of goods, services, people, and money, Europe *sans frontieres* would force CAP to compete with rival computer services firms from France, West Germany, and elsewhere in Europe for contracts in Britain. CAP Group, Smith believed, either had to grow and compete all over Europe or face the prospect of being swallowed up by the fiercer competition. His solution was a merger with Sema-Metra, the French computer services company that was in a similar position. Smith and Pierre Bonelli, Sema-Metra's chairman, created a new company, Semacap, with the size (6,400 employees, sales of $450 million a year), balance of services, management capability, and general international orientation to compete across Europe. "And we'll be able to compete with the big American and Japanese companies for contracts all over the world," Smith said.

As the EC nations begin to work more closely together, they find themselves forced to give up some of their own sovereignty and national identity. The most politically sensitive issue has been European monetary union. So far the Ecu (European Currency Unit), a monetary unit based on the floating values of a basket of EC currencies, is more theoretical than practical and is used primarily by countries and big companies to settle large debts. The movement to create a true single currency has been stalled by the reluctance of several EC nations to create a central European bank that would not only oversee the currency but set monetary policies. The British government, particularly, has been reluctant to allow the Eurocrats, rather than Parliament, the Bank of England, or the prime minister, to set its money supply and interest rates (see Chapter 11: Money Matters). Taxes are another issue. Despite the single-market movement, one study shows that tax differences are the main reason that a new Ford Fiesta with a $9,900 sticker price in Britain costs $7,400 in Germany and $6,400 in the Netherlands. The same study showed similar price differentials for a new BMW: $21,500 in Ireland, $17,000 in Belgium, and $15,400 in France.

Another facet of the auto industry highlights the hypocrisy of European unity and underscores the way in which the EC countries try to exploit the single market for their own gain. In the mid-1980s, the Thatcher government decided to try to revive the sagging fortunes of northeast England, decimated by the long demise of shipbuilding and other smokestack industries, by attracting foreign business. The biggest plum on the foreign tree in Europe at the time was Nissan, which was scouting several countries for a possible location for a new factory. Thatcher dangled an attractive package of incentives and government subsidies and Nissan bit. When the details became known years later, it appeared that the government package for Nissan was probably a violation of at least the spirit of the single market's rules against state aid to private companies.

But that didn't matter to Nissan, which built a big factory in Sunderland in northeast England and began pumping out cars. The cars were sold not only in Britain but throughout Europe. Because the Nissans were built in Britain, they were "European" cars and were not counted for the purposes of the strict import quotas that several EC countries imposed on Japanese autos. France and Italy, trying to protect Renault and Fiat sales, respectively, complained to the EC that their auto industries were being undercut unfairly. A Nissan was a Japanese car even if it was assembled in England, they argued. Britain, savoring the capital investment, factory payroll, and trade surplus that Nissan was contributing, became ardent single-marketeers and argued for the open market and free competition. Britain's position undoubtedly would have been reversed if, say, Ireland had won the new plant and started flooding the British market with Japanese cars. The EC agreed with Britain and said that France and Italy could not restrict the import of British-built Nissan cars, but softened the blow by setting up a gradual six-year phase-out so that the quotas would not completely disappear until January 1, 1999.

The political problems of true European unity and the hurdles of entrenched nationalism were underscored during the Gulf War, which demonstrated just how far apart the leading Western European countries are on foreign affairs in general and defense issues in particular. When the United States launched the first attacks on Iraq on January 16, 1991, British planes and pilots were flying alongside the American planes. French and Italian planes also flew, although they restricted their missions. France, for example, wanted to drop bombs only on Iraqi troops in Kuwait; the French were afraid that attacks on Iraq itself might hurt their chances of someday again acting as Iraq's main political and economic link with the West. And while even some of the smaller nations such as the Netherlands sent soldiers to support the American effort in the ground war, Germany refused to send troops. This was in part because of Germany's own post-World War II legal restrictions on sending any of its soldiers anywhere outside Germany ever again. It does not explain Germany's reluctance and internal political dithering on how much, if any, financial support it should provide to the allied effort. But the war produced even worse examples of Eurofriction. Belgium, for instance, refused to sell Britain the ammunition needed for some of its guns.

In the months before the Gulf War, Euro-unity supporters had been beating the drums for political integration that would go beyond a single currency and a single monetary policy. There was talk of the EC countries further aligning themselves into a single defense policy and ultimately conducting all their foreign policy through the EC—in effect, a "United States of Europe," with the individual countries filling the role of our states. Those dreams came crashing back to earth with the United States' dominant military performance and political leadership in the war. There was less talk of how a federal Europe could develop its own foreign and defense policy independent of NATO.

"Pity the small European nations like us," one Irish official told me after a couple of drinks. "We're all certainly very glad that the war was quick and successful for the allies. But it was a bitter pill of reality for all of us smaller countries in Europe that had been thinking we really could have some influence on the world stage. Before the Gulf War, in the eighties, the EC and the single market made us think that we were taking charge of our own destiny, that we were going to have a major impact on world affairs. But when Saddam invaded Kuwait, we all looked to the United States for leadership, and the United States provided that leadership. The war showed us in no uncertain terms just how powerful America still is, and how little influence we really have in the nineties. It was a humbling experience for us in Europe."

Some of the most nettlesome aspects of the single market have not been agreed upon by the member nations and may never be. Significantly, many of those troublesome issues concern not European companies, products, or money, but European people themselves. For example, the new maroon EC passport that is replacing each country's previously distinctive passports is supposed to confer the right of movement and the right to work. So doctors, lawyers, teachers, accountants, and other professionals or self-employed workers are in theory able to pursue their livelihood in any of the 12 countries. But the individual European nations have shown themselves distinctly reluctant to allow other countries' psychiatrists and hairdressers to waltz in and hang out their shingles.

In some cases, countries have set stiff professional and educational requirements for other Europeans. But even educational credentials can be difficult to come by, despite the single market's declared aim of allowing students from one country to transfer their credits to schools in other countries. A number of schools, particularly the best ones, are distinctly uncomfortable with this notion and require transfer students from other European countries to take tough exams and sometimes pass competency tests. (In one recent case, a British Ph.D. was judged incompetent to teach in France, even though the subject he wanted to teach was English.) Marriage and divorce represent another "personal" aspect of the single market that is providing headaches for some Eurocitizens. No country, it seems, wants to give up its own particular requirements either for getting married or ending a marriage. As a result, despite the theory of mutual recognition of laws, a German man married to an Italian woman had to get divorced twice—once in each country—with two sets of lawyers and their fees, two sets of court filings and fees, and two separate settlements.

Copyrights, trademarks, and patents recognized in one country are valid throughout the EC, and health, safety, and environmental rules are being standardized. But there remains a large gap between many of these rules. Regulations for drug testing in some countries, for example, fall far short of the requirements in others. The countries with the tougher standards are not about to relax theirs to allow in new pharmaceuticals that have not been tested as thoroughly in other countries where they are sold legally. At the same time, the countries with the more lenient standards don't want a tougher regimen that would put some of their home companies out of business.

Despite all the shortcomings, the drive toward the single market has indeed led to some dramatic changes, even at the cost of swallowing national pride—literally, in the case of some national foods and beverages—and eating away at national autonomy. In Germany, nothing is more sacred, or more symbolic of German pride and well-being, than German beer. That's why the *reinheitsgebot,* the "purity law" dating back to Bavaria and the year 1516, has historically required that beer sold in Germany be made solely from water, malted barley, hops, and yeast. Nothing else. No additives, no preservatives, no rice, no nothing. Across the border, Italians feel the same way about pasta, their staple, their lifeblood from the earth, their own expression of well-being and culinary excellence. As a result, Italy has its own time-honored pasta purity laws, allowing the manufacture and sale of ravioli, spaghetti, tagliatelle, and so forth only if they have been made from high-quality, hard durum wheat.

Naturally, the Germans have no purity laws for pasta, nor the Italians for beer. The Germans make and sell cheaper pasta with soft wheat, and the Italians make and sell cheaper beer with additives. So what happened when, under the rules of the single market, Germany started exporting its cheaper pasta to Italy and Italy started exporting its cheaper lager to Germany? Each country objected, and the two cases went to court. Each claimed that its particular product was such an important part of the national culture and tradition that there should be an exemption from the single market's rules on the free movement of any products legally manufactured in one EC country to all the other EC countries. The European Court of Justice, the judicial arm of the EC, disagreed with both countries. The court threw out both the German beer purity rules and the Italian pasta purity rules. German shops can sell Italian beer, the court ruled, and Italian shops can sell German pasta. There are literally dozens of similar examples throughout the EC. The French were forced to give up their laws allowing only "live" all-natural yoghurt and to reluctantly accept pasteurized imports from Spain. Belgium was forced to abandon its prohibitions on vegetable fat in chocolate and admit Danish chocolate made with vegetable fat.

For Americans, perhaps the biggest concern over Euro-unity is the concept of Fortress Europe. The fear is that while the single market offers greater opportunities for international companies with established subsidiaries in Europe, such as Ford and IBM, it will be more difficult for non-EC companies to sell their products on the other side of the Atlantic. "It might be fine for the Europeans, but it won't mean much for the United States unless they regard us with favored-nation status," said an American consultant to U.S. firms expanding to Europe. "It would be terrible if the EC sets up one wall around all of Europe to make trading and investment more difficult for international companies." The concern centers on the shape of "reciprocity" requirements that may or may not be built into the single market by the European Commission, the EC's 17-member policy-making arm. One U.S. Embassy official in Brussels said: "The Commission demands EC-wide reciprocity. Does this mean that when a U.S. bank wants to open in London or in Paris after

1992, the EC will say no because there are too few Portugese or Greek banks in the U.S.?"

Here's an example of how Fortress Europe is working against the United States, under the argument that some products and services – in this case, television programming – are too sensitive to be left to the open marketplace. Hollywood has depended more and more on overseas sales in recent years. At the same time, the European countries have been setting quotas over how much American programming can be aired, both to protect their own smaller, weaker entertainment industries and to ease fears about the cultural influence of all that Americana. As a result, the EC does not allow member nations to limit the import of programming from other EC countries, but it does allow countries to set quotas for non-EC – meaning American, almost exclusively – programming. The "guidelines" proffered by the Eurocrats suggest that member countries allow no more than half of their air time for non-EC programming, which means U.S. television and film production companies are limited in how much they can earn from the overseas sales. Because projected sales from European rights will not be as great as they might have been under a truly open market, some American companies may not be able to raise the cash to film their productions. In this way, Fortress Europe not only has an impact on the U.S. economy, but also on the quantity and quality of screen entertainment produced for American audiences.

On the other hand, there are examples of how the single market is breaking down long-existing parts of Fortress Europe. For decades, certain European countries have imposed extra import duties on bananas produced in South America and Latin America by big U.S. companies. Instead, countries such as Britain, Spain, Portugal, and Italy buy and eat the smaller, thinner-skinned, mottled-looking bananas from their former colonies in the Caribbean and Africa. Despite the interest those countries have in providing economic support for their former colonies, the tenets of the single market eventually will lead to the demise of the extra import duties on American bananas. European sales of those cheaper, bigger, yellower American bananas will undoubtedly take off.

It's still too early to see just how high the walls will be in Fortress Europe and how many cracks there will be. The Eurocrats are considering labeling restrictions that would mean the only frankfurters that can be called frankfurters are made in Frankfurt, the only hamburgers that can be called hamburgers are from Hamburg, and all champagne, burgundy, and chablis must come from the Champagne, Burgundy, and Chablis areas of France, and so forth. It remains to be seen how strictly those rules are eventually applied and how successful U.S. industry lobbyists and government officials are in winning exemptions for U.S. products using those labels. It seems altogether possible that the EC would bar American-made champagne, but not American-made hamburgers.

Americans visiting Europe are not reassured by the EC's single-market publicity campaigns. One French TV commercial shows a skinny little French businessman in a boxing ring. A Japanese sumo wrestler and an American football player climb threateningly into the ring, but the Frenchman is rescued by 11 European compatriots, dressed in their national colors, who pummel the Japanese and American. "It should be stated with extreme clarity that the single market must first offer an advantage to European companies," according to Umberto Agnelli of Fiat. Europe for Europeans, in other words, and for anyone else willing to play by Europe's rules and help make Europeans rich. But Fortress Europe implies a 12-nation stone wall, a community-wide agreement of purpose and practice. Clearly, that sort of Euro-unity is in short supply, and it remains difficult for the European countries to agree on even the simplest needs. After years of consensus over the necessity for a pan-European air traffic control system, for example, so-called Eurocontrol had only one tower—at that thriving world air hub, Maastricht.

19

Despite the movement toward a single market, Europe still has few standardized rules in any sector of business or industry. That means there are many opportunities for the creative American trader, entrepreneur, investor, or executive to take advantage of the gaps. The EC's cumbersome and often impossible decision-making process means that it is frequently difficult to get simple things done. In this setting, people used to making decisions and getting things done—like most successful Americans—are likely to be successful in Europe, too. Finally, there is one opinion Europeans share almost unanimously: no matter what else they may think of Americans, they want to do business with us.

CHAPTER 2

♦ ♦ ♦

What They Think of Us

John Hall is a gruff Scotsman who loves Americans. Hall, one of Europe's most successful real-estate developers, recalls the time he was touring the States gathering design ideas and meeting investors for the giant American-style shopping mall, the first in Europe, that he wanted to build in northern England. "It was in Cleveland, a dark, rainy morning, and I was depressed," Hall said. "Everyone in England had been telling me my project would never get off the ground, that Europeans would never go for a big American mall, especially in an economically depressed area like Gateshead. I was starting to believe them. I stepped onto the elevator in the hotel on my way down to a meeting with some potential investors, and I didn't think they'd be interested, either. I was really in a poor frame of mind."

On the way down, the elevator stopped and two Americans got on. "They were insurance salesmen of some sort," Hall recalled. "Noisy little guys. Plaid jackets. They were on their way to a meeting, too, where they had to make a presentation and try to sell somebody some of their life insurance. They started talking to each other. This is what we're gonna do. This is what we're gonna say. They're gonna like it. Yeah! Then we're gonna do this. We're gonna sell them so much insurance. This is gonna be a great deal for us. We can do it. Yeah! All right! Let's go get 'em!" By the time the elevator door opened to the lobby, Hall was fired up, too. "I tell you," he said, "I not only couldn't wait to get to my own meeting and make my pitch, I wanted to go with those guys and help them sell life insurance, too."

Business may be business around the world, but business is also personal. People make deals with other people because they believe in them. For Americans to elicit that belief from Europeans, however, it is sometimes necessary to overcome their strong—though not necessarily accurate—views of America and Americans. The stereotypes of American people and products may or may not ring true to us Americans, and we may object to the preconceptions. But like it or not, we have to deal with them. That's why I've collected examples of various characteristics that Europeans typically ascribe to Americans. Knowing what a European thinks of you in advance may help explain some of the things he or she says or does. If you recognize the pigeonhole you're being put in, that's half the battle in either getting out of it or using it to your advantage.

Since moving to London in 1984, my work as a journalist throughout Europe has brought me into contact with many Europeans who do business with Americans. I've made a point of asking many of them for their impressions of us. What impresses them the most? A surprising number of Europeans have a simple answer, but one that most Americans would never expect: our teeth. Europeans are in awe of American dentistry and the dazzling smiles it produces. A Cockney news agent once told me he doesn't even need to wait for American tourists to give themselves away with the accent; when customers approach his little blue newsstand showing what he calls "the full set of choppers, all white, all perfect," he automatically reaches for *USA Today* or the *International Herald Tribune* they are sure to ask for. At the same time, many European parents have asked me why Americans are so devoted to orthodontia for their children. "All these young American teenagers you see touring around with their parents have a mouth full of metal braces, wires, and bands. We just don't understand that," one well-educated young mother said. On the positive side, many Europeans regard most Americans as friendly, good-natured, approachable folks who are only too happy to talk about the way they do things back home. They view Americans as intelligent, sentimental, fun-loving, often generous people who love their country and won't stand for more than a little criticism of "the American system." Americans are also seen as being positive-minded, confident, and enthusiastic.

On the other hand, there are many negatives to the stereo-typical European view of Americans. For one thing, we're ob-sessed with hygiene; we demand hot daily showers, *en suite* bathrooms, and clean sheets; we send dirty tableware back to the kitchen and avoid the outdoor stands where the natives eat every day; we turn up our noses at European sidewalk rubbish, dirty canals, and downtown streets choked with diesel fumes and ever-beeping traffic. To Europeans, who regard their art and culture as superior largely because it is older, Americans are too sentimental—perhaps corny would be our word for it. They don't understand how we can be so fastidious and de-manding in so many ways, such as cleanliness, and yet so willing to swallow the American television programs and films that they see as simple-minded, cloyingly sentimental, and emotionally manipulative.

Europeans don't understand how Americans can be so puri-tanical about sex while so matter of fact about violence. On European television, for instance, nudity is not unusual, partic-ularly bare breasts. Italian TV is famous for its afternoon quiz shows where housewives who give a wrong answer must then shed an article of clothing. Throughout Europe, American films shown on television are more likely to be edited for violence than for sex. In America, of course, it's the other way. When a young misfit went berserk and shot and killed 16 people in a rampage in the English town of Hungerford, the British newspaper and TV reports all noted that this was the first incident of "American style" mass violence, and commentators were quick to blame it on the influence of Hollywood movies and television series. Even now, reruns of programs such as *Miami Vice* and *Twin Peaks* are edited to cut out simulated beatings, stabbings, and shootings.

Europeans often sneer at what they see as Americans' vanity and their fixation on health and fitness. Many European secretaries will automatically bring an American black coffee, because they have been told that Americans don't take cream or sugar because of obsessions about health. Aperitifs, wine, and liqueurs or ports are still very much a standard part of many business lunches in Europe, and an American who asks for mere mineral water is often met with stares of disbelief from lunch companions who then say, "Oh, that's right. I forgot, you're American." As if they really could forget you are American, even for a moment. Americans looking for a token drink cannot get away with light beer like they can in the States. I once went for a walk through London's fashionable Mayfair area on a summer afternoon with Ed "Too Tall" Jones when he was still playing for the Dallas Cowboys. We popped into a pub, where his 6 feet, 9 inches and 290 pounds filled the place and kept any of the ensconced afternoon ale drinkers from scoffing when he asked for a light beer. "A what?" the bartender asked. He tried to explain, but she had clearly never heard of a light beer; European breweries don't make them, and hardly anyone imports them. So Jones asked for two pint glasses, one filled with tepid lager and one with ice, and proceeded to mix up his own cold, watered-down beer. That did prompt some coughs and harrumphs from the regulars, but only behind his huge back. "My, you're tall," the bartender said as Jones drained a pint of iced beer. "Too Tall," he said.

Europeans also smoke more than Americans, particularly unfiltered cigarettes with strong tobacco, and smoking anywhere, any time is still relatively acceptable; an American who asks someone to stop smoking is likely to be jeered. This brings up one of the most nagging problems for Americans living and working in Europe. If you complain to a European about something—if you point out to a kid that it's illegal to smoke on a subway, for instance, and suggest that he put out the cigarette—the issue can very quickly shift from his behavior to your nationality. "Why don't you go back where you came from?" is the standard riposte from someone such as a subway smoker who's been called down in public for something he cannot defend. On the other hand, it's better to be accused of being an American on the Paris Metro than it is to be on the wrong end of a New York subway smoker's knife or gun.

There's also the general issue of wealth. To us, the American dream is pulling yourself up by your bootstraps, using your talents and seizing opportunities to make a better, more comfortable life. To Europeans, the American dream is too often a nightmare of greed. They see us as great strivers, but believe we often strive too much for money and power. They see the U.S. as the ultimate materialistic society, ruled by advertising and consumerism. But what Europeans really hate is this: that Americans see their wealth, both personal and national, as a symbol of success, of the absolute correctness of the American way. Many Americans don't understand that while much of the rest of the world would like a better standard of living, most of Western Europe, particularly the European Community and Scandinavian countries, has no interest in being more like America. To them, a two-bedroom apartment in a old city neighborhood is preferable to the American dream of a big house in the suburbs.

The nationalized health systems in Europe are preferable to Europeans because they know they will be taken care of eventually, even if they occasionally have to wait for some types of treatment. In the American system, they know, the quality of medical care depends on how much money you or your private insurer is willing to pay. Europeans are willing to have only one television set and one car in exchange for the assurance of government policies that prevent the wide disparities of rich and poor, the glistening mansions across town from the desolate slums that mar the American landscape. And while Americans see their country as the land of free choice and equal opportunity for all, Europeans see it as a land with tremendous cultural and economic pressures to conform, where everyone must be like everyone else, where individuality and eccentricity are punished by financial and social ostracism. It's important for Americans to remember this when doing business with Europeans: They want and need many things from us, but the American dream is our dream, not theirs.

Europeans returning from their first visit to the States often come home with strong impressions. For example, they frequently comment that so many Americans are fat, as if gluttony is a symbol or symptom of capitalist self-gratification to excess. Europeans also often comment on how American TV news carries relatively little about what's going on outside of America, while their own news programs at home are filled with news from Washington every night. One British executive loves to tell the story of how he met an American teenager who asked him, "Were the Beatles ever big in England?" Americans experienced in working in Europe avoid arguments they can't win by freely admitting that many of their fellow citizens are unsophisticated and inconsiderate of things happening in the rest of the world. We are in fact too narrow-minded and too focused on the importance of America in the world. Yet there are reasons that other countries pay as much attention to the news from Washington as from their own capitals and reasons that foreigners wear clothes from the Gap and watch *The Cosby Show* and *Dallas* reruns.

It's sometimes impossible not to remind someone who's forgotten it that the world just might be a worse place without

America and Americans. But you've got to pick your spots. Envision this ugly scene among some early-morning business travelers in a major airport, where the natives don't always respect the sanctity of lining up properly and waiting their turn at the check-in desks, especially if it's a self-important guy who's in a hurry and it's a woman he's pushing aside. "Excuse me, the queue is back there. I'm next," the woman, an American, says. The man looks shocked at being called down, but quickly recovers to chide, "Oh, you're American. I guess that means you can do whatever you want to, can't you?" The European turns to the next man behind them in the queue. "Pushy Americans," he grumbles, with a sneering grin. The man behind stares at him coldly and speaks in a perfectly genteel Virginia accent: "Get at the back of the line, asshole, and don't call us next time you're invaded." The sneer freezes and the queue-jumper shuffles red-faced to the back of the line amid the snickers of the other waiting passengers, including fellow Europeans offended by the guy's behavior but unwilling to get involved.

While Europeans often appreciate American vitality, they believe it too often builds into unacceptable aggressiveness. One European involved in a fairly straightforward, simple deal with an American was thoroughly disgusted with the way the American kept pushing him to act quickly and to make unrealistic concessions. Despite the prodding, the deal proceeded pretty much along the timetable and terms originally envisioned. Both parties were satisfied with the deal itself, but the European said he would never deal with the American again—or any other American if he could help it. The American said he had no complaints at all about the European, and said he hadn't regarded his nagging demands as aggressive at all. It was just the way he did business.

Some "aggressive" American innovations are catching on in Europe, however. One is the power breakfast. This is part of an overheard conversation:

"No, thanks, I can't go out for a drink after the movie tonight. I've got a business meeting tomorrow at 7 A.M. at the Connaught."

"Oh, you must be meeting an American."

Americans are seen as packing every possible moment with business; the British, particularly, have been horrified – their word, not mine – at the rise of the "power tea," where the traditional, ritualistic afternoon break for tea, tiny sandwiches, and sweets is ruined by talking about business. Similarly, Americans are seen as distinctly lacking in the ability to relax, or rather the ability to do absolutely nothing, even in their personal lives. When one prominent European film director returned from his first assignment in Hollywood, he was full of awe at the way the people he met there kept themselves organized, on and off the job. "Americans instinctively run their lives like businesses," he marveled.

American women working in Europe can have special problems with stereotypes. Because of feminism and the fact that many more women are managers in America than in Europe, American women are frequently seen as bossy, unfeminine, and hard-nosed. Thatcheresque, perhaps. Barbara Evans, an Oklahoma native who followed her husband to Scotland for his job in the oil business, decided to apply for a job in Aberdeen as supervisor of a janitorial team that cleaned offices. She had grown up working for her parents in a similar business back in Tulsa, and she was eminently qualified. The company's personnel director agreed, and Evans was hired. The next day, the company called and said the offer was being withdrawn. No explanation was given. Upset, she and her husband called back and pressed the company: Why? Finally, the head of the company said he was afraid the Scottish workers would not be able to understand her Oklahoma accent. "Fine," Evans said. "If they don't understand me, I'll tell 'em again. I'll tell 'em again and again until they do understand me. Jeez, it's not rocket science. It's only cleaning offices." Eventually the real reason came out: The company was afraid that the Scottish men working on the cleaning crew would resent being given orders by a woman, and particularly an American woman. Evans went to a local solicitor, who recommended that she file a formal complaint with the regional labor board. She did, and the labor board agreed that she had been denied the job unfairly. The company gave her substantial cash damages.

Many American women working in Europe say they find that European men, especially those with the best educations and from the aristocratic upper classes, have difficulty relating to women. If a woman can't talk about cricket or soccer, it doesn't matter to them that she can talk about what they should be doing to make their companies perform better. In general, American women seem to believe that the women's movement in most European countries lags at least a decade behind the States, although they almost always make an exception for the relatively generous maternity benefits mandated by European governments. Four to six months at or near full pay is typical, with a year or more common among the Scandinavian countries.

Few Europeans, despite their relative high regard for their own world views, know a lot about individual American states or cities. They know New York means money and crime, Colorado means better snow than the Alps, and Texans are big and loud. Iowa and Ohio are indistinguishable, New Orleans means Mardi Gras, and San Francisco means gays. People who tell a European they are from Chicago may well encounter a shrug and, "Is that on the East Coast? I'm sorry, I don't know U.S. geography very well." Europeans often scorn Americans and make fun of them, particularly the tourists on whirlwind, ten-day, seven-country package tours. A British newspaper once ran a contest for readers to send in their favorite American tourist jokes. The winner was about the tourist who wanted directions to the British Library because he had heard the main reading hall had a terrific echo.

Underneath the scorn, of course, is economic dependency on tourist dollars. Europeans have turned over whole cities and regions to tourism, yet they frequently complain that American visitors treat their countries like giant theme parks. Naturally, Americans who point out this obvious hypocrisy do little to further American-European relations. And it's often the same Europeans who complain about crass American tourists who are the first to whine when tourism falls off. Europeans who are more used to living with the daily threat of terrorism make fun of Americans who stay home when international tensions increase. One columnist in Britain scored points with the chattering classes when he suggested that transatlantic tourism had fallen off during the Gulf War because most Americans believe Paris is a suburb of Baghdad and London is just a little further down the road. Hollywood stars are special targets when they refuse to fly across the Atlantic to promote their movies, pick up awards, or be seen at the Cannes Film Festival. Sylvester Stallone's macho image took such a beating in the European press when his canceled trip was blamed on the threat of terrorism that he sued a British newspaper for libel and won.

Europeans chide Americans for being from such a young country and point out that they often live and work in buildings that were standing and walk streets that were paved before the voyages of Columbus. Americans, therefore, cannot appreciate the traditions, culture, and art of Europe, the reasoning goes. Yet it is often Americans who are saving the landmarks of Europe. A good example is the Globe, the London theater where Shakespeare staged so many of his masterpieces in the 16th and 17th centuries. The rebuilding of the theater, which began in 1990 as a result of a $30 million fund-raising drive, came about largely through the efforts of one man: Sam Wanamaker, the American director.

Wanamaker was shocked when he visited London as a young actor in the 1950s and found that a grimy plaque attached to a brewery was all that marked the site of the Globe, long buried beneath the brewery. Wanamaker, who has spent much of his career in Britain, initiated a drive to rebuild the theater on its original site. Surprisingly, he met considerable opposition from the British, including the theater community that should have been backing him to the hilt. Wanamaker blamed the opposition on the fact that he was American; people thought he was trying to make money on the project or that he would desecrate the memory of Shakespeare and the Globe by creating some sort of theatrical "Disneyland," the European catchall term for almost any large-scale leisure project. But when Wanamaker began getting donations from American actors, including a thousand unknowns for every Dustin Hoffman or Robert DeNiro who sent him money, the British theatrical community realized that he might really be able to pull it off. After Wanamaker enlisted the support of a top British architect whose plans mixed the authenticity of the old Globe's hardwood benches with modern restaurants, shops, and a Shakespeare museum, the British were finally convinced and even the skeptics were converted.

The term "Disneyland" has been particularly controversial in France because of the building of EuroDisneyland in the suburbs of Paris. Again, many French people criticized the plan and ridiculed the idea of Europe adopting a concept so mundane, so bourgeoise, so *American*. Disney, of course, stuck to the strong concepts and high standards that have made its "lands" successful in Anaheim, Orlando, and Tokyo, and even the French have become reluctantly convinced that this American way of having fun really is fun. Of course, there are still many French who bridle against *franglais*, the casual use of English words in everyday French. They will never approve of Mickey Mouse even if he speaks a squeaky little version of French and wears a beret, striped shirt, and neckerchief. One social commentator, Alain Schifres, observed in an influential magazine, "We can understand nothing about the United States. It is a country which is much too simple for us."

This is the 1990s version of the 1980s Cold War attitude that led one French philosopher to suggest, "Better to wear the helmet of a Red Army soldier than to live on a diet of hamburgers in Brooklyn." Ah, *mais oui*, with the French it always comes around to the food and their perception that every American lives primarily on a diet of red meat. In truth, even the most committed Parisians would probably be aghast if they ever realized how similar their own national diet is to ours, down to the Big Mac every week or two. But there are some real differences. One is that the French probably eat more cheese and vegetables because they're so commonly sold at large outdoor markets, piled appetizingly high and smelling sweet, unlike the shrink-wrapped, sell-by, sterile produce and dairy aisles of most American supermarkets. But the biggest difference is that the French drink a lot more wine. They are proud of it. They also have the highest rates of alcoholism in Europe.

Here's a typical American-in-Europe food story. In one of Amsterdam's many fine little family hotels, the European guests were settling in over their breakfasts (included with the price of the room) of tea, coffee, juice, toast, rolls, and assortments of cheese and sausage. Suddenly the peaceful chatter and clinking of cups and silverware was broken by a large American couple surveying the buffet. "Jeez," the man said loudly, "Ethel, do you think they have some cornflakes in this place?" He wasn't even interested in trying a Dutch breakfast. As it turned out, there was a big bowl of cornflakes, with smaller bowls and spoons and milk, on an adjacent table that the hotel had been putting out for years for its American guests.

One of the key aspects to better transatlantic understanding, of course, is the ability to communicate, to speak each other's languages. Americans are notoriously inept at other languages, and Europeans see this as another sign of our superiority complex and our stubbornly insular attitude toward the rest of the world. I've cringed many times, most often in tourist season in non-English-speaking countries, upon witnessing this scene: An American visitor approaches a native and blurts out some sort of request or demand in English, without even first taking the usual polite precaution of asking if the native is able to speak or understand English. When the native answers in his or her own language, the American looks temporarily befuddled and then tries once more, again in English, except this time perhaps phrasing the request differently or maybe even asking it in the exact same words *except louder.* Imagine some stranger with gaudy shorts and a huge camera confronting you and abruptly jabbering something you couldn't understand; you answer best as you can, advising that you can't help because you don't understand, and then the stranger starts shouting the same thing at you again. As I said, I've seen it many times, and I'm always embarrassed that the offender is a fellow American.

American blockheadedness over foreign languages wouldn't be so bad, of course, if so many Europeans didn't speak so many languages themselves. For instance, it's not unusual for an American to be speaking with a Dutchman in English, and then be startled as the Dutchman takes a succession of phone calls from Germany, France, or Italy, shifting to the appropriate language each time he picks up the phone. Most Americans approaching Europe have had some sort of language training, usually French, Spanish, or German, in high school, college, or both. And most of us have forgotten pretty much everything we learned. As a result, we often feel guilty, worried, at a disadvantage . . . if only we'd paid more attention to that loopy language teacher back in tenth grade.

Once in Europe, Americans quickly realize two things. First, it's relatively easy to recapture "lost" language skills from high school or college merely by taking some classes, watching local TV programming, and actually trying to speak the language at work and in local neighborhoods. Even a totally unfamiliar language can be picked up in a few months; you won't be winning any debate society awards, but you will be able to talk to the streetcorner merchants about the weather and give understandable directions to cabdrivers. One man I know chucked his office job in New York a few years back and decided he wanted to live in Paris and write fiction. To pay the bills, he got a part-time clerical job in the Paris headquarters of the Organization for Economic Cooperation and Development (OECD), a sprawling international research agency. Arriving with almost no French, he studied diligently and quickly picked up a working knowledge, although for years friends had to translate jokes – the last thing anybody understands in any language – for him at dinner parties. His main stumbling block was that everyone, including the French, wanted to speak English to him, especially at work. He finally made a deal with the French woman who sat at the next desk: He would speak only French to her, and she would speak only English to him.

The second important thing about languages that Americans working in Europe quickly realize is this: Speaking the native tongue is nice, and it's always an advantage, but it's almost never necessary. That loopy tenth-grade teacher who warned you about all the disadvantages of not speaking the language if you traveled in Europe? She lied. Or rather, she had no way of knowing that English – and particularly *American* English – would become the international language of business in much the same way it was always the international language of aviation. Any pilot who wants to make the glamorous long-haul international flights has to speak some English, and any business executive who wants to do the big international deals – the deals with Americans – has to speak it, too. Even the BBC has started using American phrases and pronunciations in its influential learn-to-speak-English videos. One European management guru put it this way: "International trade demands competence in English just as the Roman Empire and medieval Christendom once required educated people to speak Latin."

One experienced New York import-export trader told me that it can actually be a disadvantage to speak a European language, or at least to let a European business partner know that you speak it. It's better to keep it as a secret weapon, he said, to be trotted out only when absolutely necessary, such as during the critical late stages of negotiations.

Please don't misunderstand: The emergence of American English as the world language, a phenomenon of the last two decades, is not a reason to ignore other languages or to refuse to make any attempt to speak them. Even the New York import-export trader acknowledged that when working in a country where he doesn't speak the language, he at least tries to make the Europeans think he is interested in their language and that he would like to learn it someday. The most futile and comical stab at saying a few words to a Swede in Swedish or a Spaniard in Spanish is indeed appreciated and is a form of good manners that many successful cross-border deal makers perform routinely, the same way they would a handshake. Many of them can facilely and with a decent accent in half a dozen languages utter little bits of chatter limited to, "Hello, How are you. I am happy to be here. Yes, some coffee, thank you. Your city (or your office or your products) are beautiful. Can you tell me where the restroom is, please?" It's precisely because we are so poor at languages, or at least because the Europeans perceive us as being so poor, that these feeble efforts are so greatly appreciated. The Dutch, perhaps Europe's most superb linguists, are more impressed with an American who can speak German or a smattering of Dutch than they are with one of their countrymen who is at home in half the languages of the European Community.

I know one American, a travel writer, who bones up on barroom talk for whatever country he is visiting next. He learns the various ways of saying, "Cheers!" and proposing toasts to that city, country, or people. Then he finds a friendly bar and makes friends. The locals not only buy him drinks but might end up taking him home for dinner, fly-fishing in a cousin's farm stream, or on to other small adventures that travel writers thrive on to spice up their stories. I personally have been in many situations where I'm the only one speaking English and the only one not speaking, say, Czech. But even in a little neighborhood beer hall in one of Prague's grim, Russian-built suburbs, I was able to point at the plates and steins being attacked at the next table. I wasn't sure exactly what I was getting to eat when the waiter walked away, but the meat, cheese, vegetables, and pilsner that he came back with turned out to be just what I probably would have ordered if I'd known how.

Here's a word of warning, though. Even if someone seems to speak good English, don't assume that everything you say is understood. Say things over and over, in different ways, to make sure. A Texas oil engineer had a horrible experience a few years ago when he was ordered to drop everything and fly to Taranto, Italy, where his emergency expertise was needed to help with the drilling of a new well in the Ionian Sea. Every hour of delay was costing his company thousands of dollars. The engineer made the fastest connections he could for Rome, where he hurried to the ticket counter for the local airline that made the 45-minute flight to Taranto. When he asked if the agent spoke English and she said yes, he asked for a ticket on the next flight to Taranto. He paid with a credit card, never bothering to check the flying time with her or to work out how much the ticket, priced in lire, cost in dollars. Shortly after takeoff, when the stewardesses were coming down the aisle with predinner drinks and other passengers were asking about the movie, he had the sickening realization that in a few hours he was going to have to call his bosses and tell them he was in Canada, not Italy.

A quick tour of Europe might be in order to provide an idea of what to expect in the way of English. As I said, virtually everyone in the Netherlands speaks English. They're the one people in Europe who seem surprised when I ask, as I almost always do when initiating any sort of conversation, whether they speak English. "Of course," they say. Holland is a small country with a long history of trading the world over; the Dutch love their language but no one else speaks it, so they learn to speak everyone else's. For the same reasons, most Scandinavians speak English well, too, although they make the mistake of trying to translate their own somewhat suspect humor, especially puns. A good example is the Norwegian shopping center developer who once told me the Vikings started the European consumer movement. What? "You know," he said gleefully. "They came to Europe to do a little shopping. Or was it chopping?"

A fair number of the French do speak English, but many of them hate to except among themselves. The worst are minor functionaries, like the clerks in tiny rail stations who obviously understand your questions in English but refuse to answer you except in rapid-fire French. They have the best language, they reason, so why not speak it? If you apologize profusely and prostrate yourself in front of these bureaucrats, expressing your eternal regret that you were so unlucky not to be born French and vowing to start learning as soon as possible, they may deign to take pity and give you the information you need in English.

Many Germans speak English, especially in the business world. It's rare to find a German senior manager, especially one involved in any sort of dealings with Americans, who does not speak good English. An American investment banker based in Germany tells a delightful story about getting on an elevator at a Houston hotel and listening to a pair of Germans bitch to each other about the slow progress of their negotiations to raise money from an American securities house. Never even considering that someone getting on the elevator with them in Houston might be able to understand what they were saying, the Germans were stunned speechless when the doors opened at the lobby and the American banker, in his fluent German, said, "Hey fellows, stop complaining. Come and see my people and we'll swing the deal for you right away." Fluent English speakers are not especially thick on the ground in Italian business, and even those who do speak well usually give a noncommittal, "Only a little," when asked if they speak English. But it doesn't matter. The rest of the world has been doing business with Italians for centuries by smiling and waving arms the same way the Italians do when talking to each other. It still works.

A major misconception among Americans coming to Europe is that Britain, at least, will be familiar territory. But British English is quite different from American English, from the use of words to the way they are pronounced. (Studies show, incidentally, that the modern American accent, particularly as used in the mid-Atlantic states such as Virginia, is not far off the way the British themselves spoke as recently as the last century. What we now call an English accent is something the English developed relatively recently, largely a result of the upper classes trying to sound posh and the lower classes mimicking them. Accents aside, there are still more than 3,000 examples, by one academic counting, of identical words that have different meanings on either side of the Atlantic. Our "elevator," for instance, is their "lift." Our "exit" is their "way out." Our "pants" are their "knickers" or "underpants," and their "trousers" are our "pants." Their "braces" are our "suspenders," and our "suspenders" are the sexy little straps that hold up women's nylons and have yet to be as widely replaced by pantyhose as they have in America. One of the most embarrassing linguistic tumbles awaiting many new American arrivals in Europe comes in casual conversation with Britons when they describe something that made them angry. "I got really pissed," the American says. The British listeners look a little shocked and perhaps even embarrassed that the American is confessing to getting what we would describe as drunk as a skunk.

As George Bernard Shaw said, the United States and the United Kingdom share a common culture that is divided only by their common language. But that's not quite right, either. There are many cultural differences, too. Ask any American to define The Special Relationship, and the American will either ask you what the hell you are talking about or mumble something about the eternal search for true love. Ask Britons about The Special Relationship and they know, as they have known since childhood, that you are talking about political, social, and commercial cooperation between their country and the United States. Forests in Norway have been felled to print the books and periodicals in Britain and elsewhere in Europe discussing The Special Relationship: what it is; why it's important to Britain past and future; why America needs it, too; and how other European countries are jealous of it.

In truth, many British people resent The Special Relationship because it reminds them that their country is no longer the world power it once was, and because our common language has created what they view as a cultural imperialism. Perhaps the most lasting practical view was taken after World War I by Woodrow Wilson, who scoffed at the then-new notion of The Special Relationship. There is no inherent, iron-clad transatlantic bond, Wilson said; Britain and America share certain ideals and interests, which may fluctuate. When the community of ideals and interests fades, he believed, so does the so-called Special Relationship. Indeed, while the British government has worked hard to foster the idea of the relationship in recent years – largely as a means of keeping an upper hand among its European allies-rivals – many U.S. expatriates who lived and worked in Britain during this period would testify to more examples of anti-American sentiment in Britain than anywhere else on the Continent. If the British government and British corporations really believed in The Special Relationship, they would not have allowed so many American Studies programs founded in the 1960s and 1970s to fall by the wayside for lack of funding – despite continuing student interest – in the 1980s and 1990s.

The British, whose humor is based on satire and irony, feel that we Americans are particularly humorless, partly because we don't always appreciate their satire and partly because so many of us never cultivate a comparable sense of irony. The dry understatement or outlandish overstatement, in either case dripping sarcasm, is not something that comes easily to many Americans. Moreover, we are perhaps not as willing to laugh at ourselves, either individually or as a nation, as they are. I found that one of the best ways to crack the famous British reserve at either end of the vaunted class system was to poke gentle fun, although nothing too vicious or so close to the truth that it hurt. "Oy, mate, you're taking the mickey outta me, aren't you?" the grinning fishmonger said in a workingman's pub. "I say, old man, you may be the first American I've ever met with a sense of irony," a publisher acknowledged over a game of bridge.

No matter what Europeans think of Americans in general, however, they are always ready to make exceptions for us and make friends with us, as individuals, particularly if we are in a position to help them make some money. Personal appeal and compatability can indeed grease the wheels of international commerce, so it's important to think not only about the common characteristics and culture of the people you're dealing with, but also to keep in mind their preconceptions of you as an American. Then you can give them what they expect in terms of positive traits and what they don't expect in terms of negative traits, a mixture of reassurance and pleasant surprise, to create a favorable impression and a convivial atmosphere for working together.

CHAPTER 3

—————— ♦ ♦ ♦ ——————

Playing the
American Card

Lee Nordlund started the 1980s in his native California as a college student with little more on his mind than the next big party. He started the 1990s in London as the head of a successful one-man cookie business and talking about his next big party: the one for his retirement, sometime before age 40. What happened to Nordlund during those ten years—mostly by accident, by trial and error, he is quick to admit—is a classic example of how an American became Europeanized and used his American background to carve out a niche for himself in Europe. His story is about how he played the American card, blunting the negative stereotypes and capitalizing on the positive stereotypes of himself as an American.

Growing up in Newport Beach, California, Lee Nordlund knew a lot more about surfing than the cookie business or, for that matter, any other kind of business. And, like most Americans, he knew next to nothing about Europe in general or Britain in particular. At Santa Clara University, Nordlund studied biology, but he had no apparent life plan in mind. His academic career was distinguished by the stink bombs he made in lab and the cat dissections he left in roommates' beds. One summer two British women, an aunt and her niece, came to stay with some neighbors. When Nordlund met the niece, a Yorkshire girl named Bridget Fairburn, he was smitten and so was she. They fell in love. During her last three weeks in America, they spent a lot of time together, trying to figure out how to keep the flame burning once she returned to Britain. Over the next five years they conducted a long-distance romance, she working in London and he in San Francisco, both of them saving as much money as they could and then spending it on flights back and forth to visit each other.

Nordlund would have moved to London permanently, but the British immigration laws, like those of most other European countries, prohibited him from living there without a job. Between trips to Britain, he worked in San Francisco at jobs such as running a doughnut shop, painting houses, and doing market-research interviews. There was little prospect of finding an American employer who would send him to London. He couldn't simply come to Britain and find a job on his own because British companies are prohibited by immigration laws from hiring anyone without the proper residency papers. The only way they can hire a foreigner is to persuade the government that the foreigner has some skill that cannot be provided by available British workers. Nordlund was faced with the old chicken and egg: Without a job, he couldn't get a residency permit; without a residency permit, he couldn't get a job. He could, of course, get the British equivalent of a "green card" by marrying Bridget, but they were reluctant to take the big plunge without at least really living together for a while first.

Nordlund realized he needed to try something completely different. He decided he had to start his own business. An American can legally start a business in Britain without a work or residency permit. Even with a business, however, it is illegal to pay yourself a salary or to claim legal residency. As a result, Nordlund spent most of three years in Britain as a tourist. He would leave the country every few months and, when coming back, tell the immigration officials that he made so many trips for love. When it became apparent from the sequence of arrival and departure stamps that he was spending most of his time in Britain—a giveaway for immigration officers on the lookout for aliens working illegally in the country—Nordlund resorted to another strategy used by illegal aliens in Britain for decades: the requested extension. When asking to stay in Britain longer than the six months allowed by the stamp in most tourists' passports, the alien mails his or her passport to the Home Office. Such requests for extensions are almost inevitably turned down, but it typically takes weeks or months for the Home Office to do the paperwork. During that time, the illegal alien can avoid deportation by claiming that the appeal for an extension has been requested and is under review; and besides, the Home Office hasn't returned the passport.

But immigration wasn't nearly as big a problem to Nordlund as the question of how he was going to make a living in Britain. He had to come up with a product that he could manufacture and market to fill a void in the British market. In a country where they don't use cream in ice cream or cheese in cheesecake, he figured something with a good, natural taste made of high-quality ingredients was bound to be popular. He asked himself what sort of things he missed from home when he was visiting Bridget in Britain. The most obvious choice was frozen yoghurt. He did a little preliminary research and learned that he could probably get the raw materials, find a place to manufacture and package the product, and then sell it either in his own shop or to other outlets. After thinking it over carefully and spending a stretch of several months in London, including a typically long, dark and dreary winter, he decided against frozen yoghurt. "It's too cold in Britain," he said. "Too wet. Too dark. There are too many days where people just don't feel like eating frozen yoghurt. I didn't feel like eating it myself, and I love the stuff."

The other thing Nordlund missed in Britain was a decent

chocolate chip cookie. As children, he and his three younger brothers often visited their Grandma Nordlund. She was a tiny, kindly woman, everybody's ideal of a good grandmother. "She would babysit for us and make her special chocolate chip cookies," Nordlund recalled. "My brothers and I loved those cookies so much that we would end up fighting over them." As the oldest brother, ten-year-old Lee took it upon himself to end the squabbling. He asked his grandmother if he could help her make more cookies — enough so there was plenty for all four growing boys. That's how he learned her secret recipe for chocolate chip cookies. Even in his college days as a party animal, Nordlund never lost his taste for Grandma's cookies. When she died, he inherited the family mantle as chief cookie maker and keeper of the secret recipe.

Years later, visiting Bridget in London while he was living and working in San Francisco, Nordlund loved the little bakeries that are a standard feature of every British village or neighborhood shopping district, the "high street." But he never could find a good chocolate chip cookie. Nothing he tasted began to approach Grandma's recipe. Nordlund's quest for a good British cookie became something of a joke with Bridget's family. When they visited her family home in Yorkshire, Nordlund began baking the cookies for her mother, father, and other assorted relatives. "They're a bunch of the usual blunt, no-nonsense Yorkshiremen," Nordlund said. "They didn't know what to make of me for a while. An American. And a boy who would go in the kitchen. That just wasn't done. But they loved the cookies, even if they weren't sure how to handle them at first." A Fairburn family tradition on weekend mornings was for Bridget's father to make coffee and deliver steaming cups to the women in their rooms. The first time Nordlund made his cookies, Bridget's father put one on each saucer with the cup of coffee. Nordlund had to take him aside and gently explain that chocolate chip cookies are usually eaten as dessert or snacks rather than as a breakfast eye opener.

So it was logical that, after rejecting the frozen yoghurt idea, Nordlund settled on cookies. He would give Britain its first proper chocolate chip cookie, made according to his Grandma's secret recipe, and then he would get rich, sell his company and retire, preferably by age 40. Unlike many of the Americans who transplant their concepts to the other side of the Atlantic, Nordlund knew nothing about his particular business. It's much more common for Americans, particularly professionals such as bankers, lawyers, and corporate managers, to find success in Europe because they know more about what they're doing than the Europeans who are trying to do the same thing. Not Nordlund. He had never even been in a commercial bakery. But he and quite a few other Americans have not let a little inexperience (or a lot) get in the way of a good idea for doing business in Europe. They see a gap and fill it, whether or not they know anything about the product or service beforehand.

For Nordlund, the first task was to re-create Grandma's recipe in Britain and then build up a supply of dough. You'd think that would be easy: Go to the nearest high street, buy the proper amounts of flour, butter, and chocolate chips, and go back to your flat and whip it all up according to Grandma's secret. But cooking ingredients throughout Europe are different: The flour isn't milled or graded quite the same as American flour, the butter isn't quite the same as American butter, and the chocolate, especially, isn't the same as the chocolate that goes into American chocolate chips. First, it's all but impossible to find real chocolate chips; they are among the staples, like Bisquick, tortillas, and popcorn, that American expatriates living in Europe usually ask visiting friends and relatives to bring them from the States. Second, the chocolate most widely available in Europe is made from African cocoa beans, while the chocolate in America is usually made from South American cocoa beans. Nordlund found the African-based chocolate quite flavorful, delicate, and smooth, but it lost some of that flavor when baked into cookies.

45

Nordlund was determined that his British cookies were going to taste just like the ones Grandma Nordlund used to make. So he spent his life savings, about $12,000, to buy six tons of chocolate chips in the States. But none of the shippers or warehouses he talked to in Britain knew anything about chocolate chips or could give Nordlund any assurances that they would move or store the chips at less than 72 degrees, the temperature at which they would melt and not only lose their consistency but some of their flavor. A friend of Bridget's who had once been in the wine trade suggested that Nordlund contact a British company that specialized in importing California wines, which were also shipped and warehoused at cool temperatures. The wine shippers were bemused, but reacted favorably to Nordlund's plea for help.

This was the first time he played his own particular American card in direct negotiations with Europeans. Nordlund presented himself to the wine shippers, for whom his relatively small, probably one-time order was no doubt more trouble than it was worth, as an earnest young guy, nice but naive, who had a dream and needed some help with it. He wasn't demanding, he wasn't a know-it-all, he wasn't aggressive. He wasn't what many Europeans regard as American, in other words. And it worked. The wine shippers not only agreed to help Nordlund import his chocolate chips, but let him store them in one of the coolest corners in their old Victorian-era, thick-walled brick warehouse in London's Docklands.

Nordlund hauled one box of chips back to the small flat he and Bridget shared in north London and stuck them up on a high closet shelf that he figured was the warmest spot in the flat. During the more than six months that the chips were stored in the wine warehouse, London had several spells of unseasonably warm weather, with temperatures up in the mid-80s. Every morning during the warm spells, Nordlund would climb up, peer into his box of chips and breathe a sigh of relief that they hadn't started melting. Every couple of weeks or so, he would

46

make the long journey on the Underground across London to the Docklands, where he would inspect his stacks of chocolate chip boxes. "It was mostly just to let the people there know that I was really concerned," Nordlund remembered. "They seemed to like the idea of me coming around, and the chips were kind of a novelty item to them, something special in with all that wine. I'd always open up a box and hand the chips around to the warehouse boys, partly just to say thanks and partly because they wouldn't want to steal any if I gave them some."

Meanwhile, for a couple of hundred dollars, Nordlund bought an off-the-shelf company title from the Department of Trade and Industry. Using an old family name from his mother's side, and adding the word "jewel" simply because he though it added some class, Nordlund became Younglove Jewel Cookies Ltd. "Other than registering the company name, really my only dealings with the government were in filling out a few papers to get the chocolate chips shipped in," Nordlund said. Through much of 1986 and 1987, Nordlund experimented in the kitchen of his and Bridget's little flat with his American chocolate chips and with various British ingredients. "I wasn't going to be satisfied until I had the taste of Grandma's cookies exactly right," he said. When he was finally satisfied, he began looking around for a bakery that would let him mix his dough in commercial quantities. He literally started going door to door, and line by line through the phone book, in search of premises he could rent. "I think my American accent helped on the phone," he said. "Most of these small bakeries weren't used to dealing with Americans, and receptionists thinking I must be somebody important often put me right through to the boss."

But no one seemed to be interested in renting out space to someone they didn't know, someone they saw as either a complete novice who might wreck their kitchens or as a potential competitor who might someday take business away from them. Finally, after dozens of phone calls and explanations, Nordlund found two Englishmen who ran a small bakery in Holloway, a distinctly untrendy working-class area of north London. He told them about his Grandma and about Bridget and that he wanted to borrow their mixers and ovens at night, when they were closed. He said he could pay a little, but not much. The two bakers, perhaps remembering their own struggles, agreed to let Nordlund borrow their bakery – for free. It was clear that they liked Nordlund personally, his lack of pretense, his eagerness to learn, his basic plea for help for a well-meaning but ill-equipped underdog who was pursuing a dream that was far-fetched to most people but undeniably noble to a baker. Months later, Nordlund figured out what may have been the real reason for the kindness. One of the partners pulled Nordlund aside and quietly told of how he had been to the States and loved it; his secret dream – not even his partner knew it – was to sell out someday and move to the States himself. The baker told Nordlund that if and when he made his move, perhaps Nordlund could help him get started in the States, or put him in touch with people who could help him get a job or start a new bakery.

Since Nordlund had never operated or even seen a commercial kitchen before launching himself in the cookie business, the bakers had to show him how to use the big mixers and ovens they used to pump out their bread, scones, pastries, and muffins. Almost every night for six months, Nordlund arrived at the bakery at around midnight to mix 300-pound batches of what would become Younglove Jewel brand cookies. The proportions for Grandma's cookies changed considerably from the one-pound or two-pound batches Nordlund had made in his kitchen, so he had to start over in getting the measurements just right for the recipe. And the metric conversions on those large quantities were murder for a guy who had never paid that much attention in math class. When Nordlund finally did get the recipe right, he began packaging the cookie dough in 22-pound batches in white plastic buckets. The two bakers loaning him their facilities came to like Nordlund a lot. He always left the kitchen cleaner than when he came ("very un-British, they

48

really appreciated it," Nordlund laughed), and he got in the habit of surprising the bakers with the occasional gift, usually a bottle or two of good port. When Nordlund wondered aloud where he could store his mixed cookie dough, they made space for him in their own freezer – again, for free.

While Nordlund was getting his recipe right, several new American-style cookie outlets started springing up around London, including Mrs. Fields and Millie's. At first he thought this could be disastrous – somebody had beaten him to the punch. But the new arrivals turned out to be a boon because they showed Nordlund what not to do. He originally planned to start a shop or two where he could sell the cookies himself, emphasizing the American connections. But the new American-style outlets weren't doing all that well, perhaps partly because bakeries are so common in Europe; every neighborhood or village high street has at least one that sells fresh bread, cakes, muffins, scones, pastries, and so forth. Mrs. Fields was a novelty in the States, but in Europe it was just another new bakery shop, except that it didn't have the range of choice offered by the older shop down the road where the customers had been buying their bread for years and probably knew the names of the baker, the salesgirl, and their respective children.

Another drawback for the American cookie shops was that most of them were in individual shops on high streets rather than in big U.S.-style malls where shoppers are more likely to stroll in for a couple of cookies while making their way from one store to another. There simply aren't many big indoor U.S.-style malls in Europe, and the shopping patterns – and eating patterns – are much different. Americans have become grazers. When Europeans want a snack, on the other hand, they are more likely to go into a cafe, sit down, and order tea and cake that they can eat with a knife and fork. While Nordlund was trying to figure out how to market his cookies, he saw the new Mrs. Fields and Millie's outlets struggling with these unfamiliar tastes and habits. Even in the busiest shopping areas, those outlets found business irregular, often depending on the weather much more than they did in the States. Some of Millie's struggling outlets expanded into sandwiches and cakes and other noncookie items; they were designed to bring in customers, but also diluted the brand's special American identity.

Nordlund decided against trying to run his own shop. Even if the Mrs. Fields and Millie's outlets had been going well, he would have had to persuade a British bank to lend him the money to rent and fit out a shop. It would be better if he could keep the business as small and self-contained as possible. He decided against trying to market the cookies as "American," and even decided against trying to sell them to the general public under the Younglove Jewel name. Instead, he would concentrate on selling the dough wholesale to British bakeries, supermarkets, and specialty stores that could then bake the cookies on site and sell them as their own. In 1987 and 1988, Nordlund spent several more months making a new pitch on the phone and in person, this time to bakery chains and supermarket groups.

A desk in his living room became company headquarters, and from there Nordlund spent all day every weekday on the phone, going through phone books and retail directories, talking to receptionists and secretaries, trying to get the name and number of the person who had the authority to say yes, we'll try your cookies. His pitch never wavered: "Hi, I'm Lee Nordlund from Younglove Jewel Cookies. We make the best cookies in the country. . . ." He never needed to say he was American. With his accent, never affected by all those years with an Englishwoman, any further identification would have been redundant. When given the chance, Nordlund would tell the prospective buyer about his romance with Bridget, about his Grandma's secret recipe and about the advantages of baking his cookies on site and selling them still warm out of the oven. The main *American* attitude he tried to get across, however, was his unflinching, unfailing confidence in the quality of his product.

"I was genuinely naive, and I couldn't see trying to fool anyone," Nordlund reflected later. "I thought it was important to try to be friendly, though not too familiar." As an American, you can be a little more relaxed. You aren't necessarily expected to be as formal with Europeans as they might be with each other. Nordlund found that many of the British people he met "loved to think they had the corner on superiority, at least as far as Americans go. I let them have it. I didn't need for them to think I was smarter than they were or knew more than they did. I just wanted to impress them with the quality of my product and how much I believed in it." This is a popular tack used by successful Americans in Europe.

Many Americans are too quick to tell how much they know; others are more successful in admitting how much they don't know. One disciple of the latter strategy is Tom Swayne, who in the course of a few short years rose from management trainee to the head of European corporate finance for Chase Manhattan bank. After his experiences in the heady halcyon days of the corporate takeover boom, junk-bond financing, and big-money stock flotations in New York in the mid-1980s, he came to London loaded with expertise and financial products that many European corporations were eager to use to enhance their balance sheets. Yet even in situations where Swayne was seen as the investment banker who had the answers and was calling the shots, he looked for – and found – situations where the Europeans could teach him something, from employee relations to accounting methods unknown back in the States. "I try to strike a balance," Swayne said. "I want the Europeans to be aware that I know the way into town from the airport, but I don't want to act like the big American coming in and telling them they should do everything my way. It should be a partnership, with real give and take."

In British baking circles, Lee Nordlund found that as a foreigner he could ask more questions than a native who might fret about losing face; unlike Britons, whose greatest fear was showing their ignorance, he encouraged his business contacts to offer instruction and advice along the way. He found his aw-shucks willingness to listen to them to be one of the best ways of getting the British to warm up to him personally. In effect, like any salesman, Nordlund was selling himself, his own personality, as much as his cookies. That personality was usually received among his prospective customers in one of two ways. Some were skeptical of him because they are wary of all Americans, whom they regard as too excitable, too enthusiastic. Others liked the way Nordlund seemed to be caught up in his business and its promise; all they had to do was look around at the IBM computers, McDonald's arches, Ford automobiles, and Hollywood movies to be reminded that so many American ideas do work in Europe, and do make money for the Europeans who latch onto them.

In his first calls to bakery chains and supermarkets, the naturally soft-spoken Nordlund sounded nervous over the phone. That's because he *was* nervous. But many buyers and other executives responded to his unease and to the quiet halting voice that was such a contrast to braying American tourists or whip-like retorts on American TV programs. Nordlund found some potential customers trying to put him at ease. Instead of brushing him off, some allowed him to finish his pitch: ". . . I'll sell you the dough, and you can just scoop it out and bake it on site. . . . Think of the beauty of it, freshly baked cookies, the finest cookies in the country, right there in your bakery. . . . Yes, I know you already sell cookies, but they're not as good as mine. This is an old family recipe I got from my Grandma; I even brought the chocolate chips, tons of them, from America so the taste would be just right. . . ."

A few buyers agreed to try the samples, and Nordlund believes it may have been just to get him off the phone. By this time, however, the oven at his and Bridget's flat had given out. Consequently, his first sales samples were baked in an elderly neighbor's kitchen in a stove that appeared to be even more elderly. Nordlund had to use packing tape to keep the oven door closed. When a buyer turned him down in a first phone call, Nordlund rang back a couple days later and pleaded for a chance to meet face to face. "I found my American enthusiasm more effective in person," he said. "They wanted to say no again to even trying the cookies, but it was much harder for them when I was right there." Nordlund told his targeted customers that everyone in Britain who had ever tried his cookies liked them; he didn't volunteer that the sum of that market research was among Bridget's family and the couple's friends in London.

A number of buyers said they were interested, but virtually all of them wanted to know where else Nordlund was selling his cookies. When he told them they would be the first, they all balked. Nordlund realized that in Britain's insular, island economy, where consumer decisions were grounded in generations of limited, conservative choices, it was much more difficult to launch a new product than in the States, where people are relatively willing to entertain new ideas. In Britain, and indeed throughout Europe, people are more likely to say they won't try a new product simply because they've never bought it before and they've always bought another brand. Americans, on the other hand, are inclined to try something new simply because it *is* new. "In the United States, we have the notion that it is better to have tried and failed than never to have tried at all," Nordlund observed. "In Europe, it's better not to risk failure. They think they're probably going to fail, so why risk trying? In the States, everyone wants to be the leader with a new product or service. In Europe, they're afraid to be the first. They just say no, they've never done it this new way, they'll stick with the old way they've always done things." A related factor is that American society, so mobile and so fluid, yet with such a broadly common cultural underpinning, is more used to dealing with strangers. A stranger with a good idea will probably get a fair hearing in America; in Europe the same stranger might not be listened to at all.

As a stranger trying to crack the European facade of known faces and familiar brands, Nordlund realized that he was going to have to get one big-name, well-known customer before anyone else was going to buy his cookies. He began at the top with Harrods, the giant department store in the Knightsbridge district of London,' and Fortnum & Mason, a somewhat smaller store on Piccadilly with a smaller selection of specialty food and nonfood items but a similarly upmarket clientele. Instead of Harrods' "the best of everything" philosophy, Fortnum's has more of a "the best of the best things" attitude. When he approached Harrods, Nordlund found the famous Food Halls in disarray because of a massive management turnover. He decided to concentrate on Fortnum & Mason, where the entire ground floor is dedicated to champagne and other French wines, Russian caviar, Belgian chocolate, ready-to-heat-up salmon pies, quail eggs, and other such delicacies. Near the Fortnum tea and snack cafe, there is also a bakery counter. For Nordlund, all his dreams came down to whether or not he could get Younglove Jewel cookies on that counter.

After repeated attempts, he finally got the chief food buyer for Fortnum & Mason on the phone. The man was polite but uninterested. "We do everything in-house," he told Nordlund, who took this as an indication that Fortnum made its own cookie dough. Nordlund persisted, however, before the head buyer cut him off again: "Our head baker gets all the dough we need from suppliers." End of conversation. Nordlund hung up, dejected, and then thought again about what the head buyer had said. If they did everything in-house, why was the head baker buying dough from suppliers? He tried the head baker and eventually got him on the phone. "I've tasted your cookies and I know they're good," he told the man, "but mine are better, and I can supply them cheaper than you can make them yourself." There was a pause, and the man replied, "OK, bring some in and let me have a look at them." Nordlund ran over to the neighbor's, taped the oven shut, and baked up a couple of dozen cookies. When they were finished, he took the Underground to Piccadilly and made it to Fortnum's before the doors closed for the day. The baker took a bite, chewed for a couple of moments, and said, "Not bad. All right, tell you what. We'll put these out tomorrow and see how they sell." Nordlund was astonished, but quickly handed over the remaining 23 cookies, shook hands with the baker and left. Outside, it occurred to Nordlund that a friend of Bridget's worked in a nearby shop. Nordlund went into the shop, found the guy, and gave him all the money he had in his pocket, leaving just enough for a ticket home on the Underground. It was only a few pounds, but it was enough for the guy to spread around among his co-workers. The next day, they took turns wandering into Fortnum & Mason, studying the selection of cookies, choosing a Younglove Jewel, taking a bite, and telling the girl at the counter how good it was. The next day the head baker placed Fortnum's first order for Younglove Jewel.

In the following months dozens of potential outlets that had said no the first time changed their minds when Nordlund approached them again and told them that the cookies were selling well at Fortnum & Mason. Even though they hadn't bought from him the first time around, the fact that he was an American—and so positive about his product—had made many of them remember Nordlund in favorable terms. They were ready to reconsider when he gave them a new reason to buy: the fact that someone else, particularly someone as prestigious as Fortnum & Mason, had taken the plunge and proved that his quality was everything claimed. Several supermarket chains, including one with 160 stores, began selling Younglove Jewel cookies as their own in-house brand. "All of a sudden I was legitimate," Nordlund said. "Not only was I legitimate, I was suddenly an expert in the field. I started opening up my phone conversations with the Fortnum & Mason angle."

In the five years he ran his business in London, Nordlund never considered raising his prices for Fortnum & Mason, even though he actually lost money on his sales there. It was a loss leader that Nordlund believes let him sell at least eight times as many cookies as he would have without it. And once the Fortnum connection began getting him in doors, those doors stayed open. The only customer to stop re-ordering was an American-style restaurant, a place that Nordlund had counted on for good sales for years to come. Puzzled, he asked why they no longer wanted his dough. The manager eventually, reluctantly, told him: The waiters and waitresses, mostly young Americans taking a break from their college studies in the States, couldn't keep their hands off the cookies. The Younglove Jewels reminded them so much of the cookies they used to get at home that they were eating them all before they could be sold to customers.

There were few other dim spots in Nordlund's budding young business, however. The supermarket chain with 160 outlets has gone on to ask him to experiment with other American-style products for them, including muffins and fudge and other types of cookies. The chain has even put him on retainer as a consultant for producing its own British-style biscuits. "They like it that I'm relaxed, that I don't try to tell them their business," Nordlund said. "And they like it that Americans are known for working hard. That's one of the reasons, I'm sure, they wanted me as an adviser even though I know absolutely nothing about British biscuits. They know I'm a perfectionist and that I'll probably work harder and longer hours than anybody they might hire in this country. The person who is only an average worker in the States comes to Europe and is seen as having an extraordinary commitment to the task."

As business got better and Nordlund's confidence grew, he found himself playing the American card more and more —

usually at the instigation of his customers. Many of his customers, especially when they got to know him a bit, wanted to ask Nordlund about America and especially about American politics. They didn't understand this or that about American politics, in much the same way Americans cannot comprehend European politics, and they frequently asked Nordlund for an interpretation. Being from California, Nordlund was presumed to know everything about movies and movie stars. Fortunately, he had once shaken hands with John Wayne, and that anecdote served him well with a number of clients. Some customers asked about American sports, and especially American football (just plain "football" to a European means soccer), which in recent years has become one of the fastest-growing spectator sports in Europe. Nordlund, who routinely spends time in a new customer's bakery demonstrating how to handle his dough and bake the cookies, found that one head baker only wanted to talk about the National Football League playoffs. When the guy couldn't understand how quarterbacks can throw so accurately, Nordlund used loaves of bread to show the guy how to grip the ball. They ended up running passing drills, firing whole-wheat spirals to young bakery apprentices sent out on post patterns; they would head for the oven and then cut behind the mixer.

Things progressed for Nordlund's business. He stopped making deliveries personally on the Underground, and his friends no longer had to worry about being recruited to help when someone ordered more than two of the 22-pound buckets of dough. He stopped making the dough himself in the middle of the night in the little bakery in Holloway; a larger, more modern wholesale bakery in Yorkshire, not far from Bridget's family home, began mass-producing the dough to Nordlund's specifications and took over the shipping, too. Naturally, several large food corporations, both European and American, noticed Younglove Jewel's success and began sniffing around the company. After several months of bidding and negotiations, Nordlund sold his company to the British subsidiary of an

American bakery. Besides the cash payment, he was given a contract as a consultant that will give him a comfortable long-term semiretirement . . . until he starts another company, probably in an entirely different field.

Other companies are seeking him out as a consultant, too. One, for example, has asked him to help design the packaging for hamburgers, despite his up-front warning that he knows nothing about hamburgers and nothing about retail packaging. Nordlund has become a successful American businessman in Europe, and as such his advice is sought on anything remotely perceived as being American. Meanwhile, after living together in London for three years, Nordlund and Bridget were also sure that their personal relationship was going to be even more successful than Younglove Jewel. They got married, and Nordlund's immigration problems disappeared when he slipped on the wedding ring. As the spouse of a British citizen, he became legally entitled to work and live there while maintaining his U.S. citizenship. He played the American card and won.

CHAPTER 4

————————— ♦ ♦ ♦ —————————

Cultural Transfers

Brian Dwyer leaned back in his chair and waited for an answer to replace the British official's self-important smirk. Dwyer, president of Venus Wafers, Inc., a small Massachusetts manufacturer of high-quality crackers, had asked if he could keep the words "All Natural" on his cracker boxes when he started exporting to Europe. No, he was finally informed in clipped British bureaucratese; regulations forbid calling any food product "natural" unless it can be dug directly out of the ground or picked off a vine, bush, or tree. "I'm sorry, Mr. Dwyer," the official said from behind his expansive desk. "But your crackers simply don't grow on trees."

That was one of many stumbling blocks before Dwyer brought his crackers to the European market. "When you're a smaller company, it's scary to think about exporting," he recalled. "People in other countries talk different, the money looks different and you read in *The Wall Street Journal* about other companies losing $15 million on the exchange rate. We realized this was a big gamble. But with the consumption trends in Europe, it was worth the risk."

59

Venus Wafers, with annual sales of about $5 million at the time, began exploring the European market for the same reason as other U.S. companies both large and small: to grow through filling a market gap on the other side of the Atlantic. The company had been quietly selling its crackers and cookies in the northeastern United States for nearly 60 years, ever since it was founded by Napoleon Barmakian, the son of Armenian immigrants. The company's cornerstone is its whole-wheat wafer, similar to Armenian "cracker bread," but smaller and thus more convenient for snacks and *hors d'oeuvres*. Over the years, even after the founding Barmakian was succeeded as principal owner by his son Ed, the company's marketing focused on the quality and nutritional value of its crackers. Venus never tried to compete with the big cracker companies, instead remaining content with its tidy premium-priced niche. Ninety percent of its sales were in the Northeast, 70 percent in and around Boston. But the manufacturing-driven Barmakians, who had always found ways to keep production costs down while maintaining quality, found themselves being squeezed by the high-powered marketing of the bigger cracker companies. They couldn't spend millions on advertising and promotion to fight for supermarket display space alongside big brands such as Nabisco, Keebler, Sunshine, Weston, and Wasa, the five companies that control 90 percent of the U.S. market.

Dwyer became president in 1985, and over the next three years expanded Venus into other big U.S. markets such as New York, Philadelphia, St. Louis, Dallas, Atlanta, and San Francisco. Sales rose from $1 million to $5 million. Dwyer realized, however, that further domestic growth would be difficult, so he looked abroad. He took some samples to a trade fair in Cologne, Germany, and the reception from European distributors, wholesalers, and retailers "was so positive it blew my mind," he said.

Americans are used to eating crackers such as the market leader, Nabisco's Ritz, as a standalone snack. But Venus wafers are different. Rather than everyday fare, Venus crackers — crisper, drier, and "savoury rather than sweet," according to Dwyer — are typically purchased by Americans only for special occasions. "In Europe, the reaction was just the opposite," Dwyer said. "The *hors d'oeuvre* is more a part of the culture. It's not unusual for the upscale consumer to come home every day after work and have *hors d'oeuvres* before dinner. It's more civilized." Dwyer believed Venus wafers could fill a gap between two of the staples of the European *hors d'oeuvre* table: heavy, crisp melba toast and the crumbly, frail soda cracker.

Potential importers in Britain, France, Germany, and Italy expressed the most interest in Venus wafers. Dwyer decided that his first overseas target would be Britain, because it is geographically and culturally closest to the United States. (About half the American businesses making the plunge into Europe decide to begin with Britain, largely because of the common language.) Dwyer was also encouraged by his market research. Britons consume three times as many cookies and crackers per capita as Americans, but the market penetration in Britain, as in the rest of Europe, is at best 60 percent of households. In contrast, 98 percent of American households make regular cookie and cracker purchases. (Toilet paper, at 99-plus percent, is the only consumer product with higher U.S. household penetration.) Despite a few minor hiccups such as the "All Natural" labeling, Dwyer found Britain to be a receptive market. He has since left the company to become a consultant for other companies considering exporting to Europe, but Venus continues to prosper in Britain. The company would like to expand to other European countries and may eventually begin manufacturing in Europe, too. It's entirely possible, Dwyer said, that Venus could ultimately sell more crackers in Europe than it does in the States.

Venus is an example of a cultural transfer — the selling of an American product or service in Europe. Typically, cultural transfers that have made the successful jump in recent years are based on one or more of the three things that seem ultimately American to most Europeans. Those three things are quality, service, and fun. Americans are supposed to be innovative, exciting, friendly, and occasionally a bit self-indulgent – and so are American products and services. As that renowned American candelabra-and-rhinestone philosopher Liberace once said, "Too much of a good thing is *wonderful.*" American products such as Levi's jeans or Venus crackers may cost more than the local competition, but they're worth it to Europeans because of the quality they deliver and because of the lifestyle statement they make about the person wearing the jeans or serving the wafers. That's why the companies that have made successful transatlantic cultural transfers – companies as diverse as McDonald's, the Gap, Toys 'R' Us, and Merrill Lynch – have retained their strong American identities. Their shops and offices may have French or Spanish people selling their burgers, jeans, toys, or pension plans, but there is never any doubt that those products are backed by the quality and service that made them successful in America in the first place.

Why is the laundry in my London neighborhood named the American Dry Cleaners, even though it has absolutely no American connections? Why does virtually every European city feature burger joints with American names, such as Stars and Stripes Hamburgers, when they are so bad that an American couldn't be running them? Why is the big chain of British DIY (do-it-yourself home repair) stores named Texas Homecare? It's because quality and service are associated with anything that appears remotely American.

It's not hard to see why Europeans are so impressed with even the most minimal levels of American service, such as supermarket clerks who help bag your groceries. I've had European shopgirls keep me waiting, not just for a few seconds but for minutes, while they talk to their friends on the phone in an otherwise empty shop. You clear your throat and step into their line of vision. They turn their backs and continue the conversation. In Spain, I once stood at a bank window for ten minutes while the three tellers, all sitting down, had a contest to see who could smoke a cigarette the slowest. The loser resignedly had to wait on me. In an Italian post office with only one window open, I waited in line behind four people to buy some stamps. When I got to the window and asked for my stamps, the clerk said I had to go to the next window, which had no one behind it at the time. I stepped over and rang the bell for service. I waited at the empty window until the clerk at the first window finished helping three more people who had been behind me in the line. When no one else was in that line, she popped over to my window and greeted me as if I was an old customer – which in a way I was, I suppose. She sold me the stamps with a winning smile; it simply never occurred to her to sell me the stamps before waiting on the people behind me.

It's also not hard to see how American service can pay off in Europe. A good example is an American broker for one of the big Wall Street securities houses, a man who was based in London and had been traveling throughout Europe on business for several years. He was recently sent to take over and shape up the firm's Hamburg office, which had not been performing the way it should. The American, fluent in German, imme- diately set about reviewing the German clients' portfolios and the files of the German account executives who had been ser- vicing them. He was appalled at the cavalier manner in which some of the brokers in the office had been treating – or, rather, ignoring – their customers and their accounts. He noted that there had been a complaint from a client who happened to be an elderly woman, as so many German investors are. (Germany is one of the most matriarchal societies in Europe, and many of the investment decisions are made by wives. This, perhaps in connection with the typical high-cholesterol German diet, has left Germany with an unusual proportion of its private invest- ment capital in the hands of wealthy and astute widows.)

The American telephoned the woman at her home, introduced himself, apologized for the poor service, and promised it would get better. He stunned the woman by asking if he could come and see her. He further stunned her by offering to come the following day, early in the morning, even though it was a national holiday and a six-hour drive away. She agreed, he showed up, they went through her small portfolio and together mapped out an investment strategy that promised to yield both immediate and long-range benefits. The old lady was so impressed that she gave the American more business, turning her account from small to altogether respectable. She also began recommending to her rich widow friends that they call the new American. Meanwhile, back at the ranch, he sent a message through his office by firing the German who had been so lazy with the old lady's account, in spite of the fact that Germany's employment laws typically make it cheaper to keep unproductive employees on board rather than fire them.

In the business world, success breeds imitators. That's why American management training and education, from the MBA to Filofax-style organization and time management, have become common throughout Europe as Europeans embrace the concept of American business efficiency and methodology. Similarly, the financial techniques and products developed in the States in the 1970s and 1980s, from financial futures trading to mezzanine-level, junk-bond financing to management buyouts, are examples of concepts that were exported successfully to Europe. Indeed, the takeover expertise of big American financial institutions became critical to Europe Inc., with the rash of corporate reorganizing and repositioning in anticipation of the European Community's single market. American firms typically top the league tables for advising on takeovers in Europe. Even in situations where one European company is trying to take over another, it's not unusual for both to rely on one or more American investment houses and law firms for their advice.

The chairman of one leading European home-appliance company told me that he received several offers a week from

64

American securities and investment institutions that had, completely on their own, outlined various strategies for his company to buy other firms, divest part of its own operations, or otherwise restructure itself. He never asked for this advice, but the one common thread was that the deal was always designed to make him a multimillionaire many times over. (After successfully taking over several other companies, his company was itself finally taken over. Suffice it to say he did not suffer personally in any of the deals.)

That chairman and other European executives typically say the same thing about the American houses: Unlike the old-line, traditional European investment banks, the Americans went out and got the business, not only through their ideas but also through their willingness to participate with their own money. Another attraction of the U.S. firms was their ability to keep the confidentiality lid on negotiations until the deal was unveiled. There are numerous other examples of professions where American expertise has been welcomed in Europe, including the building of the Channel Tunnel. It is always billed as an "Anglo-French" project, but in truth much of the money came from American and Japanese banks, and much of the management team overseeing the actual construction came on loan from Bechtel, the big U.S. construction company that had the necessary expertise to actually run a project on a scale that neither the English nor the French had ever seen.

Many of the American products that have been transferred successfully to Europe are relatively common, everyday items, such as Venus's crackers and wafers, discussed at the beginning of this chapter, or Lee Nordlund's chocolate chip cookies, discussed in the previous chapter. Certainly one of the next big growth sectors in Europe is going to be paper products. Americans currently consume 44 pounds of table napkins, kitchen towels, toilet paper, tissues, sanitary napkins, paper plates, and other paper products per person per year. In Europe it's a mere 17 pounds per person. Even if Europeans are more conservation-minded and willing to recycle than Americans, that figure is sure to increase. Europeans follow most broad American consumer and lifestyle trends, and the big paper companies — not only American but French and Swedish, too — are aiming their marketing guns at Europe to help create a demand that will transform such products from unknown or luxury items to necessities in hundreds of thousands of households. Every time my five-year-old and her kindergarten mates in London complain about the harsh toilet paper at their school and in public restrooms at the zoo, museums, and amusement parks, I am more sure that in 20 years or so Europeans will be buying supersoft, American-style toilet paper for their own homes.

Some products are transferable to Europe simply because they are uniquely American. Authenic old American clothing, such as high school letter jackets and bowling shirts, can fetch outlandish prices in trendy second-hand shops in London, Paris, and Stockholm. And I know a Texan, an amateur pilot, who lives in a picturesque little Welsh village except for the few weeks a year he spends working — returning to the States, buying rare old American airplanes, and then flying them back to Europe where he sells them for twice as much at auctions. Sometimes Americans bringing their products to Europe are surprised at the demand. What's mundane in America can be exotic in Europe. Chrysler expected to sell about 5,000 of its cars in Europe when it kicked off a new export program in 1988. Instead, it sold 35,000, and Lee Iacocca started spending more time on the other side of the Atlantic examining the possibilities of joint ventures with European carmakers. Another example is American beer. From Britain to Germany, from Denmark to Holland to Czechoslovakia, Europeans have been doing a pretty good job of brewing their own beers for centuries. Yet Budweiser, Schlitz, and Miller are treated throughout much of Europe as upmarket imported beers, drunk by young trendy types who reject the traditional beers of their homelands simply because that's what the older generation—their fathers, uncles, and bosses—have always drunk.

Typically, what the Europeans are buying is not just American clothing, food, or methods. They are buying into the American lifestyle, the idea that everything, from work to sports to shopping to eating out, can and should be at least a little bit enjoyable. Bob Payton, a former Chicago advertising executive who was posted to London, liked living abroad so much he decided to quit and stay on when the ad firm asked him to come back to the States. Looking around for a way to make a living, he decided to open a Chicago-style pizza parlor in London, not because it was a good way to make a buck, but because—like Lee Nordlund and his grandma's chocolate chip cookies—Payton liked pizza and couldn't find a decent deep-dish pie anywhere in Britain. As it turned out, honest-to-goodness pizza, served up with smiles, bootleg NFL films on the big-screen TV, and a jukebox full of rollicking old 1960s rock 'n' roll and soul music, became a very good way to make a buck. Payton eventually expanded to more than two dozen American-theme restaurants, serving not only pizza but ribs, burgers, and other U.S. specialties, throughout Europe. Payton always says that what he is selling isn't just food, but "the whole American deal, the whole lifestyle" of good food in a fun setting.

This American penchant for mixing food and fun and business and leisure is a driving force behind some of the most successful transatlantic transfers in recent years. A fine example is the way Europeans have finally, now that they are being offered the chance, embraced the concept of big American-style shopping centers. During World War II, many downtown European shopping districts, or "high streets," were bombed. As a result, local and national governments developed postwar policies aimed at rebuilding, reviving and keeping alive those high streets. This was done largely through zoning restrictions that put roadblocks in the way of anyone foolish enough to contemplate a large edge-of-town shopping mall. All the European burghers had to do was point to the American experience and show how mall development had created a "doughnut" effect in U.S. cities, where shopping and commercial life thrived in the suburbs while the downtown shriveled and decayed. To the Europeans, the "doughnut" shape was all that mattered; they hadn't let Hitler ruin their tidy little downtowns, and they weren't going to let American malls do it, either. It didn't matter that the malling of America had helped the overall economy in many U.S. cities that were outgrowing their cramped downtowns.

Heightening the misgivings was the fact that European countries are older, smaller, and more densely populated and developed. Even if the government authorities had agreed to allow developers to build big U.S.-style shopping centers, outlying land was typically less available and more expensive than in North America. Finally, everyone seemed to believe that European consumers are inherently different from Americans; instead of a day at the mall or a big weekly grocery shop, Europeans were believed to be committed to their age-old patterns of going out each day, walking, carrying a basket, or pulling a wagon, to fetch their fresh bread, cheese, vegetables, meat, and household products at the various bakeries, butcher shops, and greengrocers lining their nearest high streets.

The old view was shattered in 1986 with the opening of the Metro Centre, a huge American-style regional mall built by John Hall, the Scottish developer who fell in love with American enthusiasm in a Cleveland elevator (Chapter 3). Previously, Hall's biggest projects had been gas stations and small commercial buildings in Spain and Portugal. For his mega-mall, Hall selected an old slagheap site outside Gateshead, a fading smoke-stack town in northern England that, along with its sister city Newcastle, was gripped by unemployment and general economic malaise. The area had been designated an enterprise zone by the government of former Prime Minister Margaret

Thatcher, meaning that Hall could get the land cheap because no one else wanted it. Through sheer force of personality, Hall convinced builders, investors, and retailers that his mall would work. And it has.

The Metro Centre was an instant success, bringing in tens of thousands of shoppers a day to its more than 250 stores and restaurants, with each visitor spending an average of $70 per visit. The Metro Centre also brought to Europe the American concept of combining shopping with leisure in the form of cinemas, amusement parks, games arcades, boating lakes, ski hills, golf courses, roller rinks, and swimming pools. Now similar regional malls are springing up elsewhere in Europe, and the American leisure concepts are being incorporated in many old high-street shopping precincts. One European wrinkle, however, is that even the biggest, most glitzy malls will be anchored not only by the usual big department stores, but also by at least one big grocery store. A middle-aged woman loading bags and bags of groceries into her car in the parking lot outside a new mall insisted that she did not miss the old daily high-street routine. "Are you crazy?" she replied. "Now that we have a mall on the edge of town, I get in my car and drive there once a week to get everything I need. I save hours and hours of time. I could never even find a place to park on the high street. Why would I want to go back to that?"

Sports is another area where the American influence is being felt in Europe. To many Europeans, the idea of spectator sports was going to an event and watching the runners, cars, or horses go round and round. They clapped politely or cheered properly for the winners. And that was pretty much it. No cheerleaders, no marching bands, no mascots doing slapstick in stupid costumes, and probably very little food or drink, either. The only exception to all this dullness was soccer, where fans at any given game might form themselves into rival gangs of hooligans, get drunk, literally piss in each other's pockets because arenas never had adequate toilets, and then beat each

69

other senseless during or after the match, win or lose. At any European sporting event, the common link was a general disregard for the spectator. Scorecards or clocks and even scoreboards were rare at many events. The queues for a cold greasy sausage, a curled-up cheese sandwich, or a cup of lousy coffee were often longer than the queues to get into the few poorly located, swamp-like toilets. Children were largely ignored. Going to a sporting event in Europe was rarely the ideal of family fun.

It's no wonder, then, that the American firms that design, build, and manage American arenas and stadiums are being asked to do the same thing in Europe. If a relatively violent sport such as football can draw large, orderly crowds that have fun and spend a lot of money because they're having fun—and because the many and varied concession stands make it easy for them to spend money—why does a relatively nonviolent sport like soccer have to suffer with fans who act like animals? Could it be because the outdated, antiquated, crude facilities make it seem as if they're being treated like animals?

Regarding football, the National Football League has had a remarkable decade in Europe, dating back to the early 1980s when rerun highlights of some games were purchased by Channel 4, the British network devoted to "minority" programming. Alongside its typical programs on religion, business, ethnic art, travelogues, gardening, and a smattering of sports programs such as sumo wrestling, Channel 4 started airing NFL highlights every Sunday evening. Condensing the typical NFL game's 3-plus hours into a tight 45 minutes of action by eliminating timeouts and huddles, Channel 4 found that it had an unexpected hit on its hands. Fan clubs for "American football" (as opposed to plain old "football," which we Americans call soccer) started popping up across Britain.

British publishers began putting out magazines dedicated to American football. Dozens of teams were formed into a series of leagues that attracted players ranging from those who liked the violence, such as prison guards and rugby players, to those who saw the game as a physical sort of chess, such as barristers and stockbrokers. More significantly for the NFL, these "instant" fans created a tremendous demand for NFL products. The American football craze quickly spread throughout Europe, and in recent years the NFL has been selling more than $60 million a year worth of officially licensed products throughout Europe. It's not unusual, from Madrid to Milan to Malmo, to see young men (and women) on the street wearing Chicago Bears caps or Oakland Raiders jackets. Teams from countries such as Denmark, Germany, Spain, and Italy have their own national leagues and then send their best teams to compete annually in the European playoffs. A few of the European clubs have ventured to the States and have generally shown themselves, despite their lack of experience, to be of good high school or low junior college quality.

For Americans based in Europe, the popularity of this "new" game made them instant heroes to friends and acquaintances. In 1985, I stopped overnight in a little rural English pub with a friend, an avid Giants fan, who was visiting from New York. After feeding us local delicacies such as his pheasant soup, the young chef popped out of the kitchen to look us over. After all, we were the only guests in the place that night, and it was rare that Americans would show up so far off the beaten tourist path. When he found out my friend was a walking Giants encyclopedia, they sat down together and talked football for hours, sustained by large quantities of Guinness. I went to bed somewhere around 5 A.M., after I heard them discussing Franco Harris' "immaculate reception" in some otherwise long-forgotten Pittsburgh Steelers playoff game. The English chef had heard about the game, but had never seen any footage, and he had my friend describe the game play by play. Americans who knew anything about football, and many who didn't, were invited to act as coaches, referees, or players. Lance Cone, a former Chicago semipro player working in London, was approached in a pub after some English fans heard his accent and asked if he knew anything about the game. He ended up becoming the first coach of the London Ravens, the team that dominated the British amateur scene for several years.

Two American commodities traders in London were asked to join the Stock Exchange Stags, a team made up of fans from the City, London's version of Wall Street. Tom Theys was a former Big Foot, Wisconsin, high school quarterback. At age 32, after not playing for 15 years, he suddenly found himself reliving the glory days as one of the most highly regarded passers in a new league. He heard cheers, gave interviews, and saw his picture in newspapers and magazines. The other trader, Mark Stanton, had never played anything but pickup football, mostly touch, on the sandlots of the south side of Chicago. Nonetheless, he became the Stags' star receiver and defensive back. Both Theys and Stanton spent a lot of time coaching their new English teammates not only on technique but on the rules. One of the toughest tasks they had was to teach all those guys who had grown up playing soccer that it was all right to use their hands; the defensive backs would go out with a receiver, get in good position, and then, instead of intercepting the ball or knocking it down with their hands, try to "head" it away with their helmets.

The culmination for the NFL, of course, has been the World League of American Football, the spring league with teams on both sides of the Atlantic, including the London Monarchs, the Barcelona Dragons, and the Frankfurt Galaxy. The league was backed by individual NFL clubs who immediately got a large chunk of their startup costs defrayed through an ABC contract to broadcast games. In its first year, 1991, the league proved more popular in Europe than in America, with average attendance of more than 30,000 per game in Europe—more than 40,000 in London—compared with fewer than 20,000 at games played in the States. If the league succeeds, it will be because of the popularity of American football in Europe rather than the popularity of springtime football in America. The guy who sweeps the streets with a broom and portable dustbin in my neighborhood in Hampstead went to several London Monarchs games at Wembley Stadium that first season, despite having to pay the equivalent of half a day's wages for a ticket. In telling me about one game, it became clear that he didn't know a cornerback from a quarterback. To him, the distinction didn't matter. He had a great time. "Forty thousand people there, and the place was rocking," he said. "The cheerleaders were great, kicking and jumping all over the place. They were hot. Nothing like that at soccer games here. The rock music was blasting out every time they stopped for a huddle or a time out. We were doing the wave all night, and we never stopped screaming."

Many of the most successful cultural transfers are American fads that just haven't caught on in Europe yet. When "paint ball" war games became popular in the States, it was only a matter of time before someone brought the concept to Europe. After all, Europe had the same sort of young achievers who paid to play in the States. In fact, in Europe it's become much more of a corporate event, where one department of a company will spend a Saturday colorfully blasting another department out of the woods, or where one accounting firm will challenge another.

Some American ideas are designed to fit in Europe but might not work in America. Tourists to London, for instance, often revel in the lively pub theater scene, jamming into the back rooms and upstairs sections of taverns to watch productions that are usually quite professional. Most visitors assume that pub theater is an old British tradition. Actually it dates back barely 20 years to when it was invented by Dan Crawford, an American backpacker who liked drinking beer, liked theater, and liked England. Deciding to try to stay in London for a couple of years, he fell back on his only working experience in the States—as a bartender and a stagehand. So he got a job at the Kings Head pub in Islington and started producing plays in the rear room. Over the years many of the plays he has produced, often by well-known playwrights such as Tom Stoppard, have been so successful that they moved to bigger legitimate theaters in London's West End, and occasionally on to Broadway. Dozens of other pubs eventually followed Crawford's example and began putting on plays, too. And thus a British tradition was born.

One of the classic case studies of an American cultural transfer involves TGI Friday's, the Dallas-based chain with more than 200 restaurants across the United States. Friday's success in the States, of course, is rooted in its strong theme of a bar-restaurant with family dining. The decor is an eclectic and appealing if sometimes goofy mix of interesting junk on the walls, such as pith helmets, sleds, and tubas. The big menu is based on simple but quick American favorites. Service is fast and informal. To many Americans, a Friday's is a fun place to get a meal and a drink, whether for singles, couples, or families. When Friday's opened talks with Whitbread, the giant British brewery-pubs-restaurants concern that wanted a franchise for the Friday's name in Europe, there was considerable worry in Dallas about whether such a distinctly American concept would go over in Europe in general and Britain in particular.

After all, Britain had no comparable family-style restaurants; maybe there was a good reason that there weren't any. There were plenty of expensive white-tablecloth restaurants, plenty of pubs that served sandwiches and meat pies, and plenty of greasy fish 'n' chips shops, but very few places where a family could sit down in a clean, airy, relaxed atmosphere, choose from a variety of meat or fish dishes, sample the salad bar, order beer or wine or milk shakes, and then have pie, cake, or a sundae afterward. No wonder people didn't eat out. At a time when studies showed that Americans were eating 55 percent of their meals outside the home, Britons were eating out only 7 percent of the time. Instead of eating out an average of once a day, they were eating out once every two weeks or so.

But those same studies showed that the number of meals being consumed outside the home was growing by as much as one-third a year in Britain, and that the only reason it wasn't growing faster was the lack of suitable restaurants.

Friday's executives ultimately chose to have faith in their concept and to believe that it was strong enough to cross borders. If anything would get Britons to eat out more, they decided, it was Friday's. They worked out a master franchise agreement with Whitbread, under which Friday's would provide the technical expertise to actually set up restaurants in Britain and, eventually, across Europe. After bearing the start-up costs, Whitbread would pay an annual royalty plus a small percentage of its profits to the Friday's home office in Dallas. Moreover, Whitbread had to do everything—absolutely everything—the way Friday's executives wanted. The British brewery wasn't even allowed to sell its own beer in its Friday's franchises. Friday's insisted that there be nothing to identify the European restaurants as foreign-owned or foreign-operated. The concept was to be kept strong and it was to be kept American.

After all, some previous attempts at transferring American fast-food restaurants had failed because they had diluted their strong American identity. One chain, responding to what it thought were British tastes, put beans-on-toast on its menu alongside the cheeseburgers. The result was disastrous. People went to an "American" place for American food and American atmosphere, not for the same bland grub and surly service they got at the fish 'n' chips shop around the corner. Friday's resolved to make all its European restaurants look as if they had been plucked from the suburbs of Cleveland; they would be indistinguishable from the American restaurants. (I once saw a tourist actually from Cleveland snapping photos in a Friday's in London. I asked him why and he said the folks at home wouldn't believe there was a nearly identical Friday's in Covent Garden.)

Whitbread executives, naturally, originally had planned to sell their own beer in their Friday's franchises in Europe. And they had figured that the menu would have to be rewritten to be more European. Friday's in Dallas said no. If Whitbread didn't want to do it Dallas's way, it wouldn't be done at all. There would be no pints of bitter at the bar and no bangers and mash on the menu. Eventually, Whitbread agreed to do everything Friday's way. Even more than selling their own beer and an English menu, Whitbread executives wanted to be at the forefront of a new trend toward family-style, leisure-oriented dining out in Europe. "If the people in Dallas told us the screws holding the clock on the wall had to be screwed in counter-clockwise, we'd do it," one Whitbread executive told me. "We wouldn't ask why. We'd just do it."

That's not to say that re-creating the American menu, ambience, or service was easy, even with Whitbread's consent. Teams of cooks, tasters, and technicians traveled back and forth for months trying to find the right ingredients and the right cooking processes to make the food at the European Friday's restaurants taste the same as the food at the American outlets. English potatoes have different textures and different sugar and starch contents than Idaho potatoes, so they have to be cooked differently to make similar french fries. It's difficult anywhere in Europe to find big Gulf-of-Mexico-sized shrimp or lean but tender and juicy corn-fed beef. And nearly all European sauces, including such standards as ketchup, mustard, mayonnaise, and Heinz 57, taste different from their American counterparts, according to the professional Friday's tasters.

In the end, after many flights of people and food back and forth between London and Dallas, the first Friday's restaurants opened in Britain with menus absolutely indistinguishable from Friday's restaurants in the States. Not only were the same items listed, but they tasted identical, too. The only major difference was the wine list; it made sense to use well-known, high-quality, lower cost French wines in Britain rather than importing California wines typically featured in the Friday's restaurants in the States. Since the first British Friday's opened in Birmingham in 1986, there has been only minor tinkering with the European menu. The main change has been to substitute a handful of spicy Indian and Pakistani dishes—familiar to Britons because of the preponderance of curry houses across the country—for some of the spicy Mexican dishes. And instead of sticking to the American custom of serving salads before the main course, the Friday's franchises in Britain now offer the option of skipping salad or having it later, European style.

This fine-tuning is not uncommon for American products, especially foods. M&Ms, for example, used a "milkier" chocolate when they started selling in Europe because that's what Europeans were used to in their chocolate candies. Kentucky Fried Chicken found that Colonel Sanders' original recipe with the 11 secret herbs and spices was too peppery for European tastes, so the batter was toned down to provide a slightly more bland taste (though it's being spiced up again in the 1990s as European tastes become more Americanized). These are examples of fine-tuning, well short of the major overhaul that may jeopardize a product's strong American identity.

Setting TGI Friday's European menu was relatively easy. Finding and training staff to work to the levels of American efficiency and enthusiastic service demanded by the chain was an entirely different matter. Just as there is little or no tradition of family dining, Britain and much of the rest of Europe have no tradition of good informal service. The change had to start with management, of course. Whitbread's point man on the Friday's franchises was Tony Hughes, who told me that the first time he ever entered a Friday's in America, on Exeter Street in Boston, he realized he had been wasting his life trying to run the brewery's English inns and pubs according to existing English standards.

One of his first assignments was to spend two weeks—which stretched into three and a half months because he was learning so much—working with and observing Friday's managers. He told me about the exact moment he realized what it would take to transplant such a uniquely American concept to Britain: "I was making out schedules in the back office of one of the Dallas restaurants when a Friday's regional manager blew in. He said, 'Hey, Tony, let's go find somebody who's doing something right.' So we did. We found a guy in the kitchen making guacamole. His ingredients were all lined up neatly, he was following the recipe exactly, his work station was clean, everything was absolutely perfect. The manager congratulated the guy, told him what a great job he was doing, shook his hand, and patted him on the back. When we walked away the guy was right back at it, and he was smiling. It was a major turning point in my life. English managers are supposed to find people doing things wrong. The thing that I admire about American companies in general, and Friday's in particular, is that they're very positive. In Britain, far too much goes into analyzing a decision instead of just making it work. We've also missed out on the service culture. We have had to close that cultural gap."

"The hardest thing for Whitbread," said Frank Steed, the Friday's executive who engineered the cultural transfer, "was adapting the American style and culture of service to the extent that it's ingrained in employees. After all, that service mentality is not a first instinct for all English employees." Friday's hit upon a novel plan for finding the right sort of employees. First, past restaurant experience in Britain was not a recommendation to work in the new British restaurants. In fact, it was usually a handicap because people with restaurant or catering experience usually had poor work habits, a poor attitude, or both. Personality was the most important thing. For the startup crew for the London restaurant, "auditions" were held in a West End theater. For another outlying restaurant, Friday's raised a circus tent to create a festive air.

The applicants walked out on the stage or circus ring and were told, "Do something." If they said, "What do you want me to do?" the Friday's recruiters said, "Thank you. Next." If they did something, they got an interview. People who sang or danced or tried to tell jokes might be trained as waiters. The most gregarious might be put into a role-playing situation where they would act as a TV talk-show host; if they did well, they might be trained as one of the receptionist-greeters who meet people at the door. Anybody who could juggle would probably get a serious look as a potential bartender who could be trained to toss ice into glasses or flip beer mugs behind the back. Those who proved themselves in a series of intricate eye-hand coordination exercises would probably become kitchen trainees as cooks or sauce-and-salad makers. "We had to ascertain who had confidence with people, who wouldn't blush or get defensive or argue or resent it when they made a mistake. They had to be able to laugh at themselves," one trainer suggested. In other words, they had to be very un-British.

I spent most of an afternoon watching British people who were wandering into a new Friday's for the first time. They looked absolutely shocked when a pert young thing would bounce up and say, "Hey, where have you been? We've been open since 11, and we've got a great table for you right over here. Been out shopping? Hey, lemme help you with all those bags. . . ." After the initial shock, however, the British customers began twittering among themselves about how different this place was. And how American. People at the bar soon got over the idea of not being able to have their favorite British beers. Bartenders were taught to say, "Sorry, we don't have any pints of bitter, but how about an American lager? Listen, try a Dixie beer, and if you don't like it, I'll buy it back from you. . . ." In a country where bartenders in even the friendliest pubs rarely buy a drink for even their best customers, this was a truly revolutionary – and American – type of sales pitch.

Waiters and waitresses were taught to take small children on tours of the paraphernalia on the restaurant's walls, to repeat orders back to the customer to make sure they're correct, to bring drinks within three minutes of taking the order, to check and see if the food is all right after it's served, to apologize for and rectify any mistakes, and to thank customers and invite them to return soon. All those things are decidedly foreign to the British restaurant world. One young British waiter told me that most people liked the American style, but a few, especially older people, were frightened away: "Many British people don't seem to be able to plug into the American hype. It's 100 percent service oriented, which is very different for this country. And British people are a lot more backward about being forward."

To make sure the British Friday's restaurants got off on the right foot, Friday's sent dozens of its own best American employees to Britain for several weeks at a time. It was a nice perk for them, and it helped the British to have someone show them how they actually talked to customers or built an enchilada. Eventually British managers took over, but over the first couple of years all the major decisions in each new restaurant were in the hands of American managers on loan to Whitbread. Brad Hanson, a Chicago native who was one of the first managers at the Friday's in London, agreed that instilling the American service mentality was the toughest part of the job—made tougher by the cosmopolitan nature of London, where Friday's staff comes not only from Britain but also from continental Europe, the Middle East, Africa, and Asia. "If you talk to Friday's staff in Chicago or Dallas or New York, they all know what you're talking about because they're all coming from basically the same place," Hanson said. "But here, if you tell the staff that they're supposed to treat customers like guests in their own home, the guy from Zimbabwe wants to walk them home after dinner and the woman from Holland is thinking maybe she shouldn't open the door in the first place." Hanson was interrupted by a waitress who said a customer wanted to talk to the manager. A retired Royal Air Force sergeant who said he was in London for the day from a rural village told Hanson, "I've eaten in a lot of London restaurants, and this is the first time I've ever felt like the staff cared about their customers. It's the first time I've been made to feel that they weren't doing me a big favor merely by serving me."

The bottom line tells the real story. The Friday's restaurants in Britain have been setting weekly sales records for the entire Friday's chain, and the royalty deal was renegotiated. In the face of larger profits than anyone expected, Friday's headquarters in Dallas readily agreed to take a lower royalty in order to free up more Whitbread capital for expansion. Whitbread and Friday's are now in the process of expanding to 75 or more franchises in the 1990s, including restaurants in Ireland, Germany, Austria, Switzerland, the Scandinavian countries, France, Spain, Italy, and Portugal. Tony Hughes, the Whitbread executive who had the most to do with the Friday's deal— including the agreement to do everything Friday's way—concluded, "The dominant lifestyle throughout Europe is going to be American. All across Europe, people are aspirational toward quality, value, friendliness, and service. Those things are associated with America, but the desire for them is universal."

CHAPTER 5

◆ ◆ ◆

Making the
Right Contacts

A Washington, D.C.-based company that publishes dozens of business and professional newsletters recently decided to expand its European coverage. So much was happening in Europe that affected its subscribers – in topics such as trade, law, banking, and the environment – that the company needed to build a network of European correspondents. With great office fanfare, one of the company's leading executives scheduled a two-week recruiting trip to several European capitals. London was the first stop and the most important, partly because many of the developments affecting America were coming out of Britain and partly because of the common language. The company hoped to recruit a small group of reliable British correspondents who would be the cornerstone of its new European coverage, providing not only British but pan-European stories.

Before setting off, the executive made contact with various British organizations, including the main journalists' trade union and the Foreign Press Association in London. He explained that he was looking for correspondents and asked those organizations to invite any possible candidates to meet with him. He then proceeded to waste several days in London in a round of often entertaining but generally useless interviews with British freelance journalists. One showed up drunk. Another said she hadn't slept in days and looked it. She told the American this was a plus because it proved she could work for him around the clock. One little old lady told the American that she was sorry, she didn't know much about law, environment, trade, investment, and things like that. She liked to write about animals; didn't he have any newsletters for pet owners? None of the dozens of British journalists who met the visiting American was remotely suited for the kind of serious, information-heavy newsletters that he produced for U.S. professionals and managers.

Merely by chance, I heard about the guy's problem late in the afternoon of his last day in London. I telephoned him, explained that I was an American journalist and lawyer, and invited him to dinner. I made a couple of quick phone calls, and two more London-based American freelance journalists joined us for the evening. The three of us provided the visiting newsletter executive with some ideas about who he should be hiring, how he should be looking for them, and what type of coverage he should be seeking from Europe. He ended up offering assignments to all three of us and went away with a short list of other Europe-based American correspondents whom we recommended because of their specialties. "It's so great to sit down with you guys, with other Americans who know what I want and what I need. All these Brits I've been meeting just don't have a clue," the visitor said.

Too many Americans trying to do business in Europe think that all they have to do is get off a plane and start making deals. Everyone needs contacts, people who can smooth the way and provide accurate, pithy information that is the basis for good business decisions. Sometimes the contacts are fellow Americans who offer to sit down over a drink or a meal, like I did with the visitor from Washington, and may or may not have anything to gain personally from offering some casual advice.

Sometimes they're consultants who expect to be paid for every-thing they do or say, whether helpful or not. Sometimes they're employees of government agencies, quasi-public advisory groups or private service organizations, and it's their job to point you in the right direction.

The whole point, of course, is to gather good information. This is done in two ways. One way is to tap into the vast framework of resources established by federal and state govern-ment agencies to help Americans do business abroad, often at little or no cost for either information or advice. The other way to gather information is through informal networking, using connections made through friends, acquaintances, and associ-ates to meet people who know more than you do about Europe, Europeans, and how Americans succeed and fail in Europe. The key thing to remember is that doing business in Europe is almost never quick and easy, and anyone who says it is should probably not to be trusted.

One New York software company found "all sorts of Euro-pean pseudo-consultants coming out of the woodwork" when it began looking for a site for a small manufacturing plant on the other side of the Atlantic. This new class of European middle-men—not all are men, although they all want to be in the middle, if only briefly enough to collect a fee—may include former diplomats, defeated politicians, failed business execu-tives, would-be entrepreneurs, moonlighting academics, and unemployed journalists. Their common characteristic is that they want to take Americans under their wing. Exclusively, of course. Usually for a flat fee, part of which is paid in advance, along with money for "expenses." Their specialty is the languid, liquid lunch, during which they will "consult" for Americans by offering long-winded but vague descriptions of the market and the insurmountable difficulties in cracking it without their con-nections. Prominent in the monologue is a lot of name-drop-ping; the consultant doesn't realize that his connections are wasted on Americans who never heard of Lord Such-and-Such or Minister So-and-So. The middleman's great hope, and his or her great promise, is to find someone with whom the American can do business. His or her secondary hope is that the American will find someone independently, and that the middleman can claim a percentage anyway.

"One of the worst things an American getting into Europe can do is hire a European consultant, unless it's for something very specific, like directed research," one longtime Europe-based American lawyer said. "Yeah, of course, big American companies might hire the management consulting division of one of the big accounting firms, one with offices both in the States and in Europe. But most of the figures and other information anyone needs are out there for free. It's just a matter of getting it, looking at it, and then deciding what you want to do. I tell my clients that if they want to use someone, look for another American, one who is used to operating in Europe. An American can tell another American about the surprises. Look at France. Say you want to sell some sort of hygiene product in France, like a toothbrush. A French consultant will show you all the surveys and they'll look great. An American familiar with France will tell you that the French are notorious for lying about their personal hygiene. According to surveys, French people buy twice as many toothbrushes as they actually do."

Americans may not be as useful as native Europeans in smoothing over cultural differences, but an experienced American will avoid those problems, or find a European to do that for him or her if necessary. If you do use a European, find one who has at least been educated in the United States. "On the other hand," my lawyer friend observed, "it's better to have a smart guy who's never been to the U.S. than a guy living off the fact that he squeaked out a B.A. from some small college in New Jersey or Michigan."

No matter where a consultant, agent, or middleman is from, an American should demand four things: commitment, responsiveness, integrity, and solvency. You want someone who can make your deal happen, but you don't want to link up with a European partner just because the middleman wanted it. You need someone you can trust, but don't absolve yourself of normal managerial decision making. The consultant should offer advice, not dictate strategy. My lawyer friend again: "Too many Americans look at going to Europe as a theoretical exercise. Big mistake. Suppose you do business in Texas, and you're thinking of setting something up in Minnesota. You go up to Minnesota and have a look. Hey, it snows in Minnesota. People eat different foods and wear different clothes. Too many Americans going into Europe think that just because they can do business in America, they can do business in Europe, too. They should get away from the theoretical aspects of the exercise and make it a practical enterprise just like they would in the States."

Long-range planning always makes things easier. Anyone thinking of doing any sort of business in Europe should arrange to visit at least once. Take the family and combine a vacation with some informal information gathering. Make lots of calls to friends and acquaintances in the States to collect European names and numbers. Ask your bank if it has European branches and if an appointment or two can be arranged over there. Ask your lawyer if he or she knows anyone or to make a call on your behalf to one of the big U.S. law firms that does have European offices. Most American law offices in Europe have only a handful of lawyers, and they're generally quite happy to get a call from a stranger: "Hi, I'm going to be in town exploring some opportunities for my business, and I wonder if I might take you out to lunch. . . ." Even Americans with whom you are sure you will never do business can be valuable sources of information about Europe and Europeans, and they're usually happy to share their experiences with another American contemplating a European plunge.

Jeff Rymer, who runs a large Chicago food-processing and supply company, is an example of a far-thinking American executive. When one of his major clients, a restaurant chain, was expanding to Europe, it ran into trouble. The meat it was getting in Europe was all wrong, both in terms of quality and cut. Would Rymer help? He took a week away from his own business, at no compensation, to visit the European suppliers, discuss how to feed and raise the livestock, and demonstrate how to butcher the meat. There was no immediate payoff, Rymer acknowledged, but the experience was invaluable background for if and when he is ready to expand into Europe himself. "I learned a lot. I made some good contacts. And I built up some goodwill," he said.

Through their agriculture or commerce departments, most U.S. states have programs aimed at helping homegrown businesses export their products and services. Through these state programs or through the U.S. Commerce Department, government money is often available for research and for exploratory trips to Europe, sometimes with fully organized trade missions. European embassies in Washington and consulates in many U.S. cities have departments or advisors that can put you in touch with people, agencies, and information. The Invest in Britain Bureau, for example, has offices in the British Embassy in Washington and in British consulates in New York, Atlanta, Boston, Chicago, Cleveland, Dallas, Houston, Los Angeles, San Francisco, and Seattle. In effect, this is a British government agency offering all manner of advice and assistance for Americans considering doing business in Britain.

European government agencies are generally eager to put you in touch with local and regional development agencies that can offer even more detailed information about specific areas. Beyond providing information, the regional development authorities often take the lead in finding attractive, low-cost sites and in arranging tax breaks and other government incentives. Apple, which has a number of computer manufacturing operations in Europe and is considering more, chooses sites in large part on the basis of the assistance it gets from these local development authorities. "We evaluate the regional development authorities," one Apple official explained at a seminar on corporate re-location in Europe. "Are they pro-business, do they have a coherent development strategy, are they selective in the countries that they take, are they consumer oriented or bureaucratic? Companies like us love people who can clear through the red tape — excessive paperwork is very costly."

American Chambers of Commerce and local chambers throughout Europe can also be quite helpful in getting started. The European chambers typically maintain lists of who does what — from consultants who help foreigners get started to importers and distributors who might be looking for American contacts — and are happy to share them. The American Chambers of Commerce in most major European capitals can be especially helpful since they are geared to assisting Americans who want to do business with Europeans, and vice versa. They sponsor regular dinners, luncheons, seminars, conferences, "business-to-business" cocktail gatherings, and other programs that grease the wheels of networking. One popular program at the American Chamber of Commerce in London brings over several hundred young U.S. executives and their spouses for four days of light tourism mixed with informal yet informative meetings about doing business in Britain. The highlights include casual meetings with young British executives in similar fields. For those with specific questions, the American chambers are usually happy to arrange meetings with their own counselors, with private consultants, or with other Americans who are already established in Euro-American business and happy to share their insights on living and/or working in Europe. They also have extensive directories, libraries, and databases for contact making, and they'll help with arranging temporary office space, clerical help, interpreters, chauffeurs, and anything else.

Brian Dwyer, who brought Venus Wafers to Britain (Chapter 4), took full advantage of all the government help he could find. When he was first contemplating exporting, he contacted

Massachusetts state agriculture officials. "Should I export? What do I need to know? What do I need to do? I don't even know where to start. Point me in the right direction," he pleaded. And they did. Besides providing basic background, the state officials referred Dwyer to U.S. Commerce Department officials who provided market information through the Washington-based Foreign Agriculture Service. The feds also arranged to help pay for Dwyer to exhibit his crackers at a trade fair in Cologne, Germany. "There's a phenomenal infrastructure in place for exporters," Dwyer marveled. "I never had any idea it was there. They are a bunch of economic bloodhounds who sniff out the information you need on how the European markets work. But they're not sales agents. They won't sell your product for you. All they do is give you the raw information. What you do with it is up to you."

The trade show in Germany, the country that is the unofficial world center for such trade fairs and shows for everything from kitchenware and computers to leather goods and medical supplies, is one of thousands listed in various international guides published by trade groups around the world. The show was a revelation to Dwyer, who dealt with hundreds of people, sometimes in English and sometimes through the German interpreter provided for him by the show. "It was amazing, purely from an investigative standpoint," he said. "There was so much interest in our product. It really opened my eyes to the possibilities. But the trade show in Europe is much different than in the States. It's a zoo. Real crowded, lots of deal making. In the U.S., a trade show is mostly for information gathering, where you go see what people are doing. Most exhibitors don't have a place for potential customers to sit down and chat. In Europe the exhibits are much more expansive, and there are rooms in back where you can sit down and have a cup of tea or a beer and really talk business. It's truly a selling environment. That's why you really need to allocate your time, and you need a show strategy. If you're a participant, you can't just grab someone's business card and say you'll call them later. You need man-power there. If you're by yourself, it's no good. You need to have people to handle the bodies that come through. If you're a visitor, start off by seeing the whole show and targeting who you want to go back and talk turkey with. If you just give them a card and call them later, they're not going to know who you are, and they're going to wonder why you didn't care enough to sit down and talk when you had the chance."

Dwyer said this is partly a symptom of European reluctance to deal over the phone. "They'd rather deal in person, if they can. The phone is used much differently than in the States, where telemarketing is an integral part of doing business. In Europe, face to face is always the preference." One other aspect of trade fairs frequently mentioned by Americans is that they are typically on neutral ground. Everyone, exhibitor and visitor alike, is from out of town, and maybe a foreigner, so it's much easier to negotiate without territorial or turf considerations.

Back in Boston, state officials recommended that Dwyer contact the Massachusetts Port Authority. Massport put him in touch with Molly MacGinnis, the young half-Irish, half-American who runs its London office. Her job, and the job of the people in the other more than three dozen state-sponsored trade offices in Europe, is to help Americans export their products overseas. "How much help was Molly? On a scale of 1 to 10, she was about a 12," Dwyer said. She helped him assemble and evaluate the official surveys and market information that led Dwyer to decide his crackers would sell in Europe and that he should start in Britain. She helped him arrange his trips to London, setting up itineraries and advising on the best way to get from Point A to Point B. She and her people went out into supermarkets and took notes for Dwyer on who was selling what kinds of crackers. He was thrilled, for example, to learn that nearly all cracker sales are off the shelf in British super-markets, rather than from the expensive floor displays that dominate U.S. supermarket aisles. "All we had to do was get on the shelf, and we'd have just as much chance as anyone else. We wouldn't have to compete with the big companies that spent so much more on marketing and promotion than we could," he noted.

MacGinnis told Dwyer exactly what he had to do and who he had to see, step by step, to get government approval. She helped guide Dwyer through the frustrating negotiations with the bureaucrat who ruled that Venus Wafers could not have "All Natural" on the label because they don't grow on trees. She helped set up appointments with distributors and retailers and advised Dwyer to tone down the aggressive American sales pitch. "She helped me develop a new attitude of going in low key," Dwyer said. He said his cold-calling approach for prospective customers was basic: "Hi, do you want to talk to a Yank?" Most of them did. "It really used to burn me back home when I'd be having trouble seeing someone, and a guy from out of town would blow in and get an appointment right away. It was nice having the shoe on the other foot. When you're from far away, people are more willing to see you on short notice. And the fact that I'm an American made them curious. They were interested in meeting me."

MacGinnis put Dwyer in touch with shippers, accountants, designers, and advertising agencies. She helped him get some magazine publicity about Venus Wafers coming to Europe. Dwyer had one big problem, but he didn't blame MacGinnis. When his crackers finally were shipped, he was hit with an 18 percent wheat import duty that he hadn't expected. He wrote it off to his own inexperience in trying to calculate all the duties and tariffs himself according to how he thought the customs people would categorize his crackers. He should have given his package to customs in advance and said, "Please tell me exactly what this will cost me . . . in writing." As it was, Venus sales in Britain got off to a fast start and the lower profit margins due to the 18 percent duty were absorbed by good continuing volume.

After shepherding Venus into Europe, Dwyer decided to use

what he had learned to help other companies. He left Venus and set up his own consultancy, specializing in American food exports to Europe. "I'm part marriage maker and part parish priest," he explained. "I help with emotional problems. I tell clients, if you expect to be in business in 50 years, you better start thinking globally. At the turn of the last century, some companies in New York said no, they didn't see any need to expand to Chicago. Those are the companies that aren't around anymore. Too many Americans think selling internationally is sexy in the 1990s. It's not sexy. It's a normal part of doing business in a bigger, different market."

The way Dwyer presents himself to prospective clients could be a guide for what Americans who want to do business in Europe should be hearing from their contacts or middlemen. A frequent obstacle when he sits down with new clients is their fear, Dwyer said. "I take an hour or so to explain to them everything that's involved. They freak out. What you don't know scares you. That's what I mean by emotional problems. They want to sell internationally as long as they don't have to do anything differently, as long as they don't have to change anything or think about anything new. Well, that's not the way it works. They ask why they can't use their same old American label in Italy. I remind them that there are a lot of people in Italy who can't read English and therefore won't buy their product."

Dwyer tries to straighten out the misconceptions common among Americans who want to export to Europe. "First, successful exporting doesn't begin overnight. You have to be committed to making it happen. One sales call ain't gonna do it. We have the gross misconception that the world wants American products. That may have been true in the late 1940s, and the 1950s and maybe the 1960s, that Americans could do no wrong. But now the rest of the world has learned that they can get along quite nicely without Americans and American products. For us, it's all a matter of education, of learning the markets. Of course, the flip side is that a little information can be very dangerous. I've got one client who has spent some time in the U.K., and he's using what he's seen to draw conclusions that aren't necessarily true. He sees things in a couple of downtown London stores, in tourist areas, and uses that as a basis for decisions about the entire U.K. market."

Another misconception is that while most American companies regard the United States as several different markets— up to 11 for many food companies, Dwyer said—those same companies tend to look at Europe as just one market. "People come to me and say they want to sell in Europe. I ask 'em what European market. They say, you know, Europe, all of it. They wouldn't sell the same way in New England and southern California, but they want to sell the same way in England and Italy. One problem is that too many companies have been sold the sizzle and sex appeal of the EC single market by slick agents and middlemen. They say they can sell your products throughout all of Europe, just give me this and that, sign here, and goodbye. You probably never hear from them again. Anyone who tells you they can sell to all of Europe is making false promises. If someone calls you from Cleveland and says, hey, he wants to sell your product, do you just tell him to go ahead? That's what some people do with European agents. Anybody can do deep enough discounts to unload a couple of containers of almost anything American in Europe. But is that how you want your product handled? Is that the image you want? This is how many small and medium-sized American companies have become disenchanted with Europe."

Another misconception grows out of Americans' fear of foreign languages and currency fluctuations. "You have to put language in perspective to your overall business. Yes, lower in the European organization you deal with, there might be people who can't speak English. But most of the people you and your top people will be dealing with will speak English. And if not, there are always interpreters. There's an infrastructure to get

93

you through. As for currency fluctuations, we all hear about big companies losing millions on the foreign exchange markets. But hey, it only takes a couple of hours in the library to learn how to protect yourself through hedging. Most people don't realize how easily this can be done through their own banks. Some companies try to protect themselves and ease their problems by saying they only want to be paid in U.S. dollars, but they're taking a risk if they do that, too. People in Europe might not want to deal with them."

In her tiny office just off London's New Bond Street, one of the most expensive shopping districts in the world, Molly Mac-Ginnis was happy to recall Brian Dwyer as one of her best pupils. He listened to what she and others said, he evaluated the information gathered from many sources, and he worked hard without trying to cut corners or grab the first offers and opportunities. "Too many Americans go with the first contacts they make," she said. "Distributors or agents find them somehow, stumble in the door, give them a sample order, and then they're never heard from again. You have to come to Europe and get to know the retailers. And you have to come back after that, again and again, to check to make sure things are working the way they should. I advise Americans who are starting to export to plan on making at least four trips to Europe in the first two years."

MacGinnis tries to prepare would-be exporters by giving them reading lists, including European trade and industry newsletters and magazines. "They can read those for six months and then come and look around," she said. "Talk to retailers and distributors, look at what's on shelves, find a trade show. Check out the competition. Talk to potential customers." It's not always necessary to be an exhibitor at a trade show. Karen Foote Richards, who has a small Boston company called Ink-adinkadoo that specializes in offbeat rubber stamps, was approached by a British greeting-card company. When it became apparent that the Brits just wanted to steal her ideas, she brushed them off and started thinking about doing the export-ing herself. "She saw how ideas like hers that were popular in the States became popular in Britain four or five years later, and how Britain could be a sister market for her products," Mac-Ginnis said. "So she came over and spent a couple of hours with me, asking what she should and shouldn't do. I told her I bet her crazy stamps would sell here, so she started making appoint-ments with distributors and retailers. She also went to a trade show, simply as a visitor. She went home with a lot of orders, including some from department stores, which she hadn't even considered until she got here and saw their stationery and notions departments."

MacGinnis tries to encourage would-be exporters to gather as much information as cheaply and easily as they can and to avoid agents and middlemen who are more interested in quick profit than a long-term relationship. At the same time, she often works closely with private consultants with good track records. An example is David Magagna, an export marketing specialist for small and medium-sized American corporate clients. Magagna complements his own quarter-century of interna-tional sales, marketing, and management with a handful of associates who specialize in geographic regions, certain types of products, or specific areas of business expertise. Magagna's own international experience began in the 1960s when, as the eager young executive trying to promote overseas sales for the Ameri-can guitar company that employed him, he went to a European trade show and introduced himself to his first prospective cli-ent, a German, and said he was from the "world famous" C. F. Martin Guitar Co. "World famous," the German repeated. "Well, if you're so famous, how come I have never heard of you?" Magagna's style has become somewhat smoother over the years, and he now offers a service that is tailored for American clients' needs.

Some companies just want Magagna to do the initial Euro-pean market research to see if Europe is ready for their products. Some want an analysis of whether their products are ready for Europe. Some want him to put them in touch with prospective European partners and distributors. Some have been approached by prospective distributors and want Magagna to evaluate them. Some want Magagna to design a complete marketing and sales program for Europe. Some want him to run the program, too. A typical client is CSP Inc., formed by Sam Lacey and a group of other current and former National Basketball Association stars, including Dominique Wilkins, Rick Barry, and Dave Cowens. Lacey had already lined up a prospective European distributor for the company's line of sports clothing when he approached Magagna for advice. "Lacey was convinced this one distributor could take care of all of Europe," Magagna said. "I told him he wouldn't have one distributor for all of the United States, so why would he have just one for a market that is more populous and more complex in Europe? You shouldn't even have one distributor for Germany, the north-south divide is so distinct there." As a result, Magagna offered to line up various distributors: two for Germany, one for each of the other major European countries, and just one to handle the Benelux countries because their markets are so similar. Magagna also set about planning promotional tie-ins and events such as exhibition basketball games in various European cities.

"Research is so much more important nowadays," he said. "We used to just get on a plane and knock on doors. Eventually, you still need to make contacts and do some wining and dining, but now there are masses of surveys and other market information available for almost every industry and product in every country. And the trade fairs are wonderful." For Americans looking for European distributors, he offered one caution: "Be careful in your correspondence, especially in the more southern countries, that you don't do anything that lets someone proclaim himself your distributor before you've made up your mind. Sometimes, if you just declare your interest and send some samples, a guy can go to his local courts and keep you from working with anyone else." Make sure the arrangements – or lack thereof – are explicitly spelled out in correspondence and that any agreement is kept open until you are ready to make a decision. Spell out the conditions and terms of exclusivity, or lack of exclusivity.

"This is part of the whole reason people come to me," Magagna said. "They don't have this sort of expertise and I do. But if I'm asked to choose a distributor, I want the client to be part of the final decision. In the end, I present choices and recommendations, and it's up to the client. But I don't insist on clients coming to Europe in the early stages. If they've asked me to set things up for them, they can only get in the way. Once they are exporting successfully, however, I insist that they come. They should get to know the distributor and the retailers and become familiar with the market." For initial market research, he typically charges a flat fee of between $4,000 and $10,000. "I don't like hourly or daily rates, and most clients don't either," he said. For this fee, he provides a report, with statistics, on market potential for the client's product, including assessments of the competition, the type of similar products already performing well, regional variations, what type of outlets do the best business, pricing information, and methods of distribution. Magagna also advises on what must be done to adapt the product and its packaging, how much shipping and duties will cost, and what other red tape will be involved.

"I give them my report," he said. "Sometimes they say thanks, they'll take it from here. Sometimes they ask what they should do next. In that case I'm put on a retainer, usually $5,000 or $6,000 a month, or on a commission of between 5 and 20 percent of their sales, or some combination of retainer plus commission. Even if I set up their entire export operation, I never handle the product myself. I'm a consultant, not an import-export operation. If you sell to an export trading company, you risk losing control of your distribution. You've got to be concerned about where your product is going and how it's being sold in Europe." Once he has established a company's relationships and procedures for exporting into a new market, Magagna likes to turn the operation back to the client. Typically, he'll train one of the company's senior managers for 18 months to take over the exporting. He may or may not stay on as a consultant after that, and sometimes he takes on new assignments for the client – perhaps ushering a different product into the same market or the same product into a different market.

To show what can happen to Americans searching for the right European contacts (and to show that not all my efforts to aid Americans have been as tidy as the dinner for the visiting Washington newsletter executive), there is the example of the Brooklyn Brewery. This microbrewery was founded by Tom Potter, a former New York banker, and Steve Hindy, a former Associated Press foreign correspondent and editor for *Newsday*. They started brewing Brooklyn Lager in 1988 with money raised from a small group of limited partners, mostly family and friends, including me. After the brewery had been on its feet for a year or so, I started mentioning it to beer and wine distributors in my neighborhood in London. One of them, Majestic Wine Warehouses, expressed interest. I telephoned Steve Hindy in Brooklyn, told him I could set up an appointment for him with Majestic, arranged a cut-rate plane ticket, and offered him my guest room. "Exporting had never been part of our business plan, but when you called and set everything up, we decided to come over and take a look," Hindy told me later. "We needed to sell beer wherever we could, and we figured selling it in Britain would certainly be good public relations for us back home. But we knew we couldn't do it ourselves. We knew we had to have an importer-distributor."

I met Hindy, jet-lagged and lugging two cases of Brooklyn Lager, at Heathrow. We took a cab straight to the appointment with Majestic's main beer buyer. Hindy went in exuding confidence. He was a former war correspondent, used to hitting the ground running in exotic and dangerous places. After thriving in Cairo and Beirut, largely through his ability to make and use personal contacts, he reckoned making a deal in London would be a piece of cake. He was wrong. "Within minutes, I knew the guy at Majestic was the same sort of hard-headed chiseler that we see all the time in New York," Hindy told me. "He had the same attitude as a discount-chain-store buyer in the States. Sure, he was interested in carrying our beer, but he didn't want to be the only one selling it. He didn't want to import it himself. He gave me a list of importers he bought beer from and told me to see if any of them would be interested in bringing in our beer. And then he asked me to buy an ad in his in-house magazine. At that point I realized I was not talking to a guy who was dying to get a great new American beer for his chain. He might buy one shipment, sell it out, and then drop it."

Obviously, I was chagrined. As Hindy's London contact, I could have sounded out Majestic and saved him a plane trip. But to Hindy's credit, he didn't seem to hold it against me. Instead, he decided to make the best of the rest of his week in London and try to learn something about the British market. He took samples around to pubs, bars, supermarkets, liquor stores, and American-theme restaurants and was encouraged by the interest. Several retailers said they would definitely place a trial order if and when Hindy found an importer. He contacted all Majestic's beer importers, and they were encouraging, too. One, in fact, was more than encouraging; he said he was eager to order a container of 1,200 cases. Unfortunately, that deal, which will be discussed in detail later (Chapter 7: Negotiations), fell through. Hindy flew back to Brooklyn empty-handed, but encouraged at the interest shown in his beer.

Then two things happened. Brooklyn Lager won the Great American Beer Tasting, one of America's top blind tastings, and the New York-New Jersey Port Authority took some samples of Brooklyn Lager – without Hindy's knowledge – to one of the biggest European gourmet and specialty food shows. Suddenly

Hindy was besieged by phone calls from Europeans who wanted to be his agent, his contact, his middleman, his consultant. Most wanted him to send free samples. Many wanted him to sign contracts making them Brooklyn Lager's exclusive agent, so that they would get a percentage of every bottle sold in Europe until the end of time. Some wanted him to ship beer to them in exchange for a promise to pay him once they sold it. Almost all of the would-be distributors wanted Hindy to make some sort of up-front payments. They themselves would take little or no financial risk while skimming off their profits before he got anything back. One Italian importer wanted Hindy to spend $50,000 to have new bottles made for an initial shipment of beer for which the Italian would pay $15,000. One Dutch importer offered to pay COD, but wanted Brooklyn Lager only as part of a one-time shipment of beers with distinctive American names, like Rattlesnake and Dixie. "We decided we didn't want our beer being sold like that, as an oddity," Hindy said. "We told them that if we ever wanted to get into Holland, we'd set up a long-term relationship with an established importer."

Then an American approached Hindy. He was an export consultant named Gregory Chesnulovitch, based on Staten Island. He was having some success exporting a couple of other quintessential New York products, bagels and cheesecake, and wanted the chance to do something for Brooklyn Lager. "He asked our permission to talk to people about us before he started doing anything," Hindy said. "He seemed earnest. He seemed honest. He promised to pay for samples himself. He didn't want anything up front from us. But he said that if he did make a deal for us, he expected to get 5 percent of everything we sold because of him. It seemed too good to be true."

Through a European contact of his own, Chesnulovitch got the name of BB Supply Centre Ltd. from the London Chamber of Commerce's directory of small British beer distributors. Chesnulovitch's contact, working for a flat finder's fee paid by Chesnulovitch, made an appointment for him with

Lynne Zilkha, the managing director of BB Supply. Chesnulovitch and Zilkha spent several hours together. She told him about her business, about how she was the main British importer of Czech beers such as Budweiser Budvar and Pilsner Urquell, and about how she was looking for a good high-quality American beer to add to her list of Japanese, Mexican, and German premium beers. She had heard of Brooklyn Lager and liked its packaging and taste. Chesnulovitch, in turn, told Zilkha what he knew about Steve Hindy, Tom Potter, and the Brooklyn Brewery.

Zilkha told Chesnulovitch about the vagaries of the British beer market and how it is different from America. "He took a lot of notes and asked a lot of questions," Zilkha, obviously impressed, said later. "I told him I wanted a commitment from Brooklyn. There was no point in simply sending us the beer and expecting us to sell it. I wanted commitments on the quantity of supplies, on the presentation of the product, on prompt shipping to protect the shelf life of the beer, and on marketing support. The taste is different for an American beer and the packaging stands out, but the marketing support from Brooklyn is the most important aspect for us. Greg took my message back to Brooklyn, and we started working through him. It was refreshing, because normally these agents come in and try to tell you what they're going to do, even though they don't know the market. You have to tear down their plan and then build a new one. Instead of trying to tell us what to do, Greg listened. Back in Brooklyn, he did the diplomacy, and the guys there listened, too. Both sides quickly came to respect Greg."

Steve Hindy certainly respected Chesnulovitch and appreciated the knowledge he was getting from him about the British market. But he didn't want to pay him 5 percent. Hindy was about to sign a deal with Gallo wine's British importer — a deal with no off-the-top percentage for a middleman — when Chesnulovitch made one last plea on behalf of Zilkha and himself. Look, he told Hindy. Gallo is a wine operation. Their distributor in Britain doesn't even deal with a lot of the beer places you want to be in. Does Brooklyn Brewery want people who don't know that much about beer handling its beer in Britain? They want to sell wine, and if somebody orders a case of Brooklyn with it, OK. Under Gallo, Brooklyn would never be more than a small, specialist product. BB Supply, on the other hand, is a beer company, Chesnulovitch told Hindy. Zilkha is a specialist in imported, upmarket beers like Brooklyn. She's placed row after row of Czech beers on the shelves of the biggest supermarkets and liquor stores in Britain.

Hindy reconsidered. It was good advice, even if it did come from a guy who was getting a cut. He made a deal with Zilkha and BB Supply, though it wasn't easy (Chapter 7: Negotiations). Chesnulovitch became Mr. Five Percent, the agent in the middle, the contact man for both Hindy and Zilkha. When they had problems, neither hesitated to bring him in. "He acted as a buffer during the negotiations, and he still does," Zilkha said. "He's an ideal agent because whenever Steve and I come to a stalemate over something, he steps in and gets us to start over. He's very calm, very patient, and works with us both." When she came to New York for meetings with Hindy and Potter, it was Chesnulovitch who picked her up at the airport.

As for Hindy, he said Chesnulovitch has more than paid his own way by taking over the shipping "dirty work" and getting rates that were at least 5 percent lower than what Hindy would have found on his own. When the original shipper went broke, Chesnulovitch dropped all his other work and literally spent night and day on the phone until he found a new one. He and Hindy have never had more than a handshake agreement, but neither feels the need for a written contract. "I wouldn't want to give someone a percentage of the deal forever if his only role was an initial introduction," Hindy said. "And if I ever feel like Greg has stopped working for us, he stops getting paid. But I don't envision that. We'll be loyal to him. As long as our deal is strong and he is there to help us as we grow and expand, there will be plenty of work for him to do."

When I asked Chesnulovitch for some general thoughts for Americans considering doing business in Europe, he offered this mini lecture:

"Successful importers and exporters have one thing in common—a long-term commitment to the international marketplace. Perhaps the most important ingredient in conducting business globally is sensitivity. Doing business varies greatly from country to country, and it is of vital importance to be well versed in the culture and traditions of each nationality you come in contact with. It has been my experience that most Americans attempting to sell their products overseas are generally viewed as individualistic, take-charge types of people. There should be no doubt that being too aggressive in many foreign markets can diminish any hopes of selling their products.

"Most U.S. manufacturers initially encounter numerous pitfalls, primarily due to a high level of excitement and a low level of experience. The enormous popularity of a product here in the United States does not ensure its success overseas. Brooklyn beer is a perfect example. Certain countries establish label requirements and content restrictions that obviously have no application here in the United States. A label alone can take weeks to investigate and properly design before approval is granted.

"The selection of a knowledgeable distributor is critical. A full evaluation of at least three potential distributors should be undertaken, paying particular attention to existing accounts and management. Another common pitfall is the failure to determine import regulations. They vary greatly from country to country, and export should not even be considered unless this has been thoroughly investigated. Sales promotion should be developed slowly and steadily in a foreign market, especially among small and mid-sized manufacturers. In my opinion, a manufacturer is better suited to find and develop a relationship with a reliable and proven distributor than to concentrate efforts and funds on promoting the product himself or herself.

"In sizing up a potential market it is always wise to review your marketing plan with an experienced trade advisor from any one of a number of government agencies. They supply a broad base of information and contacts from which to initiate research. It is an untapped resource that many manufacturers simply ignore and, as a result, they suffer the consequences. While exporting is not for everyone because it demands significant time and often significant capital, it can lead to unrivaled excitement and success—provided the ingredients of perseverance, patience, and commitment remain constant."

If you are ever sitting across a desk or table from a prospective contact or middleman who doesn't deliver the same hard-nosed logic of the sort offered here by Greg Chesnulovitch, Brian Dwyer, and David Magagna, keep looking.

CHAPTER 6

◆ ◆ ◆

The Right Europartner
or Eurorep

When a company commits to doing business in Europe, important decisions must be made as to just how that business will be done. Some Americans like to send themselves or other Americans to Europe to open branch offices and build from the ground up, hiring staff—maybe European, maybe American, maybe both—but remaining generally accountable to and run by the American headquarters. Other Americans like to establish links with local distributors, franchisees, or other representatives for each country they do business in. A few look for a master distributor, franchisee, or rep to handle regions or all of Europe. Some try to take over existing European companies, while others prefer joint ventures, partnerships, or some other sort of alliance.

Ideally, a European partner offers the right combination of attributes—cash, products, marketing expertise, or technology—that affords a comfortable synergy between the two companies. Mergers and other forms of corporate alliance might be with a company or individual in the same business, perhaps a potential competitor who would instead provide the American with a cultural bridge to Europe. Such arrangements typically work only if it is a truly two-way bridge, where both the Americans and the Europeans can benefit from each other. They may share knowledge, skills, resources, customers—and possibly profits. Other American companies look for alliances with European companies that complement or fill gaps in their operations.

An example of the latter is Spectacor Management Group, the Philadelphia-based company that builds and manages stadiums, arenas, and civic centers. The more than two dozen U.S. facilities that SMG has been involved in building and/or running include the Philadelphia Spectrum, the Los Angeles Memorial Coliseum, the Superdome in New Orleans, and Three Rivers Stadium in Pittsburgh. With the American market much more mature and American competition much greater, it was only natural that SMG turn to Europe, where countries and cities are just beginning to grasp the notion that local governments can boost their economies by spending public money on big, modern, well-appointed, and well-run arenas. Initially, SMG won contracts to operate several arenas that were either newly built or already under construction in Italy, Norway, and the Soviet Union. But the company realized that the real long-term business would be in both building and managing facilities. To further that ambition, SMG formed a partnership with John Laing PLC, one of Britain's leading contractors for large construction projects. Together, SMG and Laing, with the former's American expertise in design and management and the latter's European construction experience, won the highly prized contract to build a real European entertainment showpiece, the 20,000-seat London Dome. In its new partnership, SMG can offer other European cities the entire package for arenas and stadiums, from design to construction to management.

No matter who the partner or representative, whether a European corporation or one of your own stars sent over to run things, disappointments are always looming on the horizon.

Americans who are committed to doing business in Europe and who believe they have found the right partner or representative can do several things to help ensure success. One is to establish goals. What exactly is expected from the European venture? Should it make money? How much? By what timetable? Is volume a consideration? Are there hidden benefits from being in Europe, such as a higher public-relations profile or a better standing within the industry? Will having a European operation help promote business at home in America? What are the expectations of the European partner or representative? At what point will the European partner become dissatisfied? If you've sent Americans to Europe to represent you, what are they looking for both personally and professionally, both short-term and long-term? Can you keep them happy?

Once goals and objectives are established, a system of accountability, of monitoring the European operation, must be set up to determine whether those goals are being met. Someone has to be able to say whether or not the European operation is successful in its own right, and whether it is helping or hindering the American home base and the overall business objectives. Periodic reviews should be instituted, and from the very beginning limits should be set on how long and how far the headquarters will carry a failing European venture. What constitutes enough dissatisfaction to make changes? And from the beginning, all parties concerned should be aware of provisions for bailing out, for ending European partnerships or alliances, for closing or withdrawing European franchises, and for bringing home or replacing American representatives in Europe. Above all, any arrangement should retain adequate flexibility to accommodate whatever changes are necessary later, whether those changes are born of success or disappointment.

Often, partnership arrangements change through no fault of the partners, but through changes in the marketplace. In France, for example, Coca Cola and Pepsi-Cola both went through wrenching splits with their longtime French partners because of changes in the French market. Coke had relied for four decades on Pernod Ricard, the French drinks group, as its distributor in France. That arrangement worked well as long as the French generally disdained American soft drinks, especially colas. But in the 1980s the French market took off, with soft-drink consumption rising by 25 percent a year, and colas by 40 percent. Suddenly France was getting too big and too important for Coke to leave to an independent contractor. A long and expensive legal battle in the French courts, which were obviously sympathetic to the French company that wanted to keep its Coke franchise, was necessary for Coke to win back its distribution rights in France. Similarly, Pepsi had relied for nearly three decades on Perrier for its bottling and distribution in France before undertaking what analysts called "an acrimonious divorce." In Pepsi's case, part of the problem was that Perrier, at one time dominant in the bottled water market, had been losing share to new competitors such as Badoit and Evian, and the decline in its business affected Pepsi sales, too.

One of the most active American business sectors in seeking out European partners has been the executive search industry — headhunting, in other words. The globalization of business has created an unquenchable demand for international executives, the kind of people who have the management skills, intelligence, world view, and adaptability to run companies and do deals across borders. To service this demand, the headhunters have to be as global as their corporate clients and the executives they are recruiting. A company that is based in California but does much of its manufacturing in the Far East and sells much of its product in Europe would be foolish to insist that all its top executives be American. The nationality no longer matters as much as the ability to do the job now and to refine the job later. If the best person for the job is French or Taiwanese, then that's who should have it.

The problem is the scarcity of good international managers. They're out there, all right, but everybody who's operating across borders wants them. The challenge for the headhunters is to cast a wide enough net, particularly in Europe, where the business culture has an advantage over the U.S business culture. Historically, managers of small and medium-sized European companies, as well as individual European entrepreneurs, are much more used to doing business across borders with neighboring countries. As a result, American headhunters have found it imperative to get into Europe. Different executive search agencies have approached the market in different ways. The typical approach is to simply open a branch office in Europe. But many companies are subsequently forced to make adjustments.

"Some have started their own foreign offices from scratch, others have purchased indigenous firms in various countries, some have done both. Affiliations involving mutual referrals and fee-splitting arrangements have also been prevalent," said Paul R. Ray, Jr., president and CEO of Dallas-based Paul R. Ray and Co., Inc. His company followed other American executive search firms by opening a London office several years ago, but abandoned that strategy when the branch failed to produce as hoped. In a business where networking is everything, the Americans came to Europe with few personal connections. Rather than trying to restructure his European branch, Ray decided to try something new.

He formed a partnership with a French executive search firm, Carre, Orban and Partners, that is aimed at giving each company access to the other's European and American client bases and recruiting pools. There are no Americans managing Europeans, and no Europeans managing Americans. The Americans aren't trying to build up contacts from scratch in Europe, nor the French in America. The Americans can use their French partner's lists of European companies and executives to make job matches for American clients, and the French can do the same for their European clients with Ray's American lists. "We have both been able to keep our individual identities and operational independence in our domestic markets, for example, while benefiting from a far closer relationship than is possible through other, less binding arrangements," Ray said.

Like anywhere else, friendship can be one of the worst foundations for selecting a partner or representative in Europe. Yes, you want to be able to get along with the Europeans you will be working with, but the fact that they may be nice people should never be allowed to cloud hard business decisions. At the same time, even the most attractive business arrangement probably won't work without adequate trust and mutual respect between the Americans and the Europeans involved. TGI Friday's (Chapter 4) is a good example of how the executives from Dallas got together with the executives of Whitbread, the English brewing concern, through their respective business needs. They examined each other's companies in minute detail before they ever met face to face. Not once, in spending hours with executives from both companies while doing research on their partnership, did I ever hear anyone mention friendship as a factor in the way they made business decisions. In contrast, consider the case of Bonanza, the American steakhouse chain that saw Friday's success in Europe, examined the same market opportunities that drew Friday's across the Atlantic to Europe, and decided to make a similar international plunge.

Like Friday's, Bonanza could pick and choose among many European suitors for its overseas partner. After all, it appeared to offer the same sort of American quality and service, while filling the huge void in Europe for low-priced, family-style restaurants. Like Friday's, Bonanza decided that Britain was the place to start because of the similar language and culture. Bonanza chose Mansfield Inns, the pub-and-restaurant arm of another big British brewery, because it seemed best positioned to know how to crack the market. Unlike TGI Friday's and Whitbread, however, executives from Bonanza and Mansfield Inns seemed to base their partnership much more on the personal friendships they developed when putting the deal together. I met several of the top executives of both Bonanza and Mansfield Inns at the grand opening of the first Bonanza steakhouse in Britain, and every one of them said that they were sure the partnership would work well because they all liked each other so much. They were wrong.

If anything, Bonanza seemed to be bringing more to the party in Europe than Friday's. Its American identity was just as strong, and if its image wasn't as upscale, that could be a benefit in reaching broadly into the wide-open market. Certainly the fact that Bonanza was not as alcohol-oriented and ordinarily not as expensive as Friday's would be an advantage in filling the huge market gap for family dining. Also, Bonanza had a comparable partnership structure with Mansfield, allowing the British company a "master franchise" that envisioned 20 Bonanza restaurants initially, to be followed within a few years by perhaps 200 more. But remember, Friday's executives insisted on keeping control: They made the decisions and then demanded that Whitbread stick to them. Whitbread, despite initial misgivings, ultimately did whatever Friday's told them to do. In contrast, Bonanza's executives repeatedly applauded their own faith in their Mansfield partners, and I believe that faith led them to defer to Mansfield on important decisions. Perhaps the most critical decision was the location for the first and most important Bonanza outlet, the flagship for the entire European chain.

Mansfield put the first Bonanza in a new shopping mall. An American restaurant, they reasoned, would go well in an another American transplanted concept, the shopping mall. Naturally, that made sense to Bonanza, because so many of its 600-plus outlets in North America were in or near shopping centers. No one took into account the differences between U.S. and European shopping malls, or the reasons that people go to them. In America, people go to shopping malls for all sorts of reasons now — to shop, to eat, to see movies, to walk, to set up their tables for petition drives. The shopping mall has replaced the old town square in American life. Europe still has vibrant downtown districts, and the high-street shopping precincts are still very much alive. Europeans typically go to an American-style shopping mall (if there's one available in the area, and there's often not) only to shop and often to visit one particular store in the mall. A trip to a shopping center is an expedition, not a part of daily life, for most Europeans. They are much less likely than Americans to say, "Hey, let's all pile in the car and go over to the mall. We'll get something to eat over there." In or near the mall, they might end up in a Bonanza, which is hardly regarded as expensive.

In Europe, however, people who eat at malls are more likely to go for something really fast and really cheap—much cheaper than Bonanza. Mansfield Inns showed that it wasn't really in touch with its potential market by making Bonanza a pretty pricey proposition by American standards. A T-bone, for example, was on the menu for the equivalent of about $17. How attractive would that be to the typically British working-class family of four with a household income of not much more than $15,000 a year? Moreover, the shopping mall chosen by Mansfield for the first British Bonanza was right in the middle of London, on one of the busiest high-street shopping areas. Unlike American Bonanza customers, Britons couldn't drive into a spacious edge-of-town parking lot and then walk directly into the restaurant at ground level. You couldn't even see a Bonanza sign from anywhere on the high street. My associate Sean Kelly and I attended that grand opening in the spring of 1989. We found the entrance to the mall from the high street and then had to climb two flights of stairs to the restaurant. We passed rows of empty and unopen shops, some of them still under construction. It turned out that Mansfield, left by Bonanza to arrange the grand opening, had scheduled it for a time when the rest of the mall wasn't even open yet. It would be weeks before the rest of the shops in the mall would be open, and weeks before anyone would have any reason to come to the mall except to visit an unfamiliar and expensive American restaurant that no one knew was there anyway.

Kelly and I, along with dozens of other journalists, retail analysts, consultants, property developers, and food-and-beverage suppliers, were served steaks and champagne beneath a continuously playing video that was aimed at telling first-time British customers how to place their order, find a table, and help themselves to the salad bar. "People are really going to have to want to eat here," I said. Kelly, an American who grew up in Europe, shook his head doubtfully. "I can't see it working," he said. "Maybe someplace else in Britain, but not here." Most of the staff doing the actual cooking at the grand opening were Bonanza employees from the States who had come over to train British workers. Unlike Friday's, which went to extraordinary lengths with its "auditions" to recruit lively people who had no previous catering experience, Bonanza had allowed Mansfield to hire people who had been working in restaurants in Britain and elsewhere for years. Where Friday's could train people from scratch in the art and style of American service, Bonanza had to first teach them to unlearn bad habits and bad attitudes.

A few days after that grand opening, our Brazilian nanny's boyfriend, a personable but notoriously unreliable young German, said he had been hired to work in the kitchen of the new Bonanza. "Yah, is great job for a while," he told me about his training. "Me and the other guys make sandwiches for each other." He said that when his training ended and the rest of the mall opened—when he would have to start making sandwiches for real customers, in other words—he was going to quit. And he did. Who knows how many others like him wasted Bonanza's time and money? In the end, the Bonanza flagship led a small and sinking fleet. Only one other Bonanza was opened, in the northern England resort town of Blackpool. Neither did very well, and Mansfield quickly scrapped its plans to open others. Within two years, both had been closed. The Bonanza in

113

the London mall was replaced by a McDonald's that was doing great business.

For a final word, Sean Kelly went back to Bonanza in the States. A spokesman said Bonanza still had a master franchise agreement in effect with Mansfield; the future of the European franchises depended on Mansfield's people, however, and the Bonanza spokesman suggested that Kelly check with them. So he did. Derek Mapp, the Mansfield Inns commercial director, blamed Bonanza for not being what the British public wanted or needed. "There were conceptual problems with the product," he said, citing the shopping-mall setting and the inability of British customers to wrap their minds around the idea of a free, unlimited salad bar. "The use and value of a salad bar has been quickly understood in America," he said. "The value of money that the salad bar gives as part of the meal has been recognized there. But here, salad bars were never provided in restaurants except as an extra, at additional cost. In Britain the product looked more expensive than it actually was. We had to spend a lot of time and extra effort instructing the customer what to do." It seems hard to believe that diners anywhere would need to be persuaded to use a free salad bar with their meals, but the Mansfield official said the partnership was dead: "We have forgone our franchise interests."

The dangers of choosing the wrong European partner can be seen in the experiences of Gordon Dorrett and his design company. While still in his twenties, Dorrett developed a reputation as one of the hottest young designers in a hot new field: the blend of leisure and retail in big malls. This mixing of shopping and recreation was taking the big North American shopping malls well beyond the theme restaurants, amusement arcades, and multiplex cinemas that once summed up their "entertainment" aspects. Boating lakes, ice rinks, ski hills, indoor amusement parks, and water parks were being designed into new malls and added to old malls that were being renovated. Working for Forrec International, a Toronto-based design partnership recognized as *the* leader in this new field, Dorrett was personally responsible for some of the more spectacular and innovative leisure components in big North American shopping malls. For instance, he did the master designs for the underwater submarine ride that became a centerpiece of the amusement park in the huge West Edmonton mall. That particular mall has been studied by all manner of retail analysts, leisure consultants, and sociologists from around the world for the way it led to changes in consumer shopping and leisure patterns. The West Edmonton mall and its leisure facilities, including Dorrett's submarine ride, paved the way for the now commonplace attitude that a visit to a big regional shopping mall could be a "day out" for the entire family.

Basking in this success, Forrec International received many offers to apply its design skills abroad. Everyone who was building a big mall anywhere in the world realized that it would be more successful—with bigger, higher spending crowds and bigger, busier stores paying more rent—if it incorporated the type of leisure facilities that Forrec International could design. Besides, like many North American companies offering specialized, expensive products and services (Wall Street banks and law firms are also good examples), Forrec realized that its market in North America was relatively saturated. In Canada and the States, most cities already had all the big malls they needed. And there were plenty of other design firms competing for contracts to build leisure facilities in the malls. Forrec decided it would be foolish to ignore the opportunities in Europe, where the big regional, American-style shopping mall was a new concept, and where there were few if any designers ready or able to compete in this narrow area of expertise.

With its then unblemished track record, Forrec chose Gord Dorrett to be the firm's point man in Europe. After all, he was not only good, he was also "international." His father was a career Canadian diplomat who had served in consulates and embassies around the world, and Gord had grown up in a number of different cultures. If anyone could handle Europe for them, Forrec's managing partners reckoned, it was Dorrett. Maybe they were right. But then, maybe no one could handle Europe for them, at least not in the way they approached this new market. Certainly the way the designers tried to establish themselves in Europe is a textbook example of how not to do it. And what happened to Dorrett is a classic warning of how poor planning at home can damage companies and threaten promising young careers abroad.

The Europeans interested in building big shopping malls were all jumping on the leisure-complex bandwagon, and they were all knocking on Forrec's door. One of the firm's senior partners decided to begin investigating, and within short order he won a big contract to build an indoor amusement park at the Metro Centre in northern England, the American-style mega-mall built by John Hall (Chapter 4). All of Forrec's design work for the Metro Centre's indoor amusement park was done in Canada, but the project convinced Forrec that an office was needed in Europe. Scouting around, the Forrec senior partner who had won the Metro Centre contract made friends with an English real estate developer who had done a few smaller mall projects but seemed poised for the big time with plans for several ambitious large-scale projects. Beyond friendship, the Englishman impressed Forrec with his high-flying extravagance. He rarely took a train or car when a chartered helicopter or his private corporate jet would do. He promised to provide the money to set up Forrec Europe, which in turn would provide the design expertise to help him win contracts and build big malls. The partners back in Canada said Forrec Europe would be the firm's independent European arm, working with the Englishman to develop mall projects.

There were problems from the beginning. One was that neither Forrec International nor the Englishman had set out their goals for Dorrett and Forrec Europe. Both sides simply assumed they would do lots of business together and make

116

loads of money. But it didn't turn out that way. The Englishman, operating from one office with eight people in London's
fashionable Mayfair district, would occasionally send a simple
design query down to Dorrett, whose office was in the basement. Few major design projects filtered down the stairs. So to
get assignments and justify his existence in Europe, Dorrett had
to go out and try on his own to get a piece of projects anywhere
and everywhere. Instead of just designing shopping center facilities, his specialty, he became part of the development process,
and he was dragged into it with no experience as a developer.
He faced the prospect of helping to find and bring together the
land, investors, retailers, and builders who were all necessary
for a shopping center to get off the drawing boards.

This was made all the more difficult by the fact that Forrec
Europe had been "piggybacked" financially onto the Englishman's company. Dorrett didn't have control of his own budget,
and indeed he didn't even have a budget. What things could he
spend on? How much could he spend? No one seemed to know,
including the Englishman who was in theory paying for everything. Meanwhile, Dorrett's partners at Forrec International
back in Toronto exerted no pressure on their European operation to begin showing results. No one expected Dorrett to show
a profit in the first year, but no one ever said when he was
supposed to begin making a profit. Worse, there was no system
of accounting to see whether he was or wasn't making a profit.
There was no monitoring, no system of checks and balances, to
make sure the European subsidiary was doing what it was
supposed to do. In fact, no one seemed sure what it was supposed to do.

When Dorrett on occasion did come up with business on his
own, he didn't have the staff in London to do the designing for
it. Instead he had to send the design work back to Toronto.
Because it took so long to send the specifications to Toronto, get
the home-office designers to do the work for him, and then have
it sent back, Dorrett went to a number of presentations without

the drawings and other graphics he needed. When he did get business from European clients – mostly found on his own, rather than through the Englishman – the parent company in Canada would then invoice Dorrett for the design work. Rather than being a part of his own company, Dorrett was treated like any other developer coming to Forrec. This created an awkward conflict of interest. Should he be trying to hold down his own development costs and the costs for the clients he cultivated on his own in Europe? Or should he be trying to get as much out of his new European clients as possible in order to maximize the bottom line for the parent company in Canada? If Dorrett asked the designers in Canada to modify their bill to hold down costs, they might say, "Hey, whose side are you on?" On the other hand, if he was going to be treated like any other developer, he probably should have been shopping around at other design firms, just as any other developer would, and trying to find the best service at the best price for his clients.

Dorrett came to realize that he needed his own design team in Europe if Forrec was going to be serious about the European market. Meanwhile, fueled by easy credit and the same sort of real estate boom that boosted Donald Trump's empire in America, the Englishman's business was growing at an amazing rate. From the one address in Mayfair, he opened offices in Manchester, Glasgow, Barcelona, Frankfurt, Madrid, Paris, Majorca, Brussels, Los Angeles, and Toronto to accommodate his various developments, either real or merely hoped for, in all those areas. Unfortunately, the Englishman bit off more than he could chew. While requiring staff to read Trump's book *The Art of the Deal* and espousing the general theory that if you borrow a dollar you can use it to earn two, he vastly overextended himself, just as his hero did.

Along the way, the Englishman bought into Forrec International for $2 million, money the parent company planned to use for expansion and to buy land to launch developments of its own. Then came the worldwide property and retail slump of the late 1980s and early 1990s. The Englishman, like his model Donald Trump but on a smaller scale, couldn't meet the high interest payments on his borrowings and lost his property and his deals. His company went belly up, leaving Forrec Europe high and dry. After two years of struggling to define a role for himself and Forrec Europe, Dorrett was forced to dedicate much of his energy over several months to a damage-control and salvage operation. He tried to hang onto whatever business he could while at the same time coaxing the Englishman to pay whatever he could of the money he owed to Forrec. But besides sending his company into bankruptcy, the Englishman was deep in debt personally.

Naturally, the Englishman's financial demise caused a crisis for Forrec, which had made considerable financial commitments of its own based on the assumption that he would pay the money he owed, including the $2 million for the buy-in. There was a lot of soul-searching and second-guessing back at the headquarters in Toronto. Perhaps the senior partners who agreed to link up with the Englishman had been beguiled by his charisma. Perhaps the Englishman's friendship with the Canadian partner exploring Europe had impaired Forrec's corporate vision. Perhaps the Canadians' judgment was clouded by the Englishman's grandiose schemes, private aircraft, and lavish entertaining. Perhaps Forrec simply had been naive and not done enough homework about Europe. Whatever happened, it was obvious that Forrec had chosen the wrong European partner.

Fortunately for the Canadian designers, they had chosen the right company representative to send to Europe. When the Englishman's business was going down the tubes, Forrec's European aspirations could easily have gone with it. No one would have blamed Dorrett for telling his partners back in Toronto that it was time to pack up and head home, to cut the firm's losses and write off the whole experiment to experience. But what would his future with the firm have been after that?

Would he be forever associated with the ignominious failure in Europe? Would he be branded a loser? It's not unusual in such situations for the person or people sent to Europe to shoulder the blame for any and all problems, even if the problems are not their own fault. It's a very human response: Senior managers who send people to Europe end up blaming the Euroreps for the managers' own lack of judgment and planning. Even if such blame is unspoken, even if it's deeply subconscious, the effects can be devastating for the people who must return to their home offices after a European failure.

Dorrett, himself a partner by then, closed Forrec Europe when the Englishman's credit-dependent empire collapsed. "It wasn't doing any business anyway," he said. He could have returned to Canada then and there; his senior partners assured him he wasn't personally to blame. But Dorrett wasn't ready to acknowledge defeat and risk being branded a loser. He argued that Forrec should try again in Europe. After all, the reasons for going to Europe in the first place were as valid as ever. As Willie Sutton said when asked why he robbed banks, "That's where the money is." Dorrett and his partners believed there was still money in Europe. But Forrec had to start over, to build from the ashes of the experience with the high-flying Englishman who had crashed and burned. Dorrett and his partners agreed to abandon any grand plans to be European developers who would be the driving force behind big projects. Instead, they decided to go back to what they did best: design work for developers who already had projects in the pipeline.

Three strategies were considered. First, Forrec could start afresh, bringing over a whole new staff to build from the ground up, to create a European version of the Canadian design team. This was Dorrett's original preference. He was a designer, after all, and he wanted to head an office of designers. But his partners convinced him that such a move would be too expensive and an exercise in "reinventing the wheel," as he later described it. The second possible strategy was to buy an existing European design consultancy that could be folded under the Forrec umbrella. Forrec went so far as to look at several good medium-sized European design firms as potential takeover or merger targets, and finally identified one that was about the same size as Forrec, with the same sort of aspirations and philosophy. But the Canadians realized that just as their firm had its own distinct identity, baggage, and history, so did the European firm. Instead of Forrec being the clearly dominant partner, any alliance would be complicated by trying to mesh the two corporate cultures. Instead of making things simpler, such a merger might just double the trouble for each firm.

Finally, Forrec decided to pursue the third possible strategy for remaining in Europe: a joint venture with a small firm. Dorrett chose a two-man partnership he had worked with while still under the Englishman's wing. The two designers were young and talented, but had little experience in the large-scale retail-leisure projects that were Forrec's bread and butter. The designers were hungry for bigger and better design assignments, but weren't ambitious in the sense that they wanted to head a huge firm of their own. While they didn't have much corporate aptitude, they didn't have a corporate attitude, either. The former could be learned, but the latter could almost never be unlearned. To Dorrett, the two young designers seemed perfect. His partners in Canada agreed. The young designers, operating out of a studio in a decidedly unfashionable London suburb, were happy to be part of the new joint venture that became known as Forrec Design.

Dorrett moved out of his basement office at the Englishman's posh address and moved in with the young designers. He began teaching them what he knew about North American design concepts and what he had learned about working with European developers, retailers, and investors. The two new partners and their staff of a dozen designers went back and forth to Toronto for training and to work on joint projects. Members of the 100-strong Toronto staff who would be provid-

121

ing backup design work went back and forth to work in Forrec Design's suburban London studio. The new arrangement removed Dorrett from the conflict with his home office and with his partners. The new Forrec Design joint venture could still participate in development projects that came along, but it would primarily act as a pure design firm, bidding on any available projects. Instead of apologizing and begging for extra time because all the design work had to be done in Canada, Dorrett and his new partners could respond as quickly as their European competition. Moreover, he could offer to have the design work done either in Europe or in Canada. If it seemed like a potential client would prefer to have North American designers, Dorrett could promise that all the work would be done in Toronto. If the client seemed to prefer a European designer, then it would be done in London.

When the new Forrec Design joint venture was set up, Dorrett and his partners resolved not to repeat their mistakes. Accounting and monitoring procedures were established, including regular reviews of Forrec Design's financial performance. It was agreed that a moderate loss could be absorbed for a year or two, but after that the European operation had to at least break even. The partners agreed that having a presence in Europe was worth a fair amount of prestige, would help bring business in, and would help the overall performance of their company as long as it wasn't a financial drain. Dorrett worked with his two new partners at Forrec Design in the London suburbs for close to two years. The first year, they lost a little money. Dorrett and his senior partners in Canada reviewed the performance and decided it was working as planned. The second year Forrec Europe made a little money, and the long-range prospects were for at least breaking even for several years.

At the end of that second year with Forrec Design, after he had been in Europe for nearly four years, Dorrett returned to Toronto for good. He would have preferred that one of his

122

partners from Canada replace him as the firm's European representative, overseeing the Forrec Design joint venture with the two young English designers. But Forrec's experience in Europe had proved that the right people must be in the right slots – and they must want to be there. Of the four partners most likely to replace Dorrett, two were senior managers who were needed at the home office. Another was a technical specialist who wasn't interested in the all-round approach needed to run the European operation. And the fourth had four kids in school and a wife who loved her own job in Canada.

The firm could have sent a lower level member of the firm, an associate. But it would have cost something like $120,000, not counting taxes and air fares back and forth, to have someone there who wouldn't have the authority or the wherewithal to make key decisions. Dorrett had labored under that handicap when he first came to Europe, and he didn't want to put anyone else in the same position. So it was decided that Dorrett would still be in charge of the European operation, but from Canada. He felt the two English designers had absorbed the basics of what Forrec was trying to do and how it accomplished things. More importantly, they were continuing to learn. With frequent telephone and fax consultations and half a dozen regular trips back to Europe each year, as well as special visits to deliver or help with major presentations, Dorrett figured he could save the firm a pile of money while maintaining the kind of control needed for the European operation.

Gord Dorrett didn't slink back with his tail between his legs, with the distinction of presiding over the design firm's failure in Europe. Instead, his partners welcomed him back with an invitation to become the managing partner in charge of the day-to-day running of the office. Dorrett's partners realized that in staying on in Europe, he had proved himself in a baptism by fire. He brought back new ideas and the business acumen that had grown out of his experiences, both good and bad. He kept his head under pressure, he was a proven problem solver, and he insisted on strategic planning. As pretty much a one-man band in Europe, he had developed a well-rounded view of how a design firm should operate, from marketing to writing invoices. He maintained his loyalty and his sanity while showing management skills that no one, including himself, knew he had when he first went to Europe.

CHAPTER 7

♦ ♦ ♦

Negotiations

James A. Kiernan III was worried. Kiernan, managing partner in the Paris office of Debevoise & Plimpton, a big Wall Street law firm, had been in charge of negotiations on both sides of the Atlantic for an American corporate client's multibillion-dollar takeover deal in Europe. After months of tough bargaining, it was the deadline day, a Friday. Kiernan was certain that everything was in place. The last pending detail was the faxing of a legal certificate from the Netherlands to New York that would allow the wire transfer, by 5 P.M. Paris time, of $700 million from Paris to New York. At 2 P.M., Kiernan was told the certificate had not yet arrived in New York. He called the Rotterdam accounting firm that was supposed to send the certificate and demanded to know what had happened. The managing director wasn't sure. The accountant who had been working on the certificate, a Belgian, didn't seem to be around. No one seemed to know where he was, or where the certificate was.

Kiernan couldn't believe it. Was the whole deal going to fall apart? Hundreds of people – lawyers, bankers, investors, accountants, executives, and analysts – were waiting in offices around the world for the fax to arrive, the money to be transferred, and the deal to be announced. With minutes to spare, the missing Belgian accountant was located. He had taken the certificate, gotten in his car, and driven home to Belgium from his office in Rotterdam. He always did that on Friday afternoons, he explained. After a few choice words from Kiernan, the certificate was indeed faxed, just ahead of the deadline. The deal went through with only a handful of people knowing just how nearly it came apart because a Belgian accountant liked to be home for early *hors d'oeuvres* and cocktails on Fridays.

Kiernan's near brush with disaster was just one of many unexpected ways, despite meticulous preparations, that negotiations in Europe can go awry. If you don't like surprises, if you aren't able to adapt easily, if you aren't flexible of mind and calm of manner, if you can't read situations and react to them, if you can't go with the flow while sticking to what you know, here's some advice: Save yourself a lot of stress and strain by never undertaking negotiations in Europe or with Europeans. Things can be sidetracked for so many reasons. The Swede might not want any small talk, while the Spaniard might want nothing but. The Briton may want to hear only good things from you about his country, while expecting you to grin and bear it when he lists what is wrong with America. The French will undoubtedly be embarrassed if you bring up the financial condition of their company. The Italians often seem blithely unconcerned about profit and cannot understand why you are so interested in hard, bottom-line figures. One elderly German owner-manager who recognized that his sons weren't executive material was eager to discuss a merger, but the negotiations literally had to be conducted behind the trees in the Black Forest; he was afraid fellow villagers might find out about his plans and pressure him not to sell.

On top of the cultural and social sensibilities, a wide array of technical and procedural breakdowns can skew any European negotiations. Words are misinterpreted or misunderstood. Taxes or duties that were overlooked are arbitrarily imposed.

126

Owners come out of nowhere. Laws that no one seemed to know about suddenly come into play. Bureaucracies change their rulings on regulations. A few years ago, Skoal got permission from the British government to sell Bandits, its little pouches of chewing tobacco, in Britain. A couple of years later a different British government department announced that Bandits were a health hazard and banned them. Skoal challenged the ruling and won, but not before spending a lot of time and money on court proceedings. By then the European Community had begun talking about banning Bandits not only in Britain but everywhere in the EC.

Americans often find themselves hampered in European negotiations by the lack of available information. Many European companies don't keep track of their own or their competitors' business as well as American companies do. It's often difficult to get a handle on an entire market. And what records are available might be confusing. Accountants may keep different books for different folks: one for the tax collector, one for the bank, one for the employees, one for the management, and one for the owners. Even if an American is satisfied with a financial accounting, additional reviews, such as legal and environmental audits, are often advisable. Because so many companies have been in families for decades, and sometimes centuries, ownership structures are complicated, especially in southern European countries. Procter & Gamble thought it had signed an agreement to buy a Spanish soap company until a German group announced that it had taken over the company. The Americans belatedly learned they had been dealing with a dissident minority group that had no authority to agree to a sale. One Spanish brewery could not be sold until the purchaser tracked down all 170 family members with an ownership interest and showed them how the sale could be managed in the face of Spain's stiff capital gains tax.

Americans doing business in Europe should do as they do when negotiating in America – play to their strengths in the market: price, distribution, sales, service, or quality. Not surprisingly, people who are good at negotiating in the United States are those most likely to be good negotiators in Europe. Terry Carlson, a Los Angeles-based international lawyer who spent much of the 1980s conducting negotiations across Europe, summed it up this way: "You sit down with a bunch of lawyers from a bunch of different countries, and one says the contract has to say a certain thing under his law. Then another guy says that would be illegal in his country. And none of it works under U.S. law. So you have to find some middle ground, some new way of making it all work. If you give up easily, you don't get the deal done. It's really important to listen to people, look at the cultural reasons behind their positions, and figure out what they really need. And once a deal is done, you can always build on it next time, make it more sophisticated, add a twist or two. That's not only challenging, it can be fun. You have to be confident in your ability. You have to have a lot of patience. You have to be able to listen carefully, and ask the right questions, including why, at the right times. You also have to be able to overcome jet lag easily and be able to pick up a ringing phone in the middle of the night and make some sort of sense to your partners in the States. You have to enjoy learning about cultural differences. If you don't find something interesting, if you don't find something positive in things being so foreign, you won't enjoy the experience and you won't do well. You have to have a willingness to accept that the way we do things in America is not necessarily the right way or the best way."

Approaching negotiations with Europeans, it's often advisable to be firm, even aggressive, in setting the stage. Push to nail down the when, where, how, and why. Because holes in a diary are seen as the sign of someone who doesn't have enough to do, many Europeans need to be pressed to set dates for appointments. Their diaries are always full; everything is impossible next week, and the week after that is even worse. Unless prodded, a date for a meeting may never be found; when prodded, one is usually found fairly quickly, despite some moaning about how busy things are. Try to firm up the agenda via advance correspondence: This is what we will talk about, this is what I will bring, this is what you will bring, and this is what we will try to accomplish. Beyond good agenda-setting, which is useful in arranging negotiations in the U.S. or anywhere else, this is important in Europe because so many Europeans are not accustomed to getting directly down to business.

Traditionally, many Europeans prefer to stretch negotiations out to the point that they never really seem like negotiations. Rather than making it happen, a deal just seems to evolve as the two sides spend time together, casually or socially or in formal meetings in which little of substance is accomplished. Gradually they come to a meeting of minds, almost by osmosis. Americans are more transactional. Getting to know and like someone is a bonus in business deals, not a prerequisite. We don't want to have four meetings when one will do. "Why are we here at this concert?" Americans ask themselves. "Why do we have to have dinner again? Why can't we just sit down and hammer this thing out and go home?" Nowadays, more Europeans are happy to deal in the more abrupt, pointed *American* way, but they may be reluctant to take the lead. When arrangements are left to Europeans, the negotiations may wander for a time.

After being focused and assertive in leading up to negotiations, many Americans find it useful to back off a bit in actual face-to-face meetings. Europeans respect American decisiveness, but they don't want to be bashed over the head with American aggressiveness. They want you to blend in, to belong as much as possible. They want to feel comfortable with you. They don't want to be overwhelmed by charisma and force of personality and the brilliance of your plan or your product. If charm is part of your personal negotiating program, try to underwhelm. "Never tell them this is the way we do it in America, so this is best," one experienced American negotiator

129

suggested. "A lot of sharp Europeans will pull your chain, sometimes with digs about America, just to see if you have a sense of humor. Roll with the punches. Don't be too earnest, too eager, especially at first. Go slow. You know, out of every ten Europeans I deal with, two like Americans, two don't like Americans, and six are neutral. At first, I wasted a lot of time on the two who didn't like Americans. I considered them a challenge. I wanted to win them over, to make them like me, to persuade them to my way of thinking. It was a waste of time. Forget those two. When you come up against those two who just have it in for Americans, don't bother trying to change their minds. Concentrate on the other eight who want to do business with you."

At the same time, Europeans appreciate mild flattery. Oftentimes, merely listening and showing interest in them, their country, their company, and what they have to say is adequate flattery on the part of an American. Maintaining an air of superiority can leave you empty-handed and looking foolish. A Merrill Lynch executive warned Americans against stumbling over their stereotypes: "I've known a number of Italian corporate patriarchs who like to act dumb or crude. Some Americans will swallow it and think they're dealing with unsophisticated rubes. But these guys got where they are, to the top of big companies, through very tough family control. They've had to be far-sighted to keep that kind of control. They know what they're doing, and they know what you're doing, too."

To Europeans, an American is not a big shot just because he or she is from out of town. Almost everyone they deal with is from out of town. They've been dealing with sharp foreigners since Roman times. Moreover, they know a lot more about Europe than you do. The typical young American male executive knows a lot more about baseball trivia than he does about European history, culture, art, and languages. What did Spinoza believe? Whose side was Finland on in World War II? When was the big flood in Florence? These are things many Europeans lived through or learned in school while we were memorizing baseball stats, and they are things that many Europeans are more than willing to bring up just to test an American. Modesty, deference, and good-natured confessions of ignorance are usually the only defense.

Americans are less likely to walk away from an attractive business proposition for purely personal reasons than Europeans are. Usually, those personal reasons are rooted in loyalty. Many old European businesses prize long-term relationships more than almost anything. To consider changing a relationship, or sometimes just in opening a new one, particularly with some upstart American, they often need assurances that there will be a long-term commitment. "To us, yesterday is ancient history," one American securities lawyer observed. "To them, 500 years is yesterday. There are still some old French and British who will never do business with Germans because of World War II. There are a lot of Western Europeans who will never do business in Eastern Europe because it's too close to Russia. My American clients are companies with two-year or five-year plans. My European clients are companies with 10-year, 20-year, and sometimes even 50-year plans."

A New York-based marketing executive for a major American book wholesaler had a bitter encounter with European corporate loyalty. Negotiating a major sale of American books with a coalition of eight German cooperative library associations, she made concession after concession. "We really wanted to make this deal," she said. "It would have been a great foot in the door to what could have been a very promising market for us for years to come. They seemed to want us. They negotiated real hard on particulars like delivery and discounts. We knew they wouldn't have done that if they weren't intent on the deal. We gave in to most of their demands to get that toehold. I thought we had it locked up. Then, out of the blue, after everything was settled, the whole deal fell apart. One of the eight associations had vetoed it. They said no, and the other seven went along rather than argue. We knew that particular association had some misgivings, but we figured the approval of the other seven would put the pressure on that one to approve it, too. We had no idea that just one objection would pressure the others to drop out. There's such a spirit of concerted action in Europe, such a desire to avoid disputes that might alienate old associates, that the other seven gave up a deal that they really wanted. It just shows how Americans have to cultivate relationships across a broad base for a long time in Europe. You can't rely on the market leverage that we're used to in the U.S."

In Europe, where the centuries have been cracked by war after war over small slivers of land, territory is all-important. And most negotiations involving Americans doing business in Europe are conducted on *their* territory. Some Americans like to keep things as neutral as possible, meeting in third-party offices or rented rooms and restaurants. Or they try to gain an edge by meeting in their own hotel, in a room where they are the host. This often falls flat, however. No matter how artificially you put yourself in territorial control, no American business visitor will ever be as at home in Toledo, Spain, as in Toledo, Ohio. At the same time, it's important to avoid conducting negotiations or talking any form of serious business in settings that are too foreign even by European standards. Going to a bullfight might seem like a good idea, but the whole scene – sights, sounds, smells, excitement – are so disorienting, and sometimes so intimidating, that an American could easily end up talking about things that shouldn't be discussed at that time. It's just too easy to become dependent, even for a couple of hours, on a host who might know how to exploit that dependence. Go ahead and go to the bullfight, if you think you'd like it, but don't talk business even casually. Never, never, never talk any sort of business in a sauna with a Finn. You'll be literally naked, following their instructions, and when they turn up the heat you'll agree to anything to get out of that sweatbox.

European regulations can be maddening, particularly in recent years as the EC Eurocrats in Brussels have been flexing their new regulatory Euromuscle in imposing rules on all 12 member nations. Not that the Eurocrats have proved themselves particularly adept at negotiations so far, even with each other. Some of the most heated debates have occurred over the percentage of fat in cream and the amount of meat in meat pies. It took 14 years for the EC to finally settle on a definition for jam. When that definition said that jam must be made out of fruit, Portugal complained. It seems the Portuguese have always made jam out of carrots, too: *marmelada de cenoura*. The Eurocrats huddled again and, after only a few months, emerged to declare that for now and forever, the carrot is classified as a fruit in the EC.

Individual European countries get into the regulatory act, too. Gillette, the U.S. razor group, bought shares in and made loans to Swedish Match, a Dutch company based in Switzerland. The British government subsequently ordered Gillette to divest itself and sever all financial ties with Swedish Match. The rationale was that Swedish Match was the parent company of Wilkinson Sword, the British company that is Gillette's main rival in the British wet shaving products market. The British Department of Trade and Industry said Gillette's link with Swedish Match was therefore an antitrust violation. Gillette either had to sell or be faced with a ban from Britain, where it had 60 percent of the shaving products market compared with Wilkinson's 20 percent.

Some American companies have come up with creative ways of getting around European nationalism and protectionism. When Disney decided to build EuroDisneyland outside Paris, the French government said that the enterprise would have to be 51 percent French-owned. Disney agreed to take only 49 percent ownership, which meant that it would bring home 49 percent of the profit. On top of that, however, Disney negotiated for 10 percent of the admission fees, 5 percent of the food and merchandising revenues, and—the key to the whole thing—hefty fees for its exclusive management contract. Besides boosting Disney's profits well beyond 49 percent, the management contract virtually guaranteed Disney more control than the majority French owners. Along the way, Disney picked up millions worth of government grants, tax breaks, and other incentives, including big infrastructure spending projects on roads and mass transportation.

These incentives are the flip side of European protectionism. Although most Eurocrats would be much more willing to throw money at companies and entrepreneurs closer to home, many Americans besides Disney have taken advantage of such incentives. Ford is involved in a project with Volkswagen in Portugal for which the government and EC incentives have topped $1 billion. When Ford expressed concern during the negotiations about the availability of good Portuguese middle management, a publicly funded program was established to train managers. Ford has no financial obligation for the program and no obligation to hire the graduates. Nearly half the cost of another new plant in Portugal, this one built by Delco Remy, a division of General Motors, came from government and EC aid.

Thomas Callahan, a Frankfurt-based finance manager for TRW, the American conglomerate whose European companies are primarily in automotive parts and supplies, found that his naturally easygoing manner served him well during frequent negotiations with European banks and companies. "In the States, so much is standard, but in Europe you have to negotiate everything deal by deal. Even the commissions that you would think are standard have to be negotiated," he said. He recently suspected that one bank might be trying to take advantage of him after an Italian TRW subsidiary asked him to oversee a large payment to a German company. "The German company didn't want lire, they wanted deutschmarks, so I told the Italian bank we were dealing with to sell lire for us. In Italy, it can take anywhere from one to ten days to change money, and with large sums that can make a big difference to us in lost interest.

Well, in this case it took 10 days. I called the guy at the bank who was in charge and asked him if there was a problem."

In the States, Callahan might have raised hell, complained bitterly, and made some overt threats. In Europe, he adopted a softer approach. He made it clear that he didn't care whether someone had made a mistake or whether the bank had deliberately hung on to the money for a few extra days in order to skim off some interest for itself. Instead, he asked, "Is there anything I can do to make sure this doesn't happen again?" Callahan was afraid that any direct accusations or formal complaints to the bank's top management would have touched off a chain of recriminations through the bank, with one person after another passing the buck – or, rather, the lire. If that had happened, he reasoned, his chances of getting a refund from the bank would have been greatly diminished and held up for weeks or months even if it was approved. By not making an angry, formal demand, he ended up getting compensation quietly and quickly from the bank's foreign exchange department.

In another instance, a TRW subsidiary in Italy negotiated an attractive loan from an EC fund. The loan had to be made through an Italian state-owned bank. So Callahan set up negotiations between the bank's lawyers in Rome and TRW's lawyers in Cleveland. After the two sides seemed to get off to a good start, Callahan got a call from Cleveland. The TRW lawyers had not been able to reach the Italian bank's attorney. Would he try? Callahan spent several days attempting to make contact with her. His faxes were ignored. No one picked up the lawyer's office phone. When Callahan got through to other numbers at the bank, no one seemed to speak English. Several times when he started talking, the phone was abruptly hung up. Finally someone from the bank called Callahan. It was a replacement lawyer. The original lawyer had been injured in an auto accident and was off work. Why hadn't he called earlier, Callahan wondered. Basically, he hadn't felt like it, the lawyer said. Then the substitute lawyer started over and insisted on haggling over minor details that had been resolved weeks earlier.

Callahan had seen it all before. Europeans, more than Americans, want to negotiate for the sake of negotiating rather than for the sake of making a good deal. This Italian lawyer, like too many other European negotiators Callahan had seen, wanted concessions. It didn't matter whether they were large or small. Callahan was never sure whether this lawyer didn't like Americans or whether he handled all his negotiations so obtusely. In any event, he apparently had some personal stake in winning little self-defined victories. He had to be right, and he had to have the last word. This was particularly frustrating for Callahan and the TRW lawyers in Cleveland because the loan agreement should have been relatively straightforward. The whole thing could have been wrapped up in a couple of weeks or so. Instead, thanks to the Italian lawyer, it stretched out a full three and a half months, right up to the deadline. Each time the Italian lawyer had a new objection, Cleveland would complain to Callahan, and he would have to go back to the Italian and work out some sort of compromise, usually on wording. A typical stumbling block was the very last one, right at the deadline, when the Italian objected to some seemingly routine wording that had been in the contract but had not given any offense until then. What it boiled down to was this: The Italian lawyer threatened to scrap the whole deal unless the phrase *up until* was changed to *before,* even though it made no difference in context. Wearily, Callahan agreed.

Language is often a problem, even when no one is being intentionally obstructive. Callahan told of negotiations with a Spanish banker that centered on "discounting." In the States, this is the financial technique under which a bank provides a company with money now in exchange for receivables later. In Spain, however, discounting means presenting a future-dated draft and accepting less than face value for it. "We had a long conversation before we realized we were not talking about the same process," Callahan said. "When you're negotiating face to face in Europe, you constantly say things over and over, in different ways, to make sure the other side understands. You rephrase and rephrase and then follow up with a memo to make sure they understand before any commitments are made."

Typically, negotiations involving Americans are conducted in English. The European principals usually speak English themselves or with the assistance of interpreters. This is especially true in business sectors such as oil and computers, where English is generally acknowledged as *the* international language. (Many computer programmers argue that English is actually the second international language in their business; profanity is the first.) Larry Sullivan, a Texan who has worked for a number of American and European oil companies in recent years, became something of a specialist in negotiations in Italy because he speaks Italian. He developed a smooth routine for starting presentations in Italian and then gradually switching to English when things got down to the nitty-gritty. "Another important thing is to always to let 'em know about your university degrees," Sullivan said. "Europe isn't like the States, where 30 percent have college degrees. They're more rare in Europe, and in some countries, including Italy, a degree means a lot, especially a science degree. People know you have a science degree, and they call you doctor, *dottore,* out of respect."

Not all negotiations are conducted in English, of course. Away from the big boardrooms, small American companies and entrepreneurs often find their opportunities among people who do not speak English. This is especially true in Eastern Europe. It's always a good rule to make sure the final contract is in English, but during the negotiations it may be more convenient for Americans to work in a European language through an interpreter. A good rule: The more difficult the negotiations, the more a good interpreter is needed. An interpreter, it should be pointed out, is not a translator. Translators have time and dictionaries on their side, while interpreters have to work quickly, as quickly as people talk, and deal with the nuances of the spoken word rather than the firmness of the written word. When working with an interpreter, find and hire your own rather than relying on the other side's or using someone they offer.

Most good interpreters prefer to work from the foreign language into their own native language. This avoids the sort of problems that President Jimmy Carter had in Warsaw in 1977, when he used an American, a State Department employee, as an interpreter for a speech to a Polish audience. The interpreter stunned the Poles, according to the *International Herald Tribune,* by using the word for "lust" instead of "desire" and by twisting Carter's "When I left the United States . . ." into "When I abandoned the United States. . . ." Brief your interpreter thoroughly in advance, not only on specialized words and terminology, but also on the background of the negotiations, the characters involved, your expectations, and your goals. As the Paris-based International Association of Conference Interpreters advised: "If you are not prepared to trust an interpreter with confidential information, then don't use one." Tell the interpreter that when something comes up that may have a meaning beyond the words spoken at the time, you should be told later. Encourage the interpreter to make notes and observations for a later debriefing.

In any negotiations, patience is always a virtue. Many of the best negotiators are known as "iron bottoms" for the way they can sit forever in their chairs, listening and talking, talking and listening, wearing everyone down and out across the table. In Europe, patience is especially important because Americans are often working outside their normal cultural context. The usual touchstones are gone. In America, most successful businesspeople like to think they can size up a new acquaintance within minutes or even seconds. In Europe, you can't. All the familiar telltales—accent, vocabulary, expressions, body language, alma mater—are missing in Europeans. As a result, Americans may find themselves eager to make a deal with the first person who seems nice, speaks well, and says what they want to hear. Because Americans negotiating in Europe typically have a lot at stake, both personally and professionally, they often put pressure on themselves to come home with a result, any result, when caution might be the better option.

"And Americans often overestimate how fabulous they are as business executives," according to a Lawrence, Kansas, native who has been working in Europe for the past decade. "We tend to give ourselves an awful lot of credit. But we're not the only ones who can be creative, and we're certainly not the only ones who can be aggressive in a business deal." The best negotiators in Europe are aware that they are operating outside their normal cultural framework, but don't lose sight of the values and goals that made them successful back in the States. Look at the two U.S. restaurant chains discussed earlier. TGI Friday's said yes, things are different in Europe, but our product isn't; we're sticking with it straight down the line. Bonanza said yes, things are different in Europe, we'd better forget about the things that worked for us back home. Friday's is raking it in; Bonanza has disappeared from the European scene.

One American banker-broker (unlike the United States, you can do both in Europe) who works across Europe said he is regularly invited to pay bribes and kickbacks. It's immoral, unethical, and usually illegal in the States, but apparently quite commonplace in many European countries. "I deal with a lot of European attorneys, accountants, and bankers," he said. "I come to them with investment ideas that can make a lot of money for their clients. I want to be partners with them in bringing these opportunities to their clients. In at least 200 cases over the past five years, I've been told that I can't present my ideas to their clients unless I pay them something, or they get a percentage of whatever business I get from their clients. The Belgians, French, Germans, and Dutch seem to be the worst. I'm 200 for

200 in saying no. I ask them why they can't just play it straight. They would be doing their clients a service. But no, they want more. It's something I've never run into in the States, but I guess it happens all the time in Europe. Slowly, though, these people are realizing that I'm a straight shooter, and some of them are now coming back and asking if we can do business together, no strings attached."

Anheuser-Busch and the Brooklyn Brewery don't have a lot in common, except that both are in the beer business and both had difficulties negotiating their way into Europe. In many ways, their difficulties point out the pitfalls for U.S. companies large and small. Brooklyn first. As discussed earlier (Chapter 5), Brooklyn Brewery President Steve Hindy had several false starts in making contacts in Britain before he finally hooked up with the middleman, Greg Chesnulovitch, who put him in touch with Lynne Zilkha and her London distributorship, BB Supply, which became Brooklyn's British importer. In the course of the earlier contacts on his own, Hindy wasted a lot of time with another would-be importer in serious negotiations that eventually collapsed. At the time, this importer seemed happy to get Hindy's out-of-the-blue call. He said he had been looking for a quality American beer to bring into Britain and suggested they meet as soon as possible. Over lunch, he raved about Brooklyn Lager, praised the packaging, said he got a big kick out of the name and talked about how easy it would be to do good public relations with it. Hindy left the lunch thinking he had found his man.

The next day, Hindy visited the would-be importer's London warehouse and met a couple of the guy's customers, who both said nice things about the importer and expressed interest in buying Brooklyn Lager from him. The first discussions of payment came up, and when Hindy said he wanted cash on delivery for the first order, the importer didn't bat an eye. No problem. The day after that, Hindy took a train to the importer's office in Kent, in the hops-growing countryside south of London. They went to lunch in a pub with a man the importer introduced as "my subdistributor." Whoever the man was, Hindy didn't feel as if his role was ever sufficiently established. Moreover, Hindy was not comfortable with the man, and the man did not seem particularly interested in Hindy or Brooklyn Lager.

In this setting, with Hindy already ill at ease and wondering what was going on, the would-be importer brought up money. Instead of the $12.50 per case that Hindy had gotten from Harrods for the first shipment of Brooklyn Lager into Britain, he wanted to pay $8 a case. Never, Hindy said; he wanted to export, but he couldn't afford to lose money on it. The importer talked about how much more cheaply he could import Budweiser and other American beers. Hindy tried to explain the different economies of scale between a small super-premium like Brooklyn and a mass-market leader like Budweiser. The importer moaned about his expenses. Finally, after much haggling, they agreed on a price of $11 a case, and the importer agreed to spend a certain amount of his first profits from Brooklyn buying T-shirts and other promotional material from Hindy.

"I felt happy," Hindy recalled. "We shook hands. We had a deal. Back in New York, I faxed him an outline of a contract. Then I got the first phone call back from him, the first of many. All of a sudden he had a partner, someone I'd never met, who didn't like the COD arrangement. I hadn't realized our deal was subject to anyone else's approval. The partner wanted the same arrangement they had from a big German brewery, that they didn't have to pay until 45 days after the beer cleared customs. The blood rushed to my face. This wasn't part of our deal when I was in Britain. In a small, young company like ours, we couldn't afford to create that kind of cash flow problem."

"Think about credit," the importer urged.

"No," Hindy said.

They went back and forth over the phone for several days,

until Hindy suggested that they deal with each other by fax only. "I felt like he was whining," Hindy said. "The telephone is a deceptive medium. You hear what you want to hear in the other person's voice, and then things are somehow different when they're in black and white." Finally, the importer faxed a confirmed order for 1,000 cases of Brooklyn Lager with a promise to pay COD. But now he wanted to be Brooklyn's exclusive importer. He wanted a contract that kept Hindy from dealing with anyone else in Britain. "Not yet," Hindy said. "I want to make sure you're the right importer first. I'll send you 1,000 cases, you pay me, you sell them, you get paid, and if everybody's happy, then we'll see." He offered a contract that said if the importer paid for the beer on time and sold it all within Britain during a certain time, the importer could have exclusive distribution rights for a year.

The importer agreed, but then added another condition. He wanted his name on the labels as the importer for Britain. Hindy would have had to spend thousands on new labels. Hindy offered to stamp the importer's name on each case of beer instead, and the importer reluctantly agreed. "Then, before we could send the beer, he was back on the phone, even though I had told him faxes only," Hindy remembered. "He was whining again. The pound was weakening against the dollar, and he was suffering. How much could I come down on the $11 a case? Could we do $8 after all? He said he had already invested time and money and deserved a break. I told him I had invested time and money, too. Christ, I had flown to Britain. Up to this point, I had been doing everything I could to make the deal happen. Looking back, I realize a lot of it was that I wanted to save face. I didn't want my trip and my efforts to be a waste of time."

Tom Potter, chairman of the brewery and Hindy's founding partner, stepped in. "This guy is jerking you around," he told Hindy. "What are we doing with him? Why are we trying so hard to do this deal? Is this why we're in business? To deal with guys like this? Forget him. Bag the whole thing. We don't need this kind of aggravation." Hindy, relieved, agreed. But that wasn't quite the end of that particular importer. He called Hindy one more time a few weeks later and said he had made a deal to buy half a container of Coors and wanted to fill the rest of the container with Brooklyn Lager. "Fine," Hindy said. "Pay up front. Come and get the beer. You do all the paperwork. Those are the conditions, or there's no deal." He never heard from the guy again. But Hindy learned a lot from those ill-fated negotiations, and the lessons served him well a year later when he began dealing with Lynne Zilkha and BB Supply, his eventual British importer-distributor. "I learned that I should have asked him for a deposit when he first started talking about ordering," Hindy said of those first negotiations. "I learned I should have followed my instinct when I started getting bad signs, instead of ignoring them because I thought it was just something European I didn't understand. Most importantly, I also learned that there was considerable interest in our product and that it clearly would sell if put into the right hands."

Zilkha had the right hands. That's not to say, however, that her negotiations with Hindy went any more smoothly. They were more successful, but not necessarily smoother. This was partly because Hindy went back to Britain with confidence in his product and a determination not to sell it or himself short. He started by asking Zilkha for the $12.50 per case that Harrods had paid. She wanted to pay much less, more in the range of the $8 that the other importer had been seeking. "You don't understand," Hindy told her. "Export is not a do-or-die thing with us. We will export eventually, with someone, but we're not going to rush into anything. We are not a big-volume brewery that has a lot of capacity we're looking to take up. We're small. We have to make money on every single bottle of beer we sell. We know that by going overseas, we're also creating some good public relations for ourselves back in the States. Exporting enhances the image of our product at home. But that's no good unless we make money at it, too. If you want us, you have to realize that

143

we don't need to compromise. We can be tough on our price and our terms. If you work hard for us, we'll make concessions for you, but we're not going to do it up front."

From the beginning, Zilkha demonstrated her faith in Brooklyn Lager's future in Britain and her willingness to expend time and money to ensure that future. She paid for the required laboratory analysis of Brooklyn Lager. She bought samples. She spent money on public relations and promotions, and she laid out several thousand dollars for a party in a trendy SoHo restaurant to introduce Hindy and his beer to British retailers, wholesalers, and trade journalists. "I saw what she could do, and we made a deal for $11 a case," Hindy said. The only other major compromise was in the manner of payment. He wanted the cash up front. She wanted to pay 90 days after delivery, the way she did with her other major imported beer from Czechoslovakia. They finally agreed that she would wire Brooklyn the money on the day that Hindy shipped the beer from New York. Since it usually takes about two weeks for the money to clear and for the beer to cross the Atlantic, very often he would get the money and she would get the beer on the same day.

Like the previous negotiations, Hindy suggested dealing mostly by fax, though he and Zilkha met a number of times face to face in Britain and New York and talked on the phone once in a while. Various minor issues arose between them over cost and shipping, but the exclusivity question again caused a particular fuss. "Originally, we agreed on a one-year exclusivity deal for her," Hindy said. "Then after a few weeks, when she started reordering because the beer was selling well, she realized she was on to something, so she started asking for five years." Hindy didn't like it, but he and Potter agreed that Zilkha was working hard and doing a good job, so they rewarded her with the five-year exclusivity she wanted.

Anheuser-Busch's negotiations in Britain presented a series of larger and longer lasting problems for its Budweiser operations in Europe. "The Busches proved they are great brewers but not very good at doing business in Europe," said Harry Drnec, Anheuser-Busch's since-departed marketing director for Budweiser's initial foray into Britain. "They came to Europe wanting to be loved and wanting to fall in love," Drnec said of the St. Louis brewers. "They wanted to live happily ever after. And they could have. They've got a great product and the best packaging in the world. But they overestimated their familiarity with British culture. They thought negotiations would be a frank and open exchange of ideas with their partners, that they would agree on a course of action, and then it would happen. But they underestimated the British business acumen. They underestimated the British profit motive."

Anheuser-Busch no doubt had several reasons for choosing Watney Truman, one of Britain's biggest brewers, as its partner back in 1983. For one, Watney played up to Anheuser's view of Budweiser as "The King of Beers," the beer with the taste and marketing muscle to dominate the American beer scene. Watney's people told Anheuser that they were confident Budweiser would be the best-selling beer in Britain within a decade. Anheuser executives, naturally, wanted to believe those boasts. And why wouldn't they? Their beer was the best-selling in America, so why not the rest of the world? Furthermore, the Watney people agreed to all the quality-control demands of the St. Louis brewers.

Under the contract negotiated through much of 1983 and signed in December of that year, Watney would brew Budweiser under license at one of its British breweries. Watney had to stick strictly to Bud's recipe, however, and the taste had to satisfy the brewers and quality-control people from St. Louis. After much testing, the St. Louis brewers decided that the raw materials available in Britain and normally used in Watney's own beers, from hops to malt, were unsuitable for Budweiser. Bud just didn't taste the same with British ingredients. So it was decided that all the ingredients except the water – down to the famous beechwood chips for aging – would be imported from the States, despite great added expense. Looking back, Anheuser would probably have been better off either importing beer it brewed in the States or building a brewery of its own in Britain.

But perhaps the company's biggest mistake came in another area of the negotiations. Surprisingly for a company that has done so much over the years to promote and protect its brand and its image in the States, Anheuser agreed to leave marketing and distribution to the British brewery. Watney said, "We are the experts in this market, leave it to us." And Anheuser did. The first advertising I heard for Budweiser in Britain was a radio spot in 1985. The ad was odd, to say the least. It purported to be a conversation between a man and a woman in a trendy restaurant. It seemed that they were married, but to other people, and that they were having an affair. The upshot was that they were so sophisticated about all this that they drank the chic new imported American beer, Budweiser. Hardly a recommendation, I thought, and certainly not the image Anheuser usually cultivated.

The following year, Watney threw a drinks party for London journalists to unveil its new television advertising campaign for Budweiser. Those initial TV commercials were reportedly part of a Budweiser campaign for which Anheuser was chipping in up to $4 million a year under its contract with Watney, despite having no strategic or creative input. The ads ranged from mediocre to downright embarrassing. They seemed to represent a British advertising agency's view of what sort of American advertising might appeal to Britons. One series seemed to be about a bunch of young guys in New Jersey, including one who was fat and sloppy, getting hot and thirsty on the turnpike and then stopping for a beer. Another seemed to be set on Manhattan's Upper West Side, where two American guys were going door to door persuading people to pay them to wash their cars. After getting the money, the guys opened fire hydrants on the cars and sat back drinking Bud while the street flooded. Another ill-fated and mercifully short-lived Watney marketing ploy with Anheuser's money was to promote the beer by offering to deliver free ice to anyone, anywhere in Britain. Budweiser's marketing people back in St. Louis were never allowed to say publicly what they thought of their money being spent like this.

At the same time, Watney's method of distributing Budweiser was also a cause for misgivings in the Anheuser home office. Instead of being offered throughout Britain in the same mass-market manner as in the States, Watney's Budweiser distribution concentrated on a relatively few trendy, upscale pubs and American-style restaurants. Budweiser was getting to young drinkers who liked the packaging and the American connection and who saw the beer as something new, fresh, and different. But Bud wasn't even being offered to many of the mainstream, neighborhood pubs where it would have to become a standard if Watney's sales projections were to come true. Watney, it became clear, regarded Budweiser not as the future dominant brand in Britain, but as just one of several good imported lagers that it was handling, including Foster's, Carlsburg, and Holsten Pils.

By 1991, when Anheuser renegotiated the original contract and regained control of the marketing rights for Budweiser in Britain, the brand had already become pigeonholed. It will be interesting in the 1990s to see if the new, simpler St. Louis-managed Budweiser advertising in Britain (typically, a subway poster showing cowboys drinking Bud and shooting pool over the motto, "The Genuine Article") will reach a wider audience. In its first years in Britain, however, Budweiser made little dent in the established British beer market. Instead of the million or more barrels a year that Anheuser might reasonably have been expected to be selling in the 1990s, based on Watney's boasts that it would become the market leader, Budweiser was selling perhaps 200,000 barrels a year.

"Budweiser was never going to be more than an adopted

child," Drnec, the former Anheuser marketing man, said in looking back. He suggested that Watney, which was not using its breweries to capacity in the mid-1980s, was primarily interested in increasing production closer to 100 percent. If Watney hadn't made a deal to brew Budweiser and raise its capacity, the British brewers presumably would have looked around for another foreign brand to brew. "The Anheuser-Busch people didn't study the market to see how Watney was handling these other imported lagers," Drnec said. "If they had, it would have been apparent that Watney Truman saw Budweiser strictly as a specialty product. There were a lot of new American-style restaurants opening up at the time, and it was clear there would be some place for it. But it was never going to be more than a niche product. Watney Truman said Budweiser was going to be number one in the U.K., and the guys in St. Louis believed it for no reason other than they wanted to believe. Watney fed 'em the numbers, and they nodded their heads." When Drnec told me this, I recalled a conversation several years earlier, when I asked a Watney executive what kind of test marketing had been done for the Budweiser launch. The Briton archly dismissed the whole notion. "We've been operating quite a nice little test market here called the United Kingdom for over 100 years," he snorted.

Anheuser's original contract with Watney could have brought a lot of profits back to St. Louis — if sales had reached a million barrels a year, that is. Drnec said the contract called for Watney to pay Anheuser royalties of £1 (about $1.50 at the time) per barrel for draft beer and £2 per barrel for packaged beer. Assuming that the estimated 200,000 barrels actually sold annually in the early 1990s were evenly divided between draft and packaged beer, Drnec said, that would have given Anheuser annual revenues from Britain of about £300,000. Meanwhile, he said, Anheuser rented offices in London for £300,000. "Forget about salaries, marketing, and other expenses," he said. "There was no way they could make money."

Anheuser finally got the original contract renegotiated by threatening to withdraw from the market. But neither side really wanted that; it would have been embarrassing for both. Under the new 1991 contract, Anheuser got back its Budweiser marketing and distribution rights and a higher royalty per barrel based on revised, more realistic sales predictions that ignored Watney's previous boasts. But the prospect of meaningful profits in Britain still seemed years away for Anheuser-Busch, a legacy of the folly of falling in love with a European partner, believing everything that's promised, and not negotiating under the same principles and procedures as in the States.

CHAPTER 8

◆ ◆ ◆

Media and Marketing

Besides the myth of European unity, there is another common misconception surrounding the European Community's drive toward a single market: the myth of the Euroconsumer. Just as the "1992" movement revealed many of the continuing political and economic differences among the European countries, the single market has underscored the local, regional, and national differences in consumer tastes and preferences. Some basic necessities such as soaps and cereals can indeed be marketed on a pan-European scale, with similar if not the same packaging and advertising from country to country. But the single market has made little difference at that level of marketing; many pan-European or global products have been sold that way for years.

The EC may be creating new rules and a new bureaucracy, but European demographics haven't changed and aren't likely to change overnight just because of pronouncements from Brussels and Strasbourg. The three Bs – beer, bread, and banks – are frequently cited as examples of the sort of "home-grown" products that will continue to command local allegiance in spite of whatever competition comes as the borders melt away. Yes, southern Europeans in the so-called Garlic Belt have

150

been drinking more beer and whiskey and less wine, but it's difficult to imagine Scandinavians and northern Germans driving small, brightly colored cars with plaid upholstery. How can home appliances be marketed the same in Britain, where 43 percent have tumble driers and microwave ovens, and in Italy, where only 4 percent do?

As the single market brings down barriers in Europe in particular, and as business becomes more global in general, production and distribution for many companies are likely to become more centralized. But marketing and sales will become more localized. You can make exactly the same microwave oven for the entire world at your European subsidiary's factory in the Netherlands, but it would be foolish to try to sell it with the same marketing techniques in Britain and Italy. Americans doing business in Europe must recognize the local and regional differences and tailor their marketing programs accordingly. This extends from packaging and labeling – how *American* should a product be? – to paid advertising and promotional campaigns. The fact that a product or service is American can also generate "free" publicity, both negative and positive.

European companies that have been marketing products and services to their neighbors for decades obviously have the advantage of being experienced at European cross-border marketing. But this advantage is offset by the experience that many popular American companies have built up in selling their products and services to the vast and varied U.S. market. The differences between Americans in, say, Manhattan, Marin County, and suburban Atlanta may not be much wider than the differences in Europeans in, say, Germany, the Netherlands, and Belgium. Companies used to dealing across the American market already have an understanding of what works across a diffuse marketplace and when and how a strategy should be localized.

An added advantage is that just as English is everyone's second language, American television, movies, music, and even news (especially with the increased influence of CNN since the Gulf War) are fast becoming the common strain of popular culture across Europe. This is the Age of the Consumer, highlighted by the desire among everyday citizens to acquire the latest in worldly comfort and convenience at reasonable prices and with assurances of quality. As one European study summed it up, for most modern citizens the world over, shopping is the ultimate cultural expression. To Europeans and most of the rest of the world, consumerism is an American invention that they have been eager to embrace. In marketing to Europe, an advertisement set in France might not go over so well in Spain or Ireland, and an ad featuring Germans might not create much empathy among Greeks or Danes. But everybody can relate to Americans in the same way. The American culture is everybody's second culture, often in a much more influential way than English is everyone's second language. That's why America is such a common marketing theme, and not just for American products. A Dutch ad for Dutch radios is set in the Arizona desert, French actors dressed up as American football players demonstrate razor blades in French ads, and a pan-European campaign for electric shavers made by a pan-European electronics company was set in America and even had an American flag in the background.

American or not, however, differences persist in European culture, and different marketing techniques are sometimes demanded for different countries. A few years back, a big cosmetics company tried to market its new perfume on a pan-European basis. The emotional hook for the television advertising was the image of a boy giving a bouquet of flowers to a girl. It worked well in Britain, but flopped in France – until the sponsors changed the bouquet to a single red rose. An even older example comes from Rolls-Royce, which originally intended to call its new model the Silver Mist. But Rolls-Royce wanted to sell a fair number of those new models in Germany, where "mist" means manure. The name was changed to the

Silver Cloud. More recently, Timberland, an American company that has done well in Europe by sticking to its strong American identity, encountered a problem with a magazine ad in Europe. The ad, emphasizing the tough quality of Timberland's outdoor wear, showed a pair of muddy, cruddy boots that someone had apparently just taken off after a long, hard hike. The message of the ad was that Timberland boots wear forever and never give up. The ad went well in Italy, but when Timberland ran it in Germany there were scores of protests, mostly from housewives. "How dare you show such a dirty boot on our clean German carpets?" was the typical outraged response.

One type of common advertising in America that does not transfer well to Europe is the "denigrating" ad, the kind that promotes one brand while explicitly running down another. Although the EC is moving to allow more "comparative" advertising that borders on the denigration of brand names, the practice is still frowned upon across Europe and is still banned in some countries. An example was the ad campaign that rapper M. C. Hammer did for Pepsi. In the TV commercials that aired in the States, Hammer's high-energy dance-rap was slowed down when he inadvertently took a swig of Coke and began crooning a sentimental ballad. Appalled fans passed up an emergency Pepsi, Hammer knocked it back, and he resumed the rapping. A different version had to be shot in Europe, however. Instead of taking a drink from a clearly identifiable Coke can, Hammer was shown drinking a cola that had no brand name at all.

Sometimes Americans fail to do even the most basic research on how to reach their customers or, in one recent series of newspapers ads, how their customers can reach them. The ads were run in a European newspaper by a U.S. mail-order company that was selling jackets modeled on the flight jackets worn by American bomber pilots in World War II. The product looked good and the price was right, but the advertisement urged readers in Europe to order by telephoning a toll-free "800" number in the United States. The problem is that from most European countries, it's difficult to impossible to call a U.S. toll-free "800" number. And that was the only way to order. No other non-800 number was listed, and no mailing address was given. There must have been many would-be European buyers who picked up the phone to place an order and then gave up after failing to get through.

A company that did do its marketing homework in Europe was MTV, the American music television network. MTV was given little chance of succeeding in Europe when it first hit the market in the late 1980s. Media critics and analysts in Europe said it was too loud, too brash, too American. But MTV transformed itself into a European product in a number of ways. Veejays from various European countries were hired and did their shows in a combination of English, their native language, and any of the two or three other languages they typically spoke. The typically bright and airy American high-tech studio was swapped for a set that looked like it might be the attic of an old church, dark and comfortable. And the music was changed. Instead of the American MTV's usual diet of chart hits and heavy metal, MTV Europe reflected the European format of radio stations that are less specialized. European pop stations may air the number one rock hit followed by a classical tune followed by a folk song followed by a rock golden oldie. MTV brought a similar eclectic balance to its European programming and it paid off. Pan-European advertisers – for products such as jeans, soft drinks, and cosmetics – bought air time, while MTV conducted its own promotions on a local basis. Contests and events were conducted on a city-by-city basis, rather than on a continental scale.

The marketing of many sporting and cultural events in Europe has been transformed by the American concept of corporate hospitality, largely thanks to Mark McCormack's International Management Group. As recently as the 1970s, Wimbledon hardly lived up to its image of the world's foremost tennis tournament. Tickets were hard to get unless you were a member of the host All-England Lawn Tennis and Croquet Club or were willing to stand in a predawn queue for several hours. Facilities for spectators were almost as poor as the pay for the players. Then the All-England Club put itself in McCormack's hands. Corporate sponsorship and hospitality have become the golden geese not only for higher prize money, but also for better facilities for both players and spectators. It's not coincidental that many of the companies and individuals that made corporate hospitality work in Europe were American. These American companies found that besides being a nice perk for their own employees posted to Europe, first-class treatment at the British Open, the Monaco Grand Prix, and other cultural and sporting events was a sure-fire way to impress clients and customers, whether American or European.

On a less glamorous but no less effective scale, American growers of McIntosh apples used low-key local marketing to become successful in Europe. Several U.S. orchard cooperatives decided to start selling in northern Europe, where the season for most native varieties of apples ends well before the season for the late-maturing McIntosh strain. They started shipping apples to Scotland and northern England, but found that shoppers were reluctant to buy the McIntoshes, even when they were the only fresh apples on the shelves. It didn't take much questioning of grocers and shoppers to learn that they simply weren't used to the McIntosh's mix of coloring, 90 percent red and 10 percent green. They were more familiar with one-color varieties such as Golden Delicious or Red Delicious. Shoppers who saw a two-toned apple thought there must be something wrong with it.

In addition, the American growers had tried to break into the market by sending over prime specimens, the biggest and fullest apples they had. But the Europeans, used to smaller apples, thought they were too big. Housewives didn't want to buy an apple that might go partly to waste because their kids couldn't eat the whole thing. So the American growers printed up simple promotional literature and flyers that were distributed to shoppers at supermarkets. Besides explaining how McIntosh apples were different because they were crunchier and crisper and had thinner skins than European apples, the promotional material offered introductory price discounts. People read the promotional material and started buying. Not only were the American growers able to raise their prices when the market became established, but they were also able to use Europe as a lucrative market for the smaller, lower grade apples that were less popular back home.

Ocean Spray was another American company that had to make adjustments. When first coming to Europe, the company tried to sell its cranberry juice just like it did in the States – in those big chunky bottles emblazoned with "Cranberry Juice." The first problem was the label. Just as Venus Wafers could not have the words "All Natural" on the label because they don't grow on trees, Ocean Spray couldn't be "Cranberry Juice" because it isn't 100 percent pure cranberry; water, sucrose, and ascorbic acid (Vitamin C) are added. But that was only a minor glitch that was resolved by relabeling. "Ocean Spray Cranberry Juice" in America became "Ocean Spray Classic Cranberry Juice Drink" in Europe. The bigger problem came in the shape of those big chunky bottles. First, Ocean Spray hadn't reckoned on the fact that while Europeans drink a lot of juice, they get almost all of it out of waxed cardboard cartons. They simply weren't used to buying juice in big bottles. Second, Ocean Spray hadn't taken into account the smaller refrigerators, often half the size of big American family models, that are common throughout much of Europe. Those big Ocean Spray bottles took up a lot of room; there was no way they could fit in the typical European refrigerator door, like they do in the big standup fridge in a typical American suburban home. As a result, Ocean Spray sputtered in its first attempt to crack the European market. The company quickly realized its error, however, and moved to repackage its juice in a cranberry-colored carton of a familiar size and shape to European consumers. Sales took off, and Ocean Spray is now well established in Europe.

Part of Ocean Spray's difficulties may have come from a decision to market the juice as a distinctly American product. But juice isn't distinctly and uniquely American. Europeans get plenty of juice from their own orchards, vineyards, and groves and from countries in the Middle East and Africa. Unlike a restaurant concept such as TGI Friday's or clothing styles such as Gap or Timberland, cranberry juice carried no strong American identity to promote. This is a strategic decision that faces many Americans coming to Europe: to be, or not to be, American. In bringing Venus Wafers to Europe, Brian Dwyer for a time considered playing down the American angle. After all, crackers are crackers, aren't they? So in addition to dropping the "All Natural" claim at the insistence of the British bureaucrat, Dwyer considered changing the spelling of "fiber" to "fibre" and "flavor" to "flavour." No, Dwyer finally decided, crackers aren't just crackers the world over. He believed that in filling a gap in the European market between melba toast and soda crackers, he could capitalize on the fact that Venus Wafers were new, and that they were high quality and nutritional. That they were American, in other words. So he not only went with the American spellings on his packages, he also stuck the word "American" boldly on the front of every package, just in case anyone had any doubts. This marketing and packaging helped underline Venus's difference from the other European crackers in the market and helped sell them.

A mistake sometimes made by Americans is to view Europe as a less sophisticated market, a dumping ground for inferior products. In a way, that's how things turned out for the McIntosh apple growers, in that they were able to sell their smaller, lower grade apples in Europe. But that was a quirk, a result of European consumers being more picky about what they buy, not less. Not long ago, an American company that made cheap sweaters for discount chains decided that it was missing out by not exporting to Europe. The sweaters, it should be pointed out, were not especially appealing to the discriminating consumer, even in America. They were bulky rather than form fitting, they featured some uninspired patterns, were made of acrylic, were put together with sometimes haphazard stitching, and were in clashing multicolors.

In a word, the sweaters were cheap. The company sold them wholesale for about $14 in the States and wanted to sell them for about the same to European wholesalers. But with duties, shipping, and foreign distribution costs, that would have raised the retail price in Europe to the equivalent of $40 to $50. The company never did start exporting because it could find no one in Europe who would buy the sweaters. Europeans have been making their own sweaters for some years now, the American company was firmly informed, and any European who wanted to spend that kind of money for a sweater would be more likely to choose something from Irish wool or Scottish cashmere or with a more stylish Austrian or Swiss design.

Just as in America, quality sells in Europe. Many Americans involved in marketing in Europe find themselves targeting what the European media types call their Golden Consumer, the man or woman in the professional or management classes who cares about quality in food, clothing, transportation, vacations, and virtually every other aspect of life. These are the Europeans who are willing to spend a little more for Venus Wafers, Timberland boots, soft American-style toilet paper, or Brooklyn Lager. These are also the Europeans who, when repositioning the companies they own or manage, turn to a Wall Street investment house or law firm for corporate financial advice. They are used to the quality and prices of Italian fashion and French wine and won't accept California wine or New York designs that cannot compete on both counts.

Many Americans learn to promote themselves and their products or services in Europe through free publicity. One of my favorite Americans during his years in Europe, and a model for getting good free publicity, was J. S. G. Boggs, a young artist from Florida who specialized in drawing different types of money. Boggs would draw whimsical versions of the notes from whatever country he was in – British pounds, Swiss and French francs, Italian lire – and then use the bogus Boggs-bills to pay for food, drink, clothing, transportation, hotel bills, and anything else he could. His gallery in London would track down these transactions and then buy back the fake money for collectors at a considerable profit for the people who had accepted them from Boggs.

I once went out to lunch with Boggs. As we sat drinking beer and eating sandwiches, he put the finishing touches on a £10 note on which Queen Elizabeth II's eyes were crossed and Boggs' girlfriend, a nurse back in New York, was listed as the "Treasurer of the Artist." The motto on the Boggs-bill said, "In Art We Trust." As we finished and the waitress brought the check, Boggs presented his fake note with a flourish and asked if she would accept it. The woman burst out laughing, studied the note, laughed again, and went and got her purse so she could pay for our lunch. She pocketed the Boggs-bill, and a few weeks later sold it for £200 to his gallery, which then sold it to a collector for £300. Boggs undoubtedly had some anxious moments when Scotland Yard arrested him and the Bank of England pressed counterfeiting charges. But the trial turned into a media circus where Boggs represented himself and gave rambling, heartfelt, and altogether delightful testimony on the rights of artistic expression and free speech. The jury acquitted him and his prices went up.

Another American who promoted himself is Lee Nordlund, who started the business selling his grandmother's chocolate chip cookies (Chapter 3). Nordlund and his younger brother, who came to London to help with the business, made several attempts to write press releases that would get some interest from trade journals read by people in bakeries and supermarkets. Their news releases were admittedly less than professionally polished, but did result in some small stories in the trade journals. In search of higher profile publicity, Nordlund looked up the number of a leading British newspaper, the *Times,* and asked to talk to someone on the business staff. When the reporter came on the line, Nordlund quickly told the story of how he came to Britain to be with his English girlfriend and how he was trying to make a living out of his grandma's secret cookie recipe. The reporter bit, and a few weeks later the *Times* ran a good-sized feature, complete with a photo of Nordlund and his wife Bridget nibbling grandma's cookies. The publicity not only helped Nordlund sell cookies to several new outlets, but also sparked inquiries from big bakeries that wanted to buy him out.

One of the masters of free publicity in Europe is Bob Payton, the former Chicago ad executive who has styled himself as London's favorite American. Payton, who loves to be called Chicago's unofficial ambassador to Britain, is what other U.S. expatriates in Europe call a professional American. Besides his string of American-style restaurants across Europe, including the Chicago Pizza Pie Factory and the Chicago Rib Shack, he has purchased a rambling old English manor and turned it into a fancy $200-per-night getaway. Payton's retreat, Stapleford Park, combines elements of traditional English country weekends, from Laura Ashley decorations to almost daily foxhunts, with American standards of food and service, including hot showers that are tall enough to accommodate someone 6-foot-3, which happens to be Payton's height. The restaurants and the country estate have earned yards and yards of free newspaper and magazine stories because they are good and because they are American. But one of Payton's best brainstorms has been his whimsical annual "guide" for Chicagoans visiting Britain. Besides guaranteeing that many visiting Chicagoans will stop in one of his restaurants, the guide generates lots of free public relations thanks to British journalists who love to write stories about how their country and customs are portrayed through American eyes. Along the way, Payton has become an authority on anything and everything American. When a British journalist was assigned to write a story on a sociological study that described swearing patterns in different countries, the reporter called Payton and asked him if it was true that Americans curse more than English people. Payton didn't miss a beat. "Hell, yes," he roared. "You're goddamn right they do."

Undoubtedly much of the success of the NFL's World League of American Football in Europe was due to free publicity. All the British national newspapers and television networks, for example, covered the auditions for the London Monarchs' cheerleaders. Leggy young women in skimpy outfits may have been common on Carnaby Street in the Swinging Sixties, but Britain had never seen them prancing around doing bump-and-grind dance routines at sporting events. The TV coverage was extraordinary, and a number of young British guys told me they went to Monarchs games mostly to see the cheerleaders. In another slick move, the Monarchs signed one of the top British rugby players to a contract. He never came anywhere near getting into a game, but during the preseason British reporters and columnists followed his daily progress in practice, and the free publicity probably led thousands of rugby fans to take more interest in American football and buy a ticket or two to see the Monarchs.

Sometimes what originally seems like a European public relations dream can turn into a nightmare. Robert Heindel, a Connecticut-based artist whose illustrations are famous throughout the advertising industry and whose credits include several *Time* magazine covers, decided a few years ago to branch out into more serious art. Since he loved ballet, he decided to concentrate on painting ballet companies. Before long he was being called "the Degas of our time" and was being invited by ballet companies around the world to spend a few months in residence with them. When Heindel was finished, his paintings of dancers—many of which are now familiar on posters, postcards, calendars, and so forth—were shown at an exhibit and sale, with the profits split between Heindel and the dance company. One of the ballet companies that Heindel worked with was based in London. Its royal patron was Diana, the Princess of Wales. When she found out Heindel was painting the company, she got very excited. It turned out she had been a big fan for a long time and owned several of his posters. She volunteered to give his show a boost by appearing at the opening, thereby guaranteeing that it would be one of the highlights of the London social and cultural scene.

Heindel was extremely pleased, of course, until he discovered how disruptive Diana's presence would be. He and everyone else had to undergo strict security clearance by Scotland Yard. Exhibits had to be repositioned in a certain manner so no bombs could be hidden. Worse, the attention of everyone connected with the opening of the show, from the dancers and company administrators to the balletomanes and art collectors, was diverted by Princess Diana. Heindel himself found the princess charming, but was chagrined that the focus of the show had shifted from his paintings to her—what she wore, what she said, how she looked. To top it off, Diana let it be known that it would be simply *marvelous* if she could have one of the paintings in the show. After all, it *was* her birthday. Heindel reluctantly handed over the painting that he might otherwise have sold for several thousand dollars. "One of the things you learn the hard way about royalty," he said ruefully, "is that they don't pay for *anything.*"

Andy Grant, a native Californian who built a reputation in the States as a leisure consultant, was also involved in good publicity that backfired. His specialty was transforming old, rundown urban zoos into modern facilities that emphasized conservation in the animal world while providing enough family fun to compete with newer amusement and theme parks. After several successful European projects, most notably at Leeds Castle in southern England, Grant was hired to work his magic on the London Zoo, one of the world's oldest, largest, most prestigious and most financially troubled zoos. He was hired as a consultant, but was in effect in charge of doing whatever it took to reverse the nearly four-decade trend of declining public attendance. Grant, a natural self-promoter, seized the opportunity and made himself available for public speeches and interviews about his plans to save the zoo. Some of his proposals drew little comment, such as rebuilding animal enclosures to make them more natural-looking and upgrading the zoo's food and beverage services.

Grant ran into trouble, however, when he supported a plan for the zoo, located in Regent's Park since 1826, to take over ten acres of adjacent parkland. The zoo had been granted the right to annex the parkland many years before, but had never exercised that right. Grant also suggested dressing up the area around the zoo with floating plastic animals, illuminated at night, on the canal that ran through the park. When word of these proposals leaked out, the people living near Regent's Park were outraged. Some said they had been walking their dogs and jogging and watching their children run around on those ten acres for years. Others criticized the "typical American hype" of putting plastic animals on the canal as garish and distasteful; it just wasn't very British, they complained. "Disney-esque," some moaned. The protests reached a peak with a series of antizoo marches and petition drives. The proposals to take over the ten acres and decorate the canal were quietly dropped.

Grant, presumably on the orders of the zoo directors who had hired him, tried to maintain a low profile for the next two years, refusing interview requests that he had been eager to accommodate in the past. Suddenly, the zoo announced that it might have to close. It seems that Grant's projections for increased attendance and revenue had fallen flat, despite higher income due to his changes in the zoo shop and restaurants. In the storm of indignant publicity, Grant was a convenient scapegoat for the British press. Grant himself still refused to say anything, and zoo officials offered only a half-hearted defense on his behalf, saying that he never got enough money to do everything he wanted. But there was little doubt in the British press about just who had failed to live up to his promises to revitalize the zoo: Andy Grant, the big-talking American.

In addition to its marketing problems in Britain (Chapter 7), Anheuser-Busch was gathering bad publicity across Europe for its designs on the "other" Budweiser, the one from Czechoslovakia. In trying to sell the American Budweiser in Europe, Anheuser-Busch found that in most countries the Budweiser brand name was already reserved under trademark by the state-controlled South Bohemia Breweries. The Czech brewers, based in the town of Ceske Budejovice, which was once the German town of Budweis, had not started using the Budweiser brand name until after the Busch family had already made it the "King of Beers" in the States. But that didn't matter to the European courts when Anheuser-Busch protested. The Czechs had reserved the trademark first, and they had the right to ban the American Budweiser. Which, of course, they did, except in a handful of countries, including Britain, that allowed the sale of both Budweisers.

A new opportunity presented itself when the Berlin Wall fell and the Eastern European countries in the Soviet sphere threw off the shackles of communism. Czechoslovakia, with its Velvet Revolution under the playwright-turned-president, Vaclav Havel, was one of the models of an emerging free-market democracy. To finance these dramatic changes and to hasten capitalism, Czechoslovakia and other countries began talking about selling off their existing state industries to western partners and investors. Naturally, the best-run state industries, the ones with the most market potential in the West, were the ones that would attract the most interest and the highest bids. Anheuser-Busch let it be known that it would top all bids for the Ceske Budejovice brewery and promised that it would protect the Czech brand and even allow it to be sold in the United States.

For Havel's government, it must have been tempting. But the deal went off the rails. The Czech brewery's Western European distributors, other European brewers, and various consumer groups, led by the influential British-based Campaign for Real Ale, with tens of thousands of members across Europe, warned that eventually Anheuser-Busch would wreck the Czech Budweiser. One of the critics of Anheuser was Lynne Zilkha, the head of BB Supply, the London beer distributor handling the imports of Brooklyn Lager, the microbrewery in which I'm a limited partner. She and others told me that the European brewing industry was sure that even if St. Louis did keep the Czech brand name alive, it would be in name only; it was only a matter of time, they warned, before the commercial pressures on the world's largest brewer led to a change in the Czech brewing process, which was long, costly, and inefficient by the mass-production standards of American Budweiser.

Meanwhile, President Havel, perhaps fearing that Czechoslovakia could lose one of the few quality, brand-name products it had from the days of communist rule, stepped into the negotiations and blocked the Anheuser-Busch acquisition at least temporarily. Even if Anheuser-Busch does someday acquire the rights to sell its Budweiser in Germany and other lucrative European beer markets, the marketing people in St. Louis must overcome years of negative publicity – again, whether deserved or not, it's a widespread image – as the big, bad American giant trying to take over and ruin the poor little, high-quality Eastern European brewery.

Sometimes bad publicity can be turned around. Michael Eisner, the head of Disney, was pelted with eggs and vegetables by young anti-American protestors when he and other Disney officials went to Paris to announce the EuroDisneyland project. Eisner could easily have criticized the young French protestors and their concerns over the growing American influences on French commerce and culture. But that would only have earned him more enemies. Instead, Eisner said, "Hey, look, if it had been the sixties, that could have been me down there protesting Vietnam. They have the right, and in 20 years they'll be in our park with their children." The good-humored comment earned Eisner and EuroDisney a fair number of style points with the French for *panache.*

Not all publicity for Americans is bad, of course. In fact, most of the publicity about Americans in Europe, whether representing themselves or companies large and small, is positive. And much of it comes without large expenditures of time, energy, and money. Some American firms, for example, have raised their profiles and attracted the notice of potential clients and customers by opening offices throughout Eastern Europe. For a journalist writing about the many changes in Eastern European politics, economics, business, or society, what better source is there for the American perspective than an American lawyer, banker, or other professional-manager type who has been living and doing business in Budapest, Warsaw, or Prague? Even in such Western European capitals as London, Paris, and Bonn, where Americans are not exactly a novelty, there are a handful of Americans who consistently get more than their share of good press, both in the local media and back at home in the States, simply because they let it be known that they are available to help journalists. They are always available for a quick comment on the record, an insightful but anonymous background briefing, or – if they can fit it into their busy schedules, and they almost always can – an in-depth interview. They are also highly visible on the professional seminar and conference lecture circuit. A few even instruct their public relations people to curry favor with journalists, both in the trade and the general media, to lay the groundwork for favorable mentions.

My own limited experience in commercial promotions and public relations shows just how an American product can get a good bang in Europe for not many bucks. It started when Steve Hindy, the president of the Brooklyn Brewery, called me in London with good news and bad news. The good news was that our beer, Brooklyn Lager, was going to be on sale in Harrods, the ritzy London department store. The bad news was that Steve wanted me, as the microbrewery's only limited partner in Europe, to drum up some publicity. It was important, he said, not just because we wanted Brooklyn to sell well at Harrods; after all, Harrods' small order, an offshoot of Brooklyn Lager's come-from-nowhere victory in the Great American Beer Tasting, was for a special month-long "Best of America" display. In all likelihood, Harrods' order would be a one-time thing. However, Steve emphasized, merely having the beer in Harrods could prove to be extremely valuable in terms of public relations. It would help the brewery gain publicity and prestige back in the States, and it might pique the interest of potential European importers and distributors.

I agreed to try to help, even though Steve made it clear he could pay my expenses only. The Brooklyn Brewery investment is in effect my pension program, so it was in my interest to help if I could. ("Oh, well," I used to tell my wife back in the early days when the brewery was struggling to get started, "we didn't really want to retire anyway, did we?") But how could I help publicize the beer in Britain? Despite more than 20 years of making a living out of writing newspaper and magazine articles, I knew next to nothing about public relations. In the end, it probably helped that the brewery didn't have any money to hire a real public relations consultant or do any advertising. I decided not to try anything fancy. I know what makes a good story, and Brooklyn seemed to be a good story in

Britain, in large part because of the American angle. So I sent letters to several of Britain's leading food and wine writers, introducing myself and trying to set out the Brooklyn story and the reasons they might want to write about our beer. This is the text:

Dear ----:

I am a London-based American freelance journalist who also happens to be a partner in a New York microbrewery, the Brooklyn Brewery. My partners in Brooklyn, the guys who really run the operation, have asked me to try to get some publicity about their brew, Brooklyn Lager. Harrods has been selling Brooklyn Lager in its Pantry, and a London distributor, BB Supply, plans to begin handling the beer in the near future.

So here's my first (and I hope last) public-relations pitch. Brooklyn Lager is of interest to discriminating British beer drinkers for several reasons. The main reason is its quality. Brooklyn recently won the Great American Beer Tasting in New York, in which a number of noted American wine and beer experts chose it above other "super-premium" beers in a blind tasting. The losers included other U.S. microbrews that have been well-received in Britain, including Samuel Adams.

The beer is typically described as an amber lager, highly hopped, with a "big nose" and a "big clean taste." It's unlike the typical American overcarbonated, overadditived, overpreserved, mass-market lager, and even British real-ale fans such as Michael "The Beer Hunter" Jackson like it.

At 5.5 percent alcohol content, it's one of the strongest beers in the States, and about half again as strong as the typical British pub lager. Harrods is apparently aiming Brooklyn Lager at the "gourmet" British beer drinkers who are taking up the new wave of American micro imports, such as Anchor Steam and some of the Mexican beers. BB Supply will target a wider upscale market—pubs, restaurants, off-licenses, grocery chains. And less expensively. At Harrods, Brooklyn has been selling well despite being one of (if not the) most expensive off-the-shelf beers in Britain, at £1.95 for a 12-ounce bottle. (Still a bargain compared with Tokyo, where it goes for up to £8 a bottle.) BB's recommended retail price will be around £1.25 a bottle.

The Brooklyn Brewery was started by a former Associated Press journalist, Steve Hindy, who learned to brew his own stovetop beer during his years as a war correspondent in Beirut. Back in Brooklyn, he and a neighbor, Tom Potter, a banker, began watching baseball games together. Drinking and dreaming, they said, "How can we change our lives? Hey, let's start a brewery." And they did, borrowing $500,000 from friends and relatives. "When you borrow $10,000 from your mom that she doesn't have to lose, you've really got to make a go of it," Potter says.

The first bottles of Brooklyn Lager came out in early 1988 under Bill Moeller, a fourth-generation brewmaster for one of the big U.S. breweries. He was persuaded out of retirement by Hindy's promises that they would make the best beer in America. "I've been waiting all my life for an opportunity like this," Moeller said. The goal was a "Pre-Prohibition" beer much like the brews made in Brooklyn from the turn of the century to the 1920s. The final recipe was based in large part on the secret family brewing notebooks that Moeller's grandfather brought with him when he immigrated through Ellis Island from Germany. (Moeller is very proud that we've just started exporting to Germany.) The distinctive Brooklyn Lager packaging, including the script "B" reminiscent of the old Brooklyn Dodgers baseball team, is by the well-known New York designer Milton Glaser, also an investor.

The brewery headquarters is in the area of Brooklyn most familiar to Britons as the setting for the Spike Lee film "Do the Right Thing." In fact, Lee's office is around the corner, and he often stops in to kibbitz. Brooklyn Lager was featured in one scene in "Do the Right Thing," and Lee serves it at his company bashes.

That kind of free publicity is a big reason Brooklyn Lager has done so well. The brewery does not advertise, but does sponsor low-cost, high-impact evenings where neighborhood bars feature Brooklyn quizzes, battles of the bands, and other contests. Hindy also runs headline-grabbing surveys in neighborhood taverns, and there's an annual Winston Churchill look-alike contest (Churchill's mother was from Brooklyn . . .) that gets lots of publicity, especially since the winner usually seems to be a woman. Eventually, the brewery would like to bring similar promotional campaigns to Britain, including giveaway T-shirts, sweatshirts, baseball and cycling caps, mugs, pint glasses, openers, sports bags, and other paraphernalia with the "B" logo.

If you need any more information, if I can help put you in touch with Steve Hindy for an interview, or if you'd like to try the beer, please contact me at your convenience. Thanks.

Sincerely,

Tim Harper

This letter resulted in a surprising amount of free publicity in large-circulation publications, including a feature in one glossy Sunday magazine supplement. A writer from the newspaper we had most hoped to interest, the *Financial Times*, asked me to lunch in a nice restaurant so he could get more information. The result was a long, well-displayed feature in the Saturday paper that began: "Thirty cases of Brooklyn Lager have arrived at Harrods. . . ."

It was a public relations dream and surprised everyone, especially me. The arrival of Brooklyn Lager became an "event" in the British beer business. This strong entry into the new and untested market not only helped Brooklyn Lager sell out at Harrods, but also strengthened Hindy's bargaining position when it came down to making a deal with Lynne Zilkha at BB Supply, our eventual importer and distributor. In turn, she and her sales staff made extensive use of that early publicity in getting retailers to try the beer on their shelves. If it was good enough to get this much ink, the shopkeepers reckoned, they better give it a chance. In a number of cases, retailers who had seen the articles contacted Lynne and asked her to arrange deliveries. This publicity cost the Brooklyn Brewery about $7 to compensate me for postage stamps to send out the letters. It cost me about four hours, two to write the letter and two over the good lunch with the *Financial Times* writer.

CHAPTER 9

◆ ◆ ◆

After the Deal Is Done

How do parents choose a new rattle for a baby? To Duncan Chadwick, it's simple. The parents go to a store, hold the baby up in front of the rattles, and buy the one the baby grabs first. Chadwick was chagrined to find out that parents couldn't do that at Hamleys, the famous London toy store, after he and a small group of fellow Americans led a takeover of the venerable Regent Street institution. His cut-price $32 million buyout ended 229 years of British ownership for Hamleys, where Britain's royal family – and the rich and famous from around the world – shop for toys for themselves and their children.

The negotiations for Chadwick's takeover were long and hard, but he didn't realize just how much work was ahead of him until he walked into the store for the first time as owner and manager. Despite its longtime motto, "The Finest Toyshop in the World," it was clear that Hamleys' previous British owners had let the six-story store decline. It had lost its way. Instead of being in one place, some baby rattles were here, some were there, and yet more were around the corner. Boxes blocked aisles and fire escapes. Records of what sold and when were nonexistent. Imagine, the world's best toy shop did not

171

even have a Santa Claus on the premises during the Christmas shopping season. The previous owners had thought it was too much trouble, so they stopped having a Santa. Moreover, many of the British employees seemed to have little interest in Hamleys, in toys, or in the customers they were supposed to be serving.

Like many Americans doing business in Europe, Chadwick learned the hard way that the difficulties don't necessarily end when a deal is done. Very often there are large problems that must be addressed immediately. Even if a European operation kicks off smoothly, there are inevitable adjustments to be made later. Company structures and procedures must be realigned to accommodate growth and respond to changes in the market. Sometimes deals go sour and disputes with European partners or representatives must be resolved. And there are always headaches in managing personnel, with different sets of concerns among European local hires and American expatriate employees.

Problems, of course, are inevitable in any business venture. But problems are particularly prevalent in cross-border deals, such as those between Americans and Europeans, with the inherent cultural and communications obstacles. No matter how well the two sides get along, and no matter how much they both want their deal to work, the time to discuss failure is at the beginning. Forrec, the Canadian design company, didn't want to get into the particulars of what might happen if their deal with the flamboyant British developer turned out to be a disappointment (Chapter 6). So there were no provisions for what would happen when the developer failed to produce as much work as anticipated. And there were certainly no provisions for what would happen when the developer went broke. It's impossible to foresee all the possible areas of disagreement and all the possible ways the two parties might fail each other, but they can at least agree in advance on how they will resolve whatever disputes do arise.

Given that nobody wants to incur the time and expense of hiring lawyers, filing lawsuits, giving depositions, and going to court, alternative dispute resolution is gaining in favor throughout Europe. Arbitration and mediation clauses are becoming standard in cross-border contracts. There are innumerable ways of structuring such clauses. Typically, however, the two sides must both agree to arbitration or mediation, often before a particular tribunal or under the auspices of a particular private agency. In Britain, there's the Centre for Dispute Resolution, a nonprofit network modeled after the United States' Center for Public Resources, based in New York. Both the British and American centers, and others like them springing up in other European countries, provide flexible forms of alternative dispute resolution. Usually, proceedings are conducted in private and are completely voluntary; even if a contract allows for mediation, arbitration, or other forms of alternative dispute resolution, the alternatives won't work unless both sides submit willingly. Sometimes the two sides will agree in advance that the result will be binding. Sometimes they agree that it will not be binding, and they can still file lawsuits if they're dissatisfied with the result. Many times, however, the mere fact that an arbitrator or mediator has made an adverse decision is enough to convince an unhappy party that things would not be much different in litigation – only more expensive. One of the leading private arbitration and mediation services is IDR Europe, a subsidiary of the for-profit American service, U.S. Arbitration and Mediation. IDR Europe usually resolves the cases before it in less than two days, at a cost between $2,000 and $5,000.

Besides arbitration and mediation, another popular form of alternative dispute resolution in Europe is the minitrial. In a minitrial, each party's in-house lawyer makes a brief presentation of the heart of the case to a panel of senior executives representing both companies. Ideally, the executives on the panel are not directly connected with the dispute. A neutral panel chairperson, often a lawyer or a moonlighting judge agreed upon by both sides, then presides over negotiations among the executives as they try to reach a settlement. If and when they agree, the chairperson helps draw up a contract that would be binding in a court of law. Other alternatives include a trial before a private judge or a mock trial before a "jury" whose members then tell the two sides what they thought of their claims and how they would decide the case if they were a real jury in a real trial.

In addition to a clause that presents the option for alternative dispute resolution, many companies doing cross-border deals like to insist that any disputes will be settled under their own native country's law – the proverbial "home court advantage." When two companies both want their own respective laws to apply, they often end up agreeing to leave things to a mediator or arbitrator who will go by neither. EuroDisney, the arm of the Disney empire that built the new Disneyland outside Paris, used this tack to avoid later problems in its contracts with the French government. The French, who promised millions in incentives and infrastructure spending to entice Disney to pick the Paris site over others in neighboring countries, had a non-negotiable demand. Given the concern in general over American influences on French culture, and particularly the spread of *franglais,* the use of American terms such as "le weekend" in the French language, the government of François Mitterrand demanded that French be the "official language" of the new Euro-Disneyland. The Disney people agreed; the new park at Marne-la-Vallee would use both French and English, but French would be the "official" language.

Then, however, Disney's lawyers raised the issue of disputes. All disagreements, they suggested, should not be decided under U.S. law or French law, but rather under "international" law. The French government, being made up of good Europeans and internationalists, readily agreed – a decision that later caused a fair amount of chagrin. As the opening time for Euro-Disneyland approached, the French became concerned about

174

the use of English. EuroDisneyland was insisting that many of its workers speak English and had opened special reservation and inquiry telephone lines that would be answered only by fluent English-speaking employees. To counter the dreaded trend toward English, the Prime Minister's Delegation on the French Language demanded that Mickey Mouse should instead be called *Mickey Souris,* Snow White should be *Blanche Neige* and Cinderella should be *Cendrillon.* French lawyers tried to raise the issue, but never got very far. The contract stipulated that any disputes would be decided under international law, rather than French law, and no judge or jury outside France — and maybe none inside France, either — would be sympathic to changing the names of the main Disney characters. Mickey Mouse has been Mickey Mouse for more than half a century, in every language and in every country. Talk about your home court advantage — Mickey never plays away.

Many Americans do business *with* Europe, particularly importers and exporters who may have a European partner, distributor, or other representative but don't themselves have a regular physical presence on the other side of the Atlantic. Other Americans do business *in* Europe, establishing offices, branches, or subsidiaries on the other side of the Atlantic. Structuring the European operation, and defining its place in the overall corporate picture, offers a variety of possibilities. Sometimes the European operation is tucked into the American home structure, with employees in London or Paris working as if they were merely another department — though admittedly quite a bit further down the hall — in the U.S. office. Sometimes the European operation is a completely separate identity that shares some top management with the U.S. home office. Oftentimes, the business is organized on geographic lines, with a European division reporting to the vice-president for Europe, for example. More and more, however, led by the "transnationals" such as IBM, companies are reorganizing their global operations on business lines rather than geographic lines.

Seagram's, the $6 billion drinks group, provides an example of how companies are changing. Over the decades, the business grew worldwide on the strength of the company's distribution network for liquor. In recent years, however, Seagram's dominance has been challenged by the series of takeovers and mergers that have allowed several of its competitors to build up their worldwide distribution networks, too. Consequently, Seagram's could no longer depend solely on its distribution strength. Global marketing muscle was also needed. Seagram's restructured, moving away from its traditional geographic alignments. Under the old system, the European operation was in charge of brand management, marketing, sales, and distribution throughout Europe for all the various products: wine, liquor, fruit juices, soda, and so on. Under the new system, Seagram's was split into two global business units, one concentrating on liquor and wine, the other on wine coolers, fruit juices, and other soft drinks. The marketing for Seagram's Martell cognac in Europe no longer falls to the same people responsible for marketing Seagram's Tropicana fruit juice in Europe. The people who handle Martell in Europe also handle Martell in America. Managing brands instead of lands, Seagram's marketers now have the flexibility to tailor their specialized products to the specific needs of individual markets. Customers are better served, and Seagram's is in a better position to respond more quickly to growth opportunities.

During the boom years of the 1980s in financial services, virtually every big Wall Street investment house, and lots of smaller U.S. boutique operations, too, plunged into Europe. The globalization of the stock markets, the exporting of American takeover and corporate financing techniques, and the 1986 "Big Bang" that deregulated London's financial services industry led American investment houses to send people and money to Europe, particularly London. They rented plush offices, entertained lavishly, traveled extensively, headhunted top Europeans, and generally spent far too much money trying to compete against each other in presenting the right image. All of them wanted to be seen by both American and European clients as having the most savvy, being the hardest working, offering the most backup capital, and coming up with the most innovative financing ideas. As it turned out, there was lots of business in Europe for Americans, but not enough for everyone, particularly after the 1987 stock market crash and the subsequent decline in takeover activity and distaste for American-inspired leveraging techniques such as junk bonds.

Many American firms absorbed big losses and ended up laying off people and cutting back their European operations. One U.S. firm, however, did not fold up its tent. Instead, Goldman Sachs continued to prosper. Year after year, Goldman remained at or near the top of the "league tables" kept by the industry to gauge which firms were advising on the most merger and acquisition work, and for the most money. Goldman itself would offer many valid reasons for its success in Europe, including its financial acumen in creating and backing deals and the willingness of its people to work hard. But the firm's determination to become more "European" was also a key factor. When the boom was booming, Goldman steadily added staff, but did not rush in by throwing waves of relatively inexperienced young people at clients—something that many other banks did and regretted when it became clear that European bankers and managers were mistrustful of the youngsters. They wanted people who were older and wiser, and with Goldman that's generally who they got.

From relying on London for 90 percent of its European work in the mid-1980s, Goldman gradually spread into the rest of Europe to the point that today more than 80 percent of its work comes from the Continent. The firm avoided the "outsider" label that hampered so many other U.S. firms by setting up panels of local consultants in different countries to offer advice on cultural customs and practices and to open well-placed doors. By taking over a large former newspaper building on Fleet Street, on the edge of the City, London's financial district, Goldman underlined its commitment to and confidence in its European operation. The firm also set about expanding the number of American partners permanently assigned to Europe and building up the number of European partners. Now Europe accounts for only about one-sixth of Goldman's nearly 7,000 employees, but in any given year returns one-fourth of the firm's profits.

Whatever approach an American takes to doing business *in* Europe, the most important consideration may be communications. The people in America need to know what the people in Europe are doing, and the people in Europe need to know what the Americans are thinking. This extends beyond bosses to any member of the staff with any dealings, direct or not, with the operation on the other side of the Atlantic. Good communications lead to proper consideration, and that is often just as important at the middle and lower levels as among top managers. When an associate or junior manager working late in the Chicago home office makes a 6 P.M. phone call to a colleague or counterpart in Paris, it should be done with the awareness that it's 1 A.M. in Paris. Someone is probably being awakened, so the call had better be important. What kind of message does it send to Europe if the home office shows so little consideration?

One New Jersey executive who oversees her company's sales to European distributors describes the most difficult part of her job as getting the American side of the operation to understand the European customers' concerns. Despite America's reputation as a service-oriented society, too many U.S. companies refuse to bend their service procedures for overseas customers, she said. In her company, the service center that fills orders is based in the Midwest, and few of the people in charge have any experience with Europe or Europeans. They have set, rigid procedures for filling orders for their American customers and refuse to modify them even slightly if a European customer wants something different. One European distributor, for instance, might need delivery as soon as possible, even if it costs more. Another might be used to flexible payment terms in return for lower cost, slower delivery. But the American service managers won't budge. Their cookie-cutter system is set up to make things easy for themselves, and that's the way they want to keep it, even if it deprives the company of sales. "They want to service their overseas customers the same as their domestic customers, and they want to service all overseas customers the same as all other overseas customers," the New Jersey executive complained. "We're becoming known for being inflexible, and it's driving customers away."

If some of her customers would visit the U.S. operation and some of her managers from the Midwest service center visited the European customers, some sort of compromise would probably be worked out. Visits back and forth to Europe are expensive and time-consuming, but when the right people are brought face to face there's almost always some good fallout. They know each other's faces and each other's problems, and they're more willing to make concessions and offer assistance. This is important internally, too. Many American professional partnerships (law firms, accountants, designers, etc.) try to keep their Europe-based partners and managers in touch through regular one-on-one phone calls, periodic conference calls, and flights back home for meetings to discuss key projects that are important for the firm's long-range strategy. Isolation is always a concern, particularly among young associates and middle managers who fear that being sent abroad ("Out of sight, out of mind . . .") will hurt their chances for advancement. Consequently, some firms have quietly but deliberately adopted the policy of timing promotions for after an associate is established abroad. This does two things. It affords confirmation for the firm that the associate or middle manager will indeed be able to contribute internationally, and it sends a message to all other associates that going abroad is not a career hindrance.

Too many American companies breezily dispatch employees to Europe without really considering whether they are the right people. A lot of employees approached about a posting say, "Hey, yeah, Europe, that sounds like a good idea for a couple of years," but then fail to adjust, personally, professionally, or both. Many Americans confess to difficulties in moving to Europe, largely because they underestimated the cultural differences. This is particularly true for Britain, where people believe the so-called "common" language is a buffer that automatically smoothes out the very considerable cultural differences. After more than seven years working and living in London, I am reminded every day – although almost never in an unpleasant way – that I am a foreigner. Fewer companies are sending employees abroad for exploratory visits these days, but saving that money up front can often cost more later if the employee is never going to be happy and needs to be replaced.

Managing Europeans presents another set of challenges. They are not used to American ideas of devotion to the job or our willingness to work late or on weekends, and they are often uncomfortable with our direct manner. In some European companies, particularly in the southern countries, there is often a marked reluctance to say no. An American boss will ask a European underling if something can be done by Tuesday. The European will say yes, it is possible. Tuesday comes, the work isn't done, the American wants to know why, and the European, surprised at the indignation, shrugs and explains that the American simply asked whether it *could* be done rather than issuing explicit instructions that it *should* be done. Again, communications are extremely important. This is why so many Americans overseeing European workers try to have a European assistant or human resources manager to facilitate internal communications and mount what is in effect an ongoing internal marketing program that sells employees on the corporate objectives.

Disney, of course, is the master at this. Just as Disneyland in California and Disney World in Florida have created a working atmosphere that absorbs their American employees, Euro-

Disney in France has indoctrinated – using the word in its most positive sense – its 12,000 staffers in the Disney way of doing things. The workers, mostly French but also representing the United States and a variety of European and other countries around the world, generally applied for jobs with only the vaguest notion of how Disney combines entertainment and service into the ultimate theme park "experience." From the beginning, EuroDisney recruiters made it clear to applicants that they were not merely applying for jobs. No, they were auditioning to be cast for roles in a show, and they were all performers – from the actors inside the character costumes to the crews sweeping the walkways – who owed it to the audience to provide quality entertainment through their on-the-job "roles." (This is much like TGI Friday's stage-and-circus auditions for restaurant staff, covered in Chapter 4).

Management recruits were trained at a Disney University, and some went to Florida or California to work shifts in the kitchens or on the rides. All employees went through orientation programs underscoring Disney's history and traditions, and all went through training programs that include regular refresher courses. These sessions, along with a variety of in-house communications – in both French and English, of course – simultaneously served as training and internal marketing functions. Staffers were provided with perks such as day care, regular company outings, discounts for Disney products, and special previews of new Disney movies. EuroDisney made sure that the new staff knew its work was supposed to be fun. By making the staff customers themselves, it was much easier to reinforce the Disney messages of quality and guest service.

Americans setting up in Europe often find it easier to build from the ground up, the way Disney and TGI Friday's did, than to take over an ongoing situation with all its problems. When Duncan Chadwick took over Hamleys in 1989, he was aghast at the famous London toy store's poor organization and layout. At the same time, however, the disarray was encouraging. The

181

many changes that needed to be made, both immediately and in the long run, gave him confidence that he would be able to drag the store back from the red into the black. Hamleys had a computer system, for instance, but it wasn't being used to track which toys were selling. There was a catalog, but it wasn't generating many sales. New employees, the ones least likely to be able to answer customers' questions, were staffing cash registers. The lower floors of the store were devoted to adult sports and games, while upper floors—harder to reach with a stroller or pram—held the toys for babies and toddlers. Moreover, displays throughout the store were organized by manufacturer, not by product. In the infants' department, there was no single display or shelf of rattles. The Mattel rattles were with all the other Mattel toys, the Playschool rattles were with all the other Playschool toys, and the Fisher-Price rattles were with all the other Fisher-Price toys. Parents couldn't confront all the rattles at once to see which one their babies would grab first.

The one thing Hamleys still had going for it, owing to its long history, was a good name. That history dates back to 1760, when Cornishman William Hamley opened a shop full of tin soldiers, rag dolls, and wooden horses. In 1938, Queen Mary's shopping sprees for her little princesses, Elizabeth and Margaret, earned Hamleys the Royal Warrant that it still holds: "By Appointment to Her Majesty the Queen, Toy and Sports Merchants." Queen Elizabeth II and other British royals still do much of their toy-and-game shopping at Hamleys, sometimes coming in to browse late at night, when the store is closed. Other royals, however, including Diana, the Princess of Wales, occasionally brave the daytime crowds. And what crowds. Despite management stutters over the years, Hamleys was still drawing 75,000 customers a day when Chadwick took over.

Each December, the crush of Christmas shoppers forces bobbies from Scotland Yard to impose one-way lanes on the sidewalk outside the store. Hamleys is such a tourist mecca that foreigners account for nearly a third of total sales, which in a normal year includes a small city of teddy bears (more than 40,000) and 100 miles of toy railway track. But Chadwick believed those figures could be much better. Yes, there was still lots of traffic in the store, but he didn't think customers were spending as much as they should. Previous managers had made it more difficult to shop there at a time when competitors, notably the American chain Toys 'R' Us with its suburban shops and wide-open parking lots, were making toy shopping easier.

Beyond the problems affecting the toy industry in general in the 1980s – recession, manufacturing overcapacity, high interest rates, declining birth rates – Hamleys had developed its own special difficulties. Chadwick's takeover was the fourth change of ownership in as many years. Most of Hamleys' woes came from the fact that it was so highly regarded in the retailing business – the "Harrods" of toys, it was called – that nontoy specialists thought anybody could run it. In 1985 the Burton Group, one of Britain's leading clothing retailers, bought Debenham's, the British department store chain that owned Hamleys. The following year, realizing that Hamleys simply wasn't a good fit, the Burton Group sold it to Harris Queensway, a British retailing conglomerate based on carpet stores, for $50 million. Sir Phil Harris, chairman of Harris Queensway, set out to capitalize on the Hamleys name by opening a series of smaller outlets in smaller British cities. However, without the vast size of the Regent Street flagship, and without the huge pool of foreign and domestic shoppers in London, the Hamleys outposts bombed. By 1988, Hamleys' $4 million annual net profit had become a $7 million loss. Harris Queensway was sold to Sir James Gulliver, a London takeover specialist who set about spinning off noncore assets such as Hamleys in order to refocus on the carpet business.

Even when he heard that Hamleys was on the market in 1988, Duncan Chadwick never dreamed he had a chance at owning the most famous name in toys. At the time, he and his partner, Neil Bailey, were running an upscale Beverly Hills,

183

California, shop called Intellitoys. The two had started Intellitoys in 1981 after meeting several years earlier when they both worked for a chain of northern California toy stores. At Intellitoys, based in the prestigious Beverly Center shopping complex, they set out to follow their ideals. They would have no sexist or "violent" toys, including guns and makeup. That meant no GI Joe or Barbie dolls. Instead they would concentrate on educational toys, highlighted by a kids' computer department. "We had some fairly strong opinions at the time," Chadwick recalled, bemused. "Well, the computer thing was an absolute flop. We'd get 50 kids back there playing with the machines, and nobody was buying. We needed ten employees just to monitor them. Meanwhile, we were being undersold by computer shops. The demand was for GI Joe and Barbie. If we wanted to survive, we had to get into those areas. So we got into those areas." Stocked with the usual array of childrens' toys, plus the educational ones they personally favored, Chadwick and Bailey prospered in Beverly Hills. They also began looking to expand through an acquisition.

Sir James Gulliver put Hamleys back on the market in the autumn of 1988, but Chadwick abandoned his inquiries when told that the asking price was $70 million. Visiting relatives in London at Christmas 1988, he was surprised to learn that Hamleys had not been sold after all; no one wanted to pay Gulliver's $70 million asking price. Chadwick returned to Los Angeles and faxed Harris Queensway a note offering $35 million for Hamleys. By return fax came the acceptance in principle. Chadwick brought in his brother Tim as a silent partner. Neil Bailey, Chadwick's partner in Intellitoys, also bought in, and so did Bob Brown, the British executive who had been running Hamleys — and closing the unprofitable provincial outlets — for Harris Queensway. Working with Citicorp Venture Capital for the financial backing, Chadwick negotiated the sale price down to $32 million, and the unlikely takeover of Hamleys (annual sales $30 million) by Intellitoys (annual sales $3 million) was completed. "It was a real case of the mouse eating the lion," Chadwick said.

Chadwick, as chief executive officer, and Bailey, as chief operating officer, immediately relocated to London and set about transforming the original Hamleys. To a point, that is. They announced that they would be importing a raft of procedures, from staff training to new computer systems, but at the same time said the underlying goal was to restore Hamleys to its former glory as "an encyclopedia of toys." Chadwick and Bailey insisted they were not trying to "Americanize" Hamleys. "We're just trying to bring in good business practices," Bailey said. "It's got nothing to do with us being American." As a result, there was no British backlash of resentment at a venerable retail institution such as Hamleys falling under American control. To the contrary, retail analysts said they welcomed the fresh thinking, solid management, and commitment to toys that Chadwick exhibited.

Chadwick has done much to reorganize the Regent Street store. He set about restoring the number of different toys carried by Hamleys to its peak level of 35,000. Previously, the number of different products on the store's shelves had dropped to 12,000. "That's not enough for a store of 40,000 square feet," Chadwick said. In contrast, his Beverly Hills shop carried more than 20,000 items in only 4,500 square feet. Chadwick banned the previous management's storewide sales featuring markdowns on most toys. He reasoned that customers come to Hamleys for quality, service, and the wide range of choice. During the store's desperate special-sales periods before he took over, business actually went down. With all the changes, it took less than two years for Chadwick to get Hamleys' profit margins back where he wanted them.

Much of the revitalization focused on service. Chadwick instituted a free gift-wrapping service. Clerks were taught that when a customer was considering an item, the sale could be closed by saying, "You know, the cost includes free gift wrapping if you'd like." And, of course, the most experienced staffers were made the most visible, working the cash registers. Chadwick was stunned when he learned why the most famous toy shop in the world had abandoned the traditional Santa's grotto during the Christmas shopping season. Previous managers had done away with Santa because the long queues to see him were blocking the aisles. Chadwick ordered Santa reinstated and worked out a way to keep the lines down and out of the store's main traffic flows. "It was an example of how Hamleys had lost its way," Chadwick said. "For too long, managers were just putting out fires. They solved problems as quickly and easily as they could, instead of trying to work out good long-range solutions."

To improve the store's layout, Chadwick put younger children's toys on the lower floors, and the older children's and adults' departments on the higher floors. The customer service department was moved from its hideaway on the fifth floor to a prominent spot on the ground floor. Toys, including rattles, were grouped by product rather than manufacturer. Chadwick also revamped the store's internal structure to improve shoppers' traffic patterns. One thing he didn't change, however, was the ground floor, where red-coated doormen welcome shoppers in from Regent Street, and where Hamleys has its seasonal displays of the newest and most popular toys. Even on weekday mornings when most shops are quiet, Hamleys' ground floor is a noisy whirl of toys. Red-shirted employees demonstrate them on the floor and children squeal in delight as their parents break into wide smiles at the latest singing flower or diving-dolphin bath toy. To inspire staff to get more involved in demonstrations, and to increase personal interaction between staff and customers, Chadwick and Bailey frequently get down on their knees themselves, surrounded by chattering kids and buzzing toys. Another fixture on the ground floor, right inside the main entrance, is a Hamleys staffer standing on a box to demonstrate little cardboard airplanes that, with a proper flick of the wrist, loop-the-loop around the room and come right back to the launcher. The little planes sell for less than $2 apiece, and Hamleys moves close to a quarter-million of them a year. Chadwick reckons the box where the staffer stands is the most profitable square foot of retail space in the world, and he's not going to change anything to jeopardize that claim.

To upgrade the Hamleys staff, Chadwick instituted mandatory training programs that emphasize helpful, courteous service. His regular morning training sessions include role-playing in which staff are confronted by various difficult personalities, and Chadwick has a crew of undercover "professional shoppers" who work the store and report back with criticisms and suggestions. Chadwick's training sessions include manufacturers' instructional videos explaining their toys and recommending how they should be sold, but in general he is trying to reduce the influence of the big toy manufacturers on Hamleys' operations. In recent years, much of Hamleys' operational authority was forfeited by disinterested owners. Manufacturers told Hamleys what to order and how to display it. The manufacturers also offered more and more of their own employees to work as Hamleys' staff. Chadwick was dismayed to find that the 150 sales staff he inherited included 45 clerks who wore the red Hamleys shirt but were actually hired and paid by toy manufacturers, not the store. He vowed to phase out the manufacturers' reps and replace them with Hamleys' own employees. "We couldn't have staff with two bosses. It was too confusing, and even though they meant well they didn't do right by either of us," he said of the manufacturers' reps.

In the back rooms, Chadwick brought in a new computer system that keeps track of purchases on a daily basis and helps translate that information into strategy for efficient shelf-stocking. Now he can tell not only how well red balloons sell, but on which shelf and which corner of the shelf they sell best. The computer can tell what people are buying today, of course, but it can't tell what people are going to buy next month or next year. That's another reason Chadwick and Bailey can often be found down on the floor, playing with the toys the manufacturers are trying to sell them for the next season, and showing the new models to young customers for their reactions. "You have to have a certain feeling for toys, sure," Chadwick allowed. "And you have to be aware of all the other outside factors that impact on toys—fashion, science, the economy, world events. It's the sociology of the market. The easiest thing is to pick a hot item. The hard part is guessing how hot it will be. And in the end, nobody makes that choice but the customer."

Another change is a new catalog and mailing list. "The suppliers are going to pay for the new catalog, and it's going to be available on newsstands, too," Chadwick said. "Before, no one ever called people on the mailing list. The year before we took over, Hamleys sent out 70,000 catalogs and got 1,800 responses. I say let's send it to people who buy toys." To bring a wider choice to Hamleys customers, Chadwick is cutting out the wholesale distributors, the "middlemen" of the toy business, and moving toward direct purchases from manufacturers, including factories in the Far East. He's hoping that lower prices on bulk orders will let Hamleys set its own price for toys instead of relying on the manufacturers' suggested retail.

Toys are a fun way to make a living, Chadwick admitted, but "it's still a business." Ultimately, he envisions dozens of Hamleys outlets across the United States, either in the form of smaller Hamleys stores in shopping malls or substantial Hamleys departments in existing department stores. And he plans to expand the business with more large flagship-type stores in other world capitals. "Toys are totally international," he said. "Kids are kids and toys are toys throughout the world. A set of blocks in Japan is the same as a set of blocks anywhere else."

CHAPTER 10

———————— ♦ ♦ ♦ ————————

Eastern Europe

Monika Stopczynska is a wide-eyed, vivacious young Polish woman who, like many Eastern Europeans, has hope for the future. Hope. A future. Those are two things that most of us in the industrialized West take for granted, but seemed out of reach for most people in Eastern Europe until the dramatic political and economic changes that lifted them out of the Soviet sphere.

I met Monika one evening in her hometown, Lodz (pronounced *whoodge*), a grim industrial city with a shameful history of mistreatment of local Jews during World War II. With a population of more than a million, Lodz is Poland's second-largest city. It is characterized by bleak Russian-style high-rise apartment buildings that stand hard by dirty, smoke-belching factories. Monika lives with her parents in one of those buildings. Her boyfriend lives with his parents in another. Monika and her boyfriend are in their mid-twenties and want to get married, but they have no place to live. Long waiting lists, a hangover from the old communist regime, mean it could take years for local authorities to assign them an apartment. Even then, it would be just like their parents' cramped little flats in one of the dreary high-rises.

So Monika has decided to build a house. A proper house, with two stories, a front yard and a back garden. But to do that, she first must make some money, a lot of money by Polish standards. Along the way, she has joined thousands of other enthusiastic, optimistic young Poles who are helping change their country's entire political, economic, and legal structure. Monika is in many ways representative of a new generation trying to impose its hopes and aspirations onto the emerging democracies of Eastern Europe. Her experiences also provide insights for American business executives, entrepreneurs, and investors considering the risky and often literally lawless business climate of Central Europe, Eastern Europe, and the former Soviet republics.

What is happening in Eastern Europe today has some distinct parallels with China's newly opened doors a few years ago. America, Inc., became enamoured of the idea of a billion new consumers for our fast food, Barbie dolls, and computer games. But the same sort of disappointments that many Americans encountered in China in the 1970s and 1980s may be looming for those who believe that Eastern Europeans are eager to buy whatever we have to sell them in the 1990s. From an American business standpoint, Eastern Europeans share several disadvantages with the Chinese. The biggest disadvantage, of course, is that they are poor. As some marketing genius once pointed out, the only problem with poor people is that they don't have any money. Even among the scant few Eastern Europeans who might have some money to spend on our products and services, it's nearly impossible at this point to tell exactly what they will spend it on. There is little history of reliable market research in Eastern Europe; what government figures do exist for spending and consumption should not be taken as gospel, and sometimes they shouldn't be taken as anything more than someone's optimistic but amateurish guess. In the past, people simply bought what was available. "How do I know which one to buy?" a befuddled Polish housewife asked when several new brands of household detergent appeared on the shelves. The new markets of Eastern Europe are not only poor, they are immature and unsophisticated. One analyst pointed out that while Hungarians may be eager to try some types of new food available from the West, they are years away from a high-margin product such as Lean Cuisine.

Real changes are happening in Eastern Europe, but they are happening slowly, and it is far from certain that Americans will be comfortable doing business in the political, economic, and legal systems that evolve. Even more than in Western Europe, Americans need to be careful in approaching Eastern Europe. Flexibility is important, and so is patience. The successful Americans in Eastern Europe are not likely to be those who are looking for quick profits, but rather those who are committed to the long haul despite all the obstacles. The institutions and systems of Eastern Europe are being rebuilt from the ground up, and so are the attitudes of the people of Eastern Europe. Some aspects of the rebuilding will be positive in the eyes of Americans, some not. But for Americans willing to be part of these grand experiments, the rewards could be great – someday.

Just as there's a myth of unity in Western Europe, there are wide differences – again, political, social, economic, and cultural – among the countries that are generally regarded as part of Eastern Europe. Here's a good example. For nearly two years in London, our family and several other American expatriate households depended on a delightful young Polish couple who cleaned for us, did babysitting, and acted as general home-help handypeople. They were terrific. They came to Britain simply because they could make more money there. Their goal was to save enough to build a really nice house back in Poland, and they did it by working incredibly hard and spending incredibly little on themselves. They lived the Puritan work ethic that history books tell us is what made America great. I once asked

191

them just how they were going to build this dream house. I knew they had been buying bricks and lumber all along, stockpiling materials against inflation. But would the two of them actually do all the work? Oh, no, they said. They would hire Russians who came to Poland for the same reasons that our Polish couple had come to Britain—because they could make more money to take home.

Russia and the other former Soviet republics are still going through traumatic changes, and it's too early to tell just how things are going to shake out in terms of business opportunities for Americans. Certainly some Americans did business successfully in the Soviet Union for years, despite the many limitations. Pepsi, for instance, reaped great rewards when it bartered soda pop for Russian vodka at a time when the market for vodka was growing in the West. To me, however, after repeated visits to the Soviet Union, tours of most of its major cities, and talks with dozens of civic leaders, the new commonwealth remains one large question mark. It is very different, for many reasons, from the rest of Eastern Europe, and the people who venture there need to know more about Russia and Russians than about Europe and Europeans. Even in Latvia or Lithuania, where natives tout their pre-World War II independence and bridle at any suggestion that they are remotely like Russians, the chains of 50 years of communism cannot be shaken off lightly. Capitalism must be re-learned. Similarly, countries such as Romania and Bulgaria have moved away from the Soviet sphere, but have not proven themselves to be sufficiently welcoming or attractive to American business.

The former East Germany offers many opportunities, but most of them are being seized by or reserved for former West Germans. Since reunification, the Germans have given the rest of the world the distinct impression that while they can use help, they're quite capable of solving their own problems. But Americans have made some tentative inroads into eastern Germany, particularly in mass-market products. The Philips tobacco company, for example, moved quickly to bring Marlboro cigarettes into East Germany because the East Germans, thanks to West German reunification payments, jobs, and welfare, had more money than other Eastern Europeans. Similarly, Woolworths, with a long history of retailing in Eastern Europe, was one of the first American companies to announce an expanded chain of stores in East Germany after the Wall came tumbling down.

The countries of Eastern Europe where Americans have the most opportunities are Hungary, Poland, and Czechoslovakia. Indeed, those three countries have been waging a sometimes sharp competition to attract Western investment. The Hungarians argue that they are the most sophisticated, Westernized, consumer-oriented of the three, only five hours from Vienna by hydrofoil on the Danube. Budapest is closer to Munich than London is to Manchester. The Czechoslovaks point out that they are the most industrialized and have the most skilled labor force. The Poles maintain that their 38 million people make up the biggest potential national market and offer the cheapest labor and that its eastern location makes Poland a logical gateway to the Soviet Union.

Differences aside, Hungary, Poland, and Czechoslovakia have much in common, including the problems they present for Americans who are considering doing business in Eastern Europe. They all need money to finance their new democracies, to erase the legacy of the communists, and to pave the way for Westernization. They need money for unemployment compensation programs for the many workers who are left jobless as old, inefficient state-run industries close down. They need money to build schools, roads, and communications systems to bring their infrastructures from the standards of 30 and 40 years ago to the standards of the 21st century. They need money for new factories that will produce the sort of goods that can compete on the international export markets. They need money for environmental programs to clean up pollution damage from communist factories.

Beyond money, Czechoslovakia, Poland, and Hungary need new technology, new management, and the entire range of business skills, such as marketing and accounting, that are taken for granted in the West. Tony O'Reilly, an Irishman and chairman of the board of Pittsburgh-based H. J. Heinz, is extremely qualified to comment on both American and European business. He has said repeatedly that Westerners must keep reminding themselves how much they don't understand about Eastern Europe. Nothing should be assumed in Eastern Europe, and nothing should be counted upon. This is especially true for Americans because we are farther away, not only geographically but also socially and culturally. Because of their closer background and greater ease in understanding the makeup of Eastern Europe, Western Europeans typically have an advantage over Americans. Eastern Europeans are often more comfortable with Western Europeans than with Americans, and Western European products and companies are often more familiar than American products and companies. After years of distrust, during which two generations of young people were taught that Americans are the enemy, it is perhaps not surprising that Eastern Europeans retain misgivings about dealing with Americans. In Eastern Europe, Americans face many of the negative stereotypes of the rest of Europe (Chapter 2), except that fewer Eastern Europeans have had any personal experience with Americans. Therefore, fewer of them have been able to dispel the indoctrinated notions that we are money grubbers who will use them any way we can to make ourselves richer.

Even Americans who have been successful in Western Europe might find themselves floundering in the unfamiliarity of Budapest or Warsaw. In Prague, I managed to squeeze into the office of the beleaguered Czech government official who was in charge of coordinating Western business contacts. Chain-smok-

194

ing and chain-drinking coffee, he stared at me with a sagging face and exhausted eyes across a desk nearly submerged beneath stacks of business proposals that flowed onto an adjoining conference table and onto the floor around his feet. "I'm beat," he told me. "I don't eat or sleep anymore. I don't see my family. Nothing but letters and files and meetings. I was in London last month for 48 hours and I had 44 business meetings. In Prague, I'm here at the office 18 hours a day dealing with thousands of people from Western Europe, America, and Japan who want names, numbers, and information. They want to sell things here. They want to buy things here. They want to set up factories. They are all going to make our people rich." The man sighed and put out one of the two cigarettes he had going. "The problem is, many of these people come in like cowboys. They tell us what they are going to do. They tell us how they have millions to spend. They tell me they are going to be in town for 48 hours, and they expect to leave with something all signed. I tell you, 48 hours isn't enough time in this town to find a good restaurant and a girl for the evening."

From a practical standpoint, there is little recognizable business infrastructure in much of Czechoslovakia, Hungary, and Poland, especially outside the capital cities where it can be difficult to find a good hotel room, a competent interpreter, a working fax machine, or a clear phone line to the West. Under the communists, Poland's 38 million people shared a mere 3 million phones. That's changing rapidly as more phones and better lines are put in, but it can still be difficult to make a good connection to Poland from overseas, and it can be impossible to make a quick overseas connection from Poland. Internal domestic calls can be worse. In Warsaw, I once phoned for an hour trying to get a government office just on the other side of town. Finally, a Polish woman took pity and did what the Poles do. She called a friend who lived near the middle of town, in a district between mine and the one I was trying to reach. She gave my message to the friend. The friend then called the office

I was trying to reach and passed along my message. Such communications difficulties can confound even travelers with the foresight to bring along a portable fax or computer and modem.

Budapest is relatively well set up for visitors, but suitable places to stay and even to have dinner can be hard to come by in Prague and Warsaw. In planning a trip to Prague, I tried to book a room several weeks in advance, but was told none were available. Through friends of friends, I was able to arrange to take over someone's flat in a drab suburban high-rise for $20 a night. It served my purposes on that particular trip, but was hardly the sort of accommodation that most business travelers want. In booking hotels, make sure there's a restaurant in the hotel and that guests have priority in booking tables. Restaurants are often few and full, especially in summer. More and more Eastern European hotels are putting in fax machines and making photocopiers available to guests, and some have established business centers that can provide meeting rooms and translation, transportation, and clerical services. The obvious problems in just getting started in Eastern Europe explain why so many Americans – and the Eastern European governments themselves – have proved willing to put money into restaurants, hotels, and other aspects of tourism and business travel.

The Eastern European countries are struggling with strategies for their currencies as they move away from the state subsidies and artificial price supports. Poland, Czechoslovakia, and Hungary have all moved to make their currencies convertible, first internally and then on the international exchanges. The price of hardening their currencies has been inflation; people are paying what things really cost instead of the cheaper prices set by the government. In Poland, where the 1990 "shock therapy" made the zloty convertible virtually overnight, inflation in the first month was more than 70 percent. But the Solidarity government held firm and kept the exchange rate at a steady 9,500 zlotys to the dollar for that entire year. In a few months, the inflation rate settled down to a more manageable range, around 3 percent a month. Some Americans joked that they should substitute small zloty notes for toilet paper because the money was worth so little and good toilet paper was so expensive.

Another common problem in Eastern Europe is that the laws and legal systems became misshapen by the years of communism. As a result, the new democratically elected parliaments are overburdened by pressures to come up with legal mechanisms for doing business in the Western, capitalist style. This isn't merely a matter of enacting legislation to allow the selloff of state-run industries to private concerns or to allow foreign investments for the first time. These are nations where the entire concept of owning property – by anyone – was discouraged. A whole new legal foundation is needed to protect private investment: ownership, copyright, trademark, and so forth. Foreign investors need to be allowed not only to bring in money, but to take out profits in hard currency. Western managers need to be able to hire and fire people, instead of being stuck with unproductive loafers who could not be fired, even for failing to turn up for work, under the leftover communist laws. Similarly, employee "councils" that had the right to fire managers or veto management policy are being outlawed. New laws are needed for collecting debts and, eventually, for bankruptcy. Imagine: There was no law of contract as we know it in the old regimes. And after years of state monopolies, new pro-competition, antitrust, antimonopoly laws must be passed. For the new stock exchanges, securities laws must be passed.

Ownership of property posed one of the most serious obstacles. Who would be able to reclaim property that was nationalized by the communists? What if someone else had a claim? I recall a seminar in Helsinki attended by American property developers, retailers, and investors who were interested in building shopping centers in Eastern Europe. They seemed startled when a banker bluntly told them he wasn't interested in loaning money for any project until ownership issues were cleared up once and for all. "You'll feel pretty silly," he warned, "when old Friedrich pops up in the middle of your million-square-foot shopping center to claim his historic allotment." Hungary, Poland, and Czechoslovakia have all moved to restore property to rightful owners or their heirs, with one eye toward fairness to their citizens but the other toward settling things quickly so that private investment is encouraged. The important thing for the would-be American investor is that all the past property claims are being cleared away. It's still a good idea to make title searches, of course, and to talk about old ownership claims with sellers before buying property. In general, however, new investments can be made with reasonable assurances that no "old Friedrich" is going to pop up with a legal claim that could stall a project in Eastern Europe.

English is fairly widely spoken in Eastern Europe. As in Western Europe, it is the language of business. But because of the lack of a business culture in Eastern Europe, there are often more language difficulties. Many Eastern European businesspeople, even in high places, don't understand the words – let alone the concepts and technology behind them – that we use every day. Subsidiary loans. Poison pills and white knights. Electronic mail. Swaps. Shrink-wrap. Offshore. Focus group. Enterprise zone. Golden handcuffs and parachutes. Hedging. Factoring. Video conferencing. Mezzanine financing. Mailshot. Food court. Arbitrage. Officials and traders from the Chicago Board of Trade and the Chicago Mercantile Exchange have made several trips to help a number of Eastern Europe capitals put together commodities exchanges of their own. On one trip they were contacted by someone from a remote rural town. "Can you help us set up an exchange, too?" the caller wondered. "We already have a computer. . . ." As if a little desktop PC was all that it took to open a commodities exchange.

Even if laws change, people sometimes don't. In many cases, the same bureaucrats who ran government agencies in the communist days are still in charge – and trying to run things the same way. They don't want to do things any differently because that's not the way they did them before. Two days after Pizza Hut opened in Moscow amid great public fanfare, a government car pulled up in front. Out came a heavyweight bureaucrat who announced that her department was required to do inspections. She found that the Americans working there had not had the venereal disease test required of all foreigners in the old days, so she ordered the restaurant closed. She even locked a chain across the front doors. It only took a few hours and a few frantic phone calls to have the chains removed, but it was a stark reminder to the Pizza Hut people – and all Americans doing business in Eastern Europe – that not all vestiges of the bad old days are gone.

Some of the old communist-era bureaucrats were managers of state businesses, and some of them are still clinging to their positions. Most are being phased out, and the sooner the better. They are part of a "lost generation" of Eastern European management. Generally between the ages of 30 and 55, they are schooled in the Soviet style of central planning, speak Russian as their only foreign language, and cannot wrap their minds around capitalist principles that would have been criminal in the old days. Under communism, accounting and bookkeeping were geared to the requirements of the state, not to gauging performance. No one cared about the bottom line because there wasn't one. There were no private investors for the managers to worry about pleasing. Most businesses had large orders that they filled for a few big customers, mostly other state companies. Managers were often told what supplies they would receive and in what quantities. They were told how much to produce and where to ship at what prices.

Under this system, it was hard to tell what anything was really worth. It still is today. Determining values is one of the most difficult aspects of doing business in Eastern Europe. Even if you manage to come up with a reasonable figure about what a business and its assets are worth, the figure may not mean a thing in the real world because of uncertainty over future markets, inflation, and currency devaluations. Many Eastern Europeans have little comprehension of real values for companies or property; in the past, something was worth whatever the government said it was worth. When one Western airline decided to take over and renovate a state-run hotel in Eastern Europe, it found that the construction would cost $11 million. Fine, the government said, that's exactly the value of the old broken-down hotel—$11 million. We put up the old hotel, you put up the cash, and we'll call it a 50-50 joint venture, the government suggested. Ultimately, the airline decided to go into the joint venture on that basis, but only if it had complete control and did not have to suffer any input from Eastern European managers.

All the Eastern European countries have moved to harden their currencies so that they are convertible on the international money exchanges. They have also moved to allow Western investors to repatriate their profits. But there are still the dangers of wildly fluctuating exchange rates and hyperinflation. Suppose you put $100,000 into a business in Czechoslovakia, and the business shows a 20 percent profit in the first year. A good start, yes. But your investment isn't worth $120,000—the original capital plus profit—if there were adverse currency fluctuations over the year. If the Hungarian forint is only worth half what it was against the dollar when you originally went in, your investment after a year may be worth only $60,000. (See Chapter 11 for further discussions.) Or suppose you start a business in Poland that will rely on local suppliers, and you plan on breaking even the first year despite forecasts of 30 percent inflation. You're not going to break even if inflation is 60 percent. Shortly after Pizza Hut opened in Moscow, its suppliers' prices tripled and the restaurants had to double their prices, which undoubtedly discouraged many potential customers. Until some sort of stability and reliance on economic forecasting is part of the picture in Eastern Europe, Americans can be forgiven for regarding any venture in the region as extremely risky. Adding to the financial uncertainties is the fact that Eastern European banks are just learning to operate like banks as we know them. Loans of any form, including those for corporate financing and home mortgages, are a new concept.

In a way, Pizza Hut was lucky; at least it kept getting the cheese, flour, and other ingredients it needed from its local suppliers. Some businesses that try to "live off the land" find that their suppliers inexplicably go out of business, or suddenly start selling all their supplies to a competitor. It's going to keep happening until the law of contracts is well established, which could take years. McDonald's was so intent on avoiding supplier problems – both in terms of quantity and quality – that it spent $45 million to build a new plant that would produce the hamburger patties and bake the buns for its first restaurant in Moscow. Of course, McDonald's never said it intended to make a quick profit from that first Moscow shop. Instead, the company will spend its ruble profits, if and when there are any, on opening new shops in Russia and perhaps elsewhere in what's left of the former Soviet republics.

The cornerstone of the move toward the open market in Hungary, Poland, and Czechoslovakia is privatization – the selling off of state-run companies. Most of the buyers, naturally, are foreign investors, although efforts are being made to allow natives, and particularly employees of privatized companies, to take up shares while putting down little or no cash. Some companies are being privatized outright, simply sold off to the highest bidder. Often, the buyer has a prior claim, such as family ownership before nationalization by the communists, that may shut out the competition from other bidders. Some are sold off as joint ventures, and it is not unusual for governments to keep a large ownership share initially. The government share may then be gradually diminished in further share selloffs until the company is fully private.

The scale of the privatization efforts can be seen in the fact that Czechoslovakia alone wants to sell off 4,000 state-run industries. When the Czechoslovak government unveiled the first stage of its privatization, the government said that 50 of its largest industrial manufacturers would be sold off. The government said it was hoping to raise $1.5 billion, an average of about $30 million a company. The government also added, as a caution to investors, that each newly private company would require an average of $50 million in investments, for everything from new machines to pollution cleanup, over the first three years of private operation.

Even for Western companies with the best claims and connections, privatization in Eastern Europe can cause major headaches. After the broadly based citizens' group Civic Forum led the so-called Velvet Revolution in Czechoslovakia in 1989, the dissident poet Vaclav Havel was proclaimed president. Havel's new government let it be known that Czech and Slovak political exiles would be welcomed back. We need your expertise and your investments, the new administration said, and we want you to resume the businesses that you lost when you either fled or were forced out. One of the first to reclaim the old family business birthright was Tomas Bata. The Bata family had been making shoes in Czechoslovakia for ten generations when they fled to Canada in 1932. Under Tomas Bata, Sr., the family business was re-based in Toronto and grew to become the world's largest shoemakers, producing 300 million pairs of shoes a year at 40 factories around the world. The company has 70,000 employees and sells its shoes in more than 6,000 shops in 70 countries. The old Bata factories in Czechoslovakia continued to turn out shoes under the communists, but the company was nationalized in 1946 and its name was changed to Svit. Most of its shoes were sold in Eastern Europe, the Soviet Union, and the Third World, largely because the quality was not of export standard for the West. From North America, the Bata family retained its strong Czech identity, and during the Cold

War Tomas Sr. was often heard addressing his homeland on Radio Free Europe and the Voice of America. His message, like that of so many other successful exiles, extolled the virtues of democracy and capitalism and tried to let the people left behind know that they were not forgotten in the West and that there were people working for their freedom.

After the Velvet Revolution, Tomas Bata, then 76, immediately began making plans to return to Czechoslovakia. When his Lear jet landed in Prague, he was given the welcome of a returning hero, part prodigal made good and part saviour bearing the gifts that would make his countrymen rich and free. But Bata's honeymoon with Czechoslovakia didn't last long. He announced that his family wanted its property returned – land, homes, factories, and so forth. It was his, he reasoned. It had been illegally seized by the communists, with no compensation. The Havel government agreed with the unfairness of what had happened to the Bata family, but could not simply return the property. Svit represented one of Czechoslovakia's largest industrial enterprises. It also had considerable potential for becoming a major exporter. Svit was important not only to the Czechoslovak economic future in general, but to Havel's government in particular. It could have been one of the plums of the privatization selloff, the profits of which would help pay the massive costs of transforming the economic system and modernizing the country. If Havel's government simply gave back property worth millions to the Bata family, other exiles with all sorts of claims, real or imagined, would come flooding back. What little flesh that was left would be stripped from the bones of the old Soviet-sphere state, and Havel's new government would be broke.

Tomas Bata flew home disappointed. But he didn't give up. He sent top Bata executives from around the world into Czechoslovakia to provide technical and managerial assistance. Bata also enrolled dozens of young Czechoslovak technicians and managers in company training courses. Slowly, gradually,

Tomas Bata, Sr. and his son and successor, Tomas Bata, Jr., neared agreement with the Havel government. Finally, after 18 months of negotiating, a compromise was worked out. A new company, Bata Czechoslovakia, was formed. Czechoslovakia's contribution was existing Svit factories, offices, and shops, along with the people who worked in them. Much of the production operation was worthless, however, and most of the administrative processing had to be scrapped. Some factories were still using the same machines Tomas Bata had left behind nearly 60 years earlier. Production forms were exactly the same as before, except that instead of one form the communists had swelled the red tape to seven pieces of paper. In return for the Svit assets, Bata brought his company's administrative structure, including computerized record-keeping, its marketing know-how, the Bata trademark, and the money – shoeboxes full of it, undoubtedly – to upgrade the technology and improve the quality of the shoes produced in Czechoslovakia so that they could be sold in the West. Will the Bata family make money in Czechoslovakia? Given the family's track record, yes. Eventually. Would Tomas Bata have worked so hard on the deal if he had been trying to take over a factory in Africa or South America or anywhere other than his native Czechoslovakia? No.

When considering a joint venture or other form of partnership or alliance in Eastern Europe, it's important to recognize what you want and what the Eastern Europeans want. The Americans are looking for local insight, the cultural bridge. We are also looking for cheaper labor and production costs; that, after all, is the main thing the East has to offer. We are also looking for profits that can be taken out and will still be respectable in terms of the dollars originally invested. The Eastern Europeans in any joint venture want access to our technology and our money to help them modernize and become competitive. They are looking for us to use our management skills to expand their export markets and bring them profits in their local currency. We can't expect them to do things they are not equipped to do, such as contribute to product development. Developing products that people want or are willing to pay for was not part of their culture for half a century, and we can't ask them to suddenly know what their citizens want or how much they can pay. The citizens themselves don't yet know what they want or what they are willing to pay. We can't expect Eastern Europeans to hand over a framework for joint distribution because they haven't had an efficient or logical distribution system of their own. Adidas is a company that could have hooked up with any number of existing wholesale-retail distribution networks in Eastern Europe – what Eastern European shoe company wouldn't have wanted to hook up with Adidas? – but chose instead to set up its own network from scratch.

Some say the best way to stick a toe into Eastern Europe is to be an advisor or consultant. Certainly U.S. law firms, with the mad dash among Eastern European governments to come up with legal systems that are comfortable to us, have been among the high-profile entrants since the democratization processes began. Some say the best way is to limit capital outlays as much as possible and take a piece of the future action. In other words, to do business *with* Eastern Europe instead of *in* Eastern Europe.

In any event, making a deal in Eastern Europe typically has several requirements regarding communications, both within and between the two companies. A respected, influential senior figure, probably the big boss, is usually needed from each side to inspire a can-do attitude that senior managers pass along to the middle managers. There has to be somebody who says, "It's going to happen, no matter what the obstacles," in order to get things moving and keep them moving. In American business, fierce competition has always put information at a premium. We have a lot of secrecy, and information is parceled out on a "need-to-know" basis, just so our competitors don't find out what we are doing and use it to their advantage. Eastern Europe is different. Much of the knowledge that a competitor might be interested in was never available, such as the profile of a typical customer. Those workups were never done because the economies were based on central commands instead of local demands. Information that was available, such as the number of units produced, was of little value because it was produced not for internal use in improving operations, but only for the external purpose of appeasing the central planners. Today, when Eastern Europeans are told by Americans that they must do things differently than in the past, they often want to know why. They have a different type of need to know. And even if something is explained to them in terms of the American business culture, they may not understand. When it comes down to whether a joint venture works or not, the communications question is perhaps even more critical than currency fluctuations, inflation, or other larger, more easily explained reasons for failure.

At this point, I've got a few comments for personal investors, people with an ethical or ethnic agenda or who want to do a little risk-taking for the possibility of high returns down the road. The Eastern European privatization programs are all supposedly aimed at anyone who wants to invest, including Americans with a few thousand dollars to put into shares of the Czechoslovak national airline or the best Polish truck manufacturer. But it's very difficult to make such investments, they're very risky, and they're very hard to manage even if completed. For several of Poland's early privatization offerings, the government announced on a Monday that bids would be accepted on the following Friday. How much information could prospective American investors gather in four days? Even with the information, who could get through on the Polish phone system? Even if they got through, would the person on the other end speak English well enough to distinguish "thousands" from "millions"?

Poles themselves have had problems acquiring shares to which they are entitled at little or no cash cost. The offerings are typically oversubscribed, and the banks are typically understaffed, to the point that only a minority of the would-be stock purchasers ever actually end up with certificates for newly privatized companies. Even in a country used to standing in line, the queues at the banks handling public offers are too long for many people. For Americans daunted by these obstacles, as most should be, an attractive alternative may be investments in American or Western European mutual funds or unit trusts specializing in Eastern Europe. Another possibility is Western companies that are already in Eastern Europe. These are the companies that are already locked into their joint ventures, building the hotels, extending the communications networks, and manufacturing the steel needed for upgrading the national infrastructures.

Some observers of Eastern Europe believe that the problems may be insurmountable. They believe that the changes will come too slowly and that the citizens of countries such as Poland, Czechoslovakia, and Hungary will become impatient with the time and energy required to achieve democracy and free markets. Indeed, many Eastern Europeans have told me that they are now working hard not to improve their own standards of living, but to give their children and grandchildren the chance to enjoy the modern Age of the Consumer. I disagree with those who say that inflation, unemployment, and other social woes will lead the countries of Eastern Europe back to the relative security of political dictatorship and state-dominated economies. But that's because I've met people such as Monika Stopczynska, the young Polish woman who has become an entrepreneur in her home town of Lodz.

I met Monika during a two-day visit to Lodz. She was my interpreter. As she translated the conversation with my host over dinner in his apartment, it became apparent that she had a lot to say for herself, too. As the evening wound down, over vodka and sweet wine, I asked her to tell me about herself. "My boyfriend and I live with our parents," she said. "We want to get married and have a house together, but the only way we can do it is by making money in the private sector." So after she graduated from Lodz University she rented a small (600 square feet) shop in a decidedly unfashionable side street near one of Lodz's many tower-block public housing estates. Like most everything else in Lodz, her shop was in the shadow of one of the big smokestack companies. Monika rented the space from a large state trading company that once had a shop there. The previous shop always had trouble selling its stock of inferior clothing made in state-run factories. Monika used her meager life savings of dollars to buy a few items of imported women's clothing and some paint to dress up the place.

She sold the clothes quickly—at a 20 percent markup, modest by Western standards—to the women who live in the tower-block apartments and immediately used the money to buy more clothes. By plowing every zloty back into the business, she gradually built up her inventory, although she often had to buy clothes from Southeast Asia or the Middle East because she couldn't find anyone importing the French, Italian, British, and American fashions she preferred. When she told me this, I would have given her the Levi's I was wearing if I'd had another pair along. "No one person in the neighborhood can buy a lot," she said, "but everyone wants one or two nice things." The shop has no name. Monika laughed when I asked what was written on the sign outside. "There is no sign," she said. "People just find the shop. You see, things are much different here. We have almost no advertising, not even signs over many shop doors. If you have something good to sell, people will find you." She wants to buy the shop outright from the state trading company that owns it, but is afraid that the company—which will eventually go out of business or be privatized under Poland's economic reforms—will sell it to someone else or that someone else with a claim from before World War II will be awarded the deed. "I'm doing absolutely everything I can to make the place my own, but we still don't have clear property rights," Monika said.

To fix up the shop, which she said was "a wreck" when she moved in, Monika persuaded a Lodz government bank to grant her a rare loan in the grand sum of $1,800. The terms were that if she paid it off in one year, the interest rate would be 32 percent; if two years, 62 percent. "Our banks are not prepared for what's happening in the country," Monika said. "It's a big problem for small businesses and for the future of the country."

She applauded the idea of Western ideas and money coming into Poland and welcomed the day when Lodz has a McDonald's and an American-style shopping mall. "But that is some years away," she said. "Because of the uncertainty over our laws, it's very difficult for Westerners to come here to do business. We need stability first." Monika's goals, and the opportunities and obstacles in her path, offer a vivid example of what is happening in Eastern Europe today. Her sincerity, her intelligence, and her idealism – tempered by the pragmatism of growing up amidst the communist bureaucracy – offer great hope for the countries of Eastern Europe, and great hope for the Americans who are willing to help people such as Monika.

CHAPTER 11

———— ♦ ♦ ♦ ————

Money Matters

After a two-week business trip through Eastern Europe, I returned home to London particularly impressed with Poland's determination to seize democracy and free enterprise. The Polish people, it seemed to me, had an especially realistic view of just what sacrifices they might have to make, and how hard they might have to work, to become a Westernized, industrialized, consumer-oriented nation. A few months later, I heard that Polish banks were offering extraordinary interest rates, partly due to high inflation and partly due to the government's policy of encouraging people to save money in their own country instead of converting it to dollars and investing outside Poland.

Polish acquaintances confirmed that, yes, Warsaw banks were paying up to 80 percent interest for one-year deposits. But there were risks. For more than a year, ever since the Solidarity government's January 1990 "shock therapy" made the Polish zloty convertible against the dollar and wiped out the currency black market, the official exchange rate had been 9,500 zlotys to the dollar. But there was always a danger of devaluation now that the government was about to embark on its massive privatization program. If I changed $100 to 950,000 zlotys and invested them at 80 percent, I'd have 1.7 million zlotys at the end of a year. But if the government in the meantime devalued the zloty – cut its value in half, say, to 20,000 zlotys to the dollar – my pile of 1.7 million zlotys would be worth only $85. Not much of a deal. If the devaluation was smaller, of course, I could still end up making money. If the exchange rate dropped to 11,000 zlotys to the dollar, for example, my $100 invested at 80 percent would be worth more than $150 at the end of a year. On the other hand, my Polish friends said interest rates seemed to be dropping rapidly; one bank had already lowered them from 80 percent to 70 percent a year.

I decided to go ahead and invest, hoping that the devaluation would be small enough and the interest rates hold high enough to make a good profit. Along the way, I told myself, I would give the Polish economic system a small injection of currency to help with the transformation toward a market economy. I ended up investing $5,000. Just before I actually converted my dollars to zlotys and made the deposit, the devaluation came, and it was 14.4 percent. This was good news. Not only was the devaluation small, the Solidarity government was saying it did not envision another devaluation for at least a year. Second, and more important for my investment, by a lucky stroke of timing my dollars were changed at the new rate, and thus fetched about 54 million zlotys. A day earlier, under the old rate, I would have gotten about 47 million zlotys. My zlotys went into the Polish equivalent of a six-month Certificate of Deposit paying an annual interest rate of 60 percent. I could have gotten a higher interest rate by putting the money into a one-year CD, but my Polish friends said the government was considering a new law that would have automatically withheld taxes from interest earnings during the second half of the year. At the end of the six months, I had about 87 million zlotys in my Polish bank account, worth $8,000 US. I took a chunk of profits out in dollars and reinvested in another zloty CD.

This is the kind of extraordinary investment – short-term, risky but rewarding, and not requiring huge capital – that Americans are likely to stumble onto as they internationalize their personal and business finances. It typifies the opportunities and dangers in making such investments in foreign countries. After all, Poland could still devalue at any time and wipe out my profits. Or somebody's tanks could roll in. That could be the end of democracy, and of my CD. Doing business in Europe opens a whole new set of possibilities and problems, both personally and professionally, that challenge the way Americans handle their money.

Most Americans know little about exchange rates until they begin traveling abroad. "How much is that in real money?" we all ask each other, as if the pounds, francs, and marks are handed out when we pass GO. One American, an executive who should have known better, landed in Europe and asked to change his American dollars into Eurodollars. In fact, "Eurodollar" is simply the term for U.S. dollars deposited in any bank anywhere outside the U.S. Even if they know about exchange rates, Americans can be confused by the different currencies floating around in other countries. Different regions and even different banks sometimes issue their own notes within one country. They may be worth the same, but they look different. A Merrill Lynch executive from New York visited Scotland and then went into the London office with a pocketful of Scottish notes. Not realizing the Scottish pounds were worth exactly the same as the English pounds, he asked his colleagues in the London office if they would change them for him. Someone gladly made the swap for the equivalent of about 50 cents on the dollar, and the visiting New Yorker was the butt of office jokes – "Oh, yeah, that shrewd American currency trader . . ." – for years to come.

The dollar's worth in the rest of the world depends on a number of factors, but is supposed to represent the health of the U.S. economy. When the economy is good, foreign money comes into America. Foreigners change their money for dollars in order to invest in America, and the demand drives up the value of the dollar on the foreign exchanges. When the dollar is strong, Americans pay less for European money and the European things they buy. A strong dollar means that Europeans, in turn, must pay more of their own money to buy dollars or American products. A strong dollar provides higher profit margins for American exports, but it also discourages foreigners from buying those exports. So American exporters sometimes cut their prices in Europe when the dollar is strong; they maintain their profits while not pricing themselves out of the export market. When the dollar is weak, everything is reversed. Americans must pay more dollars for European products, which discourages imports to the United States. Europeans pay less of their currency for American products, which encourages U.S. exports.

Since more than half of the U.S. investment into Europe in recent years has been into Britain (in some years more than 60 percent), this discussion of exchange rates will be restricted to dollars and pounds. But the principles of exchange-rate movements are the same for the dollar against all European currencies. Let's look at the past decade or so. In the early 1980s the dollar was worth up to $2.40 against the pound. But then Reaganomics set in. The Reagan administration financed its tax cuts in large part through deficit spending and raised money by increasing the interest rates on Treasury bonds, Treasury bills, and other U.S. government securities. Foreign money poured in. With the high interest rates, the stability of the U.S. economic and political system made the dollar the safest and smartest investment in the currency world. The more demand for the dollar, the stronger the dollar got on the foreign exchanges. The stronger the dollar, the more expensive U.S. exports were for the rest of the world. Hence we got a trade deficit alongside our budget deficit.

When I moved to London from New York in late 1984, the

dollar was very strong, bubbling along in the $1.25 range. Some luxury items were selling in London for half or a third of what they cost in Manhattan. In the next few months, the dollar continued to strengthen, perhaps as an aftershock of the administration's efforts to further expand and stimulate the U.S. economy in the weeks before the November 1984 election. Reagan, you'll recall, was reelected in a landslide by asking Americans, "Are you better off today than you were four years ago?" Thanks to the budget and tax cuts financed by deficit spending and foreign investments, most Americans were indeed better off at that moment. By March 1985 the dollar had dipped to $1.04 against sterling, and Americans were flying across the Atlantic, some on one-day shopping sprees, to gobble up bargains on crystal, china, works of art, Savile Row clothing, jewelry, and other luxury items. One group of young professionals from Washington, D.C., flew over to buy an English country estate in the same way – and for about the same amount of money – they might have gone in together on a country house in Virginia or a beach cottage in Maryland. Some Americans bragged that they saved enough on the purchases to pay for their flights, even on the Concorde.

Gradually, the Reagan economic miracle lost its sheen, however, and the return of the dollar to more normal levels (back in the $1.50 range by 1986) was accelerated by the world stock market crash of 1987. The dollar dropped to nearly $1.90 within a year, by late 1988, before recovering to close to $1.50 in mid-1989. By late 1990 it was back down below $1.90. By mid-1991, however, it was back to just over $1.60. These are tremendous swings, with a huge scope for making and losing money for those who changed money.

Overall, a weaker dollar is good for United States exporters. In 1990, the U.S. registered its first trade surplus in eight years, and the share of American manufacturing exports increased above 20 percent for the first time. After years of record sales in America in the mid-1980s, the early 1990s brought big U.S.

sales dips for European companies such as the carmakers Jaguar, Rolls-Royce, Volvo, and Saab; the luxury products group Louis Vuitton-Moet-Hennessy; and the crystal-and-glass manufacturers Waterford Wedgwood. Other European companies such as Bayer, the German chemicals conglomerate, had record U.S. sales but saw their profits decline because of the exchange rates. This shift, along with publicity about the European single market and the maturing of their own domestic sales bases, led small and medium-sized American companies to begin thinking of exports as never before. But many of those American companies tempted to take the European plunge were put off by the wide and sometimes wild exchange-rate swings of the past few years. Brian Dwyer of Venus Wafers (Chapter 4) was daunted at first, but tried to coordinate his plunge into Europe with a time when the dollar was relatively strong. That way, the lump of upfront costs – travel, initial shipments, packaging, advertising, and other promotions – could be paid out more cheaply than when the dollar was weak and bought less in Europe. Ideally, an American spends money in Europe when the dollar is strong and brings the profits home when the dollar is weak.

For there to be profits, people must pay. Americans who are selling their products in Europe typically want to be paid in advance. Europeans naturally want to pay as late as possible. When payment is for products that may take weeks to be shipped across the Atlantic, the two are often weeks apart on when they think payment should be made. Even cash on delivery terms can be treacherous. A New England seafood supplier recently agreed to ship some lobsters to France. The French importer said he would pay COD, but added that he would refuse to pay for any dead-on-arrival lobsters. The New England company agreed and suggested a small trial shipment. As soon as it arrived, the French importer paid in full and asked for another, larger order in time for Christmas, when lobster is a traditional holiday treat. The New England company sent off $100,000 worth of lobsters and waited for payment. And

waited. When the American company called France, the importer said sorry, all the lobsters arrived dead and had to be thrown
away. With no way to verify what happened, the New England
company had to swallow the losses—whether or not someone
actually swallowed the lobsters.

Regarding the manner of payment, increasing sophistication
in European banking circles has led to more payments by wire,
when funds are electronically transferred from the importer's
European account to the exporter's American account. In some
northern European countries, particularly Germany and Scandinavia, checks are sacred, and it is extremely rare for a company to try to bounce one. Many northern European importers
like to pay with corporate checks drawn on U.S. banks or
cashier's checks, both of which are more than welcomed by
most American exporters. In other countries, particularly in
southern Europe, American exporters are more likely to demand letters of credit before they put their products on a boat.
Letters of credit are expensive, time-consuming, and often confusing, but they are one of the safest ways to ensure payment,
and many Americans insist upon them whenever dealing with a
new European partner.

Many American exporters require their European purchasers to make all payments in dollars. That relieves the Americans of much of the administrative hassle of dealing with
foreign currency, but it rarely allows an exporter to escape the
many ramifications of money movements. The Brooklyn Brewery is again a good case study. When Steve Hindy, the brewery
president, negotiated with Lynne Zilkha, head of the British
distributor BB Supply, the dollar was at $1.96 against the
pound, its lowest level in years. Hindy wanted $11 a case for his
beer, and Zilkha agreed. For her first 600-case container, she
changed pounds at $1.96 and paid £3,367 for the container.
Three weeks later, when it became obvious that the beer was
going to sell well in Britain, she ordered another 600-case con-

tainer. But by then the dollar had strengthened to $1.88, and Zilkha's cost rose to £3,510.

Sales continued to take off and so did the dollar. By the time Zilkha placed her seventh and eighth orders, the exchange rate was approaching $1.60 and she was paying more than £4,000 for 600 cases, an increase in cost – and a loss in gross profits – of £700, or more than 20 percent from her original purchase. "I was naive," Zilkha said. "Within Europe, we're not used to big swings like that. I thought the dollar might go up to $1.85 eventually, but I never expected it to change so much so fast. We're losing all our profits. We can't absorb this. I'm going to have to go back and ask Steve to do something about cutting the price. I can't tell my Brooklyn buyers in Britain that they have to wait until the dollar weakens to get more beer in. I should have made a hedging arrangement with my bank, or changed a lot of money when the dollar was so weak, but I didn't. I made a mistake." Unfortunately, her mistake means trouble for Steve Hindy, too. His choice, in the face of her dilemma, is to either cut his $11 price or risk losing her business.

Once in Europe, some American companies and individuals simply ignore exchange rates. They change dollars to European currency when they need to spend money in Europe, and they change their profits in European currency back into dollars whenever they are available. Over the long run, that's entirely reasonable; things in general even out over the years. But for companies or individuals making relatively big investments, it makes sense to hedge. In managing money, whether personal or company funds, you're automatically taking a position if you don't hedge. You're saying that the currency you're putting your money into, or taking your profits in, is going to strengthen.

Historically, importers and exporters, even relatively small operators, hedge against unfortunate currency movements through the financial process known as *forward cover*. They go to their banker and agree to a forward exchange rate. This forward rate locks in the exchange price on a certain date. Suppose an American agrees on March 1 to buy £200,000 worth of smoked salmon from Scotland on June 1. On March 1, when the deal is signed, the dollar is trading at $1.70 against the pound. Suppose the American has already made a deal to sell the salmon in the States for what would be a 25 percent profit if the exchange rate stays at $1.70. To lock in the profit, the American makes a contract with his or her bank to buy £200,000 on June 1 at a rate as close as possible to $1.70. Even if the dollar weakens by June 1, which could mean less profit, or if it strengthens, which would mean more profit, the dealer is unaffected because the $1.70 exchange rate and 25 percent profit is assured. When large sums are involved, it makes sense to arrange forward cover for even a few days in advance.

Obviously, arranging forward cover through your local bank is a lot less intimidating than trying to plot out a commodities contract on the financial futures exchanges. As a result, more and more internationalized Americans are using this quick and easy form of hedging in their personal finance. An American in London, an art dealer, was recently given six months' notice by her gallery that she was needed back in New York for a bigger and better job. She immediately put her London flat, purchased several years earlier, on the market. At the time, the dollar was around $1.90, one of its weakest levels in years. The art dealer knew that the sale of her flat would give her at least £80,000 to take back to the States, but what would it be worth in dollars? If the exchange rate held at $1.90/£1, she would be taking home $154,000. If it returned to a more normal $1.60 level in the four to six months it would take to sell the flat, however, her £80,000 would fetch only $128,000.

The art dealer, on the advice of a friend who happened to be a financial futures trader, went to her local bank branch manager and said she wanted to arrange a forward foreign exchange transaction. The bank said it could offer her an exchange rate of $1.89 on £80,000 on a specific date in six months. The bank's fee would be one-half of one percent. In fact, the exchange rate did drop to $1.60 by the time the art dealer sold her flat. But her forward contract allowed her to take home just over $150,000 from her £80,000, compared with the $128,000 she would have taken home if she hadn't locked in the higher exchange rate.

An indirect way of hedging, both for companies and individuals, is to make capital investments in, say, real estate in the European countries where they are living and doing business. By investing in capital improvements, a company not only lays the groundwork for expansion but also takes advantage of improving local economic conditions. This will be an increasingly popular strategy in Europe as the national economies grow with the single market, and especially in Eastern Europe where the scope for rapid growth is even greater. By investing profits earned in Czechoslovakia back into Czechoslovakia, for instance, the payoffs—increased business activity, increased property values—may be greater in the long run than in taking the profits out of the country in dollars.

The same principle applies to individuals. An American lawyer, paid in dollars, rented a flat for the first couple of years he was in London. Two things happened, however. He and his wife had a baby. And the dollar, which had been lingering around $1.40 against the pound, began to weaken slowly but steadily. So he bought a house, bringing dollars from the States and converting them at $1.55 against the pound. Over the next few years, he changed money whenever the exchange rate got near or below $1.55. Each time, he converted enough to retire a good slice of the mortgage and leave a cushion so that he wouldn't be forced to change money at $1.80 or $1.90. Even if the exchange rates went way up or way down and stayed there for years, the lawyer reasoned that home ownership was a built-in hedge in anticipation of his eventual return to the States. If the dollar was strong, his salary bought more in Britain. He would have to use fewer dollars to pay off his mortgage, but he would get less money back in dollars if and when he sold the house and converted the weak pounds back into dollars. If the dollar was weak, his salary would buy less in Britain. He would have to pay more dollars for his house, but the pounds received for the eventual sale of the house would bring more dollars back in the States.

Housing purchases can't be guaranteed to work out well, of course. In 1987, an American architect in London decided to buy a flat after renting for a year. The dollar was at about $1.50 and getting stronger, and the market for upscale flats in London's prime residential neighborhoods had been increasing dramatically. Most buyers were seeing their homes increase in value by 20 percent or more a year. So the architect, who reckoned that the rising dollar would make his payments cheaper as the property gained in value, bought a flat for £100,000 ($150,000). A few days later, the stock markets crashed. Over the ensuing months the bottom fell out of the upscale housing market, in part because American financial institutions began cutting costs by laying off people at home and scaling down their operations abroad. As more American expatriates were called home and fewer were sent abroad, the pool of potential buyers for expensive flats became smaller. Then the architect took another job back in the States. His flat stood idle for several months as he continued to pay the mortgage. Meanwhile, the dollar declined past $1.70 at times, and his mortgage was costing more and more for an apartment he wasn't using. Finally, he found a buyer for £80,000. He absorbed a loss of more than $30,000.

"Trading foreign currency is like sex," someone once said. "You do not fully appreciate the pleasures and the frustrations unless you've done it." That's not meant as a comment on those who buy and sell currency for a living, but nobody who does business in Europe remains a foreign-exchange virgin for very long. Look at what it costs just to move around Europe. Let's say someone started with $100 in Madrid and went on a 12-nation tour of the European Community, changing the money into local currency at each stop. Upon arriving back in Madrid, our traveler would have only $28 left. The rest would have gone to commissions and the rates "spread" under which currency exchanges buy the dollar lower than the official exchange rate and sell it higher. In my local bank in London, if the official exchange rate is $1.70 to the pound sterling, I'm likely to be offered a rate of $1.75 if I'm buying pounds and a rate of $1.65 if I'm buying dollars—plus a 3 percent commission for each exchange, of course. So if I bring $100 in and change it to pounds and then hand the sterling back for dollars, I'll end up with about $88. Many travelers try to avoid changing money in airports, but they are often cheaper than banks. Sometimes there are bargains, as when big banks sell their travelers' checks fairly close to the official exchange rate and for little or no commission. The banks that cash such checks may tack on an additional charge, but there still may be a substantial savings.

One of the best ways to save money is to change the right amount of money from the start, so it's not necessary to pay additional commissions when returning for more currency or changing "left over" foreign currency back into dollars. Rather than changing all foreign currencies back into pounds or dollars when I return home to London after a trip on the Continent, I keep small amounts of "left over" francs, marks, crowns, and so on to use on the next trip. If you have to go in a hurry, it's always handy to have enough money to at least pay for a cab from the airport to the hotel. Some people try to avoid using their U.S. credit cards in Europe, but in many cases the card companies offer comparable and sometimes even cheaper exchange rates than banks or *bureaux de change*. I've found American Express to be especially fair. Credit cards are also fast; there's no standing in queues to change money. Remember, though, the applicable exchange rate is the one on the day that the transaction is posted or reaches the credit card account, not the day the purchase is made.

Some companies, and many individuals, try to balance out

the currency swings and keep down the nagging erosion of exchange commissions by keeping bank accounts in different currencies. This flexibility allows bills in dollars to be paid in dollars, bills in francs to be paid in francs, and so forth. Similarly, payments received can be accumulated in those accounts and then moved in strategic lumps when and where necessary. I have dollar accounts on both sides of the Atlantic and keep a variety of sterling accounts in Britain for receiving and paying out bills in sterling. My bank charges essentially the same handling fee, no matter how large the transaction, for electronically moving dollars from New York to become pounds in London. When getting established with a European bank, it's worth it to make whatever arrangements in advance for such electronic transfers. The arrangements – often no more than a letter of authorization that is in your file or that you can present to the bank each time – can take several days, but once in place, such electronic transfers can save days of waiting for money from the States to clear and be converted into pounds through the traditional method of putting a check in the mail.

One American businessman who has been in London for years moves money whenever he sees a favorable trend. "The trend is your friend," he maintains. Since he is paid in pounds but has occasional dollar expenses, he waits for trends in which the dollar looks like it is gaining strength. At one point, when the dollar was at $1.95 against the pound, he and his wife planned an extended vacation in the States, with some investment possibilities while he was there. Since the trip was several months away, there was no need for him to change money immediately. So he waited to see if the dollar would weaken further, but it didn't. Instead, it started gaining strength: $1.92, $1.90, $1.85. At that point he swapped several thousand pounds for dollars. So he got $185 for every £100, compared with $195 if he had made the change when first considering it. He made a mistake, some might say. But the $1.85 swap looked pretty good compared with the $1.62 exchange rate when the businessman and his wife eventually took their trip. By paying attention and relying on the trend as his friend, he got $23 more per £100 than if he'd waited until he needed the money to make the change.

When moving around different European countries, it's wise to remember that some do not accept credit cards as readily as America or Britain. In Germany, for instance, most restaurants and even many hotels do not accept credit cards of any kind. In contrast, many places that do not accept credit cards will happily take a personal check in payment. For people traveling around Europe, it's often advantageous to have a Eurocheque account. Issued by most major European banks, this account allows you to use one checkbook to write checks in the different European currencies. The fees are modest, a few dollars a year plus a commission of around 2 percent per check, and the accounts typically include a Eurobank card that allows automatic cash withdrawals in local currency from tens of thousands of bank machines.

Clerical quirks and mistakes can cause huge banking and accounting snafus. In some countries, people writing the number 1 often use a symbol that looks to us more like a 7. Their 7 also looks like a 7 except that it has a small horizontal bar across the belly. So don't forget to dot your *i* and cross your 7. The other quirk is that in some countries, a period is used instead of a comma in big numbers. Consequently, there is occasional confusion over whether 1.000 means one or one thousand. One big New York law firm's London office had a costly embarrassment when representing a European client in one of the biggest proposed corporate takeovers in history. In transcribing complicated financial documents, a clerk typed in a dollar sign instead of the pound sterling sign, so that £30 million became $30 million – a $20 million discrepancy at the time, since £30 million was then worth about $50 million. The mistake could actually have caused the law firm's client to lose $20 million, but the other lawyers involved – acknowledging that it could happen to them some day, too—allowed a correction without penalty.

If there are two rules to follow in handling money across borders, they are these: be consistent and be cautious. Don't try to pick the high and the low. Lock in sure profits or interest rates when and where possible. Be consistent, and don't change your currency-exchange philosophy or strategy just because rates seem particularly high or low at the moment. Of course, much of the fretting about currency fluctuations within Europe could disappear within a few years if the EC carries out its plans for a single European currency. Many of the movers and shakers in Europe believe that a single currency is the most important foundation for a true single market. After centuries of the Germans using marks, the Dutch guilders, the Italians lire, and so on, all the individual countries would scrap their historic currencies. They would simply cease to exist. Instead, all 12 EC member nations, and any other nations that join, would all use a common currency. Maybe it would be called the Eurodollar (except that term already means something else in financial circles), the Euronote, or the Ecu, for the European Currency Unit already in use. My own personal nominee is the florin, a gold coin that originated in Florence in the 13th century and became popular across Europe.

Whatever it is called, the single currency, issued by a central European bank that would set monetary policy for the EC much like the Federal Reserve does for the United States, would reduce the costs of doing business across the EC. Its main advantage is that it would eliminate exchange-rate variables and transaction costs. Those transaction costs in recent years have skimmed off between 0.5 and 1.5 percent—the figures vary in different studies—from each EC country's gross national product. By eliminating those commissions and fees for changing money passed between EC member states, the 12 countries would give themselves an immediate and significant jump in economic performance. Moreover, a single currency would wipe out the last little bit of uncertainty over exchange-rate variables in trade among the EC countries.

The European Monetary System (EMS), through its Exchange Rate Mechanism (ERM), has for years regulated most of the EC currencies to the point that they do not swing by more than 2.25 percent against each other. Despite this degree of stability, some European companies have been reluctant to do cross-border business for the same reasons that some American companies are reluctant to venture abroad — because they are afraid of losing money on currency fluctuations. An International Monetary Fund study showed that before World War I, when the industrialized world followed the Gold Standard and was therefore operating on what was in effect a single currency base, more than 3 percent of the world's wealth was invested across borders. Since World War II, with world currencies floating against each other, only 1 percent of the world's wealth has been invested cross-border. With a single currency, there will be no fluctuations at all within the EC. Prices will stabilize, and all aspects of production and distribution will be forced to become more efficient in order to compete.

Here's an example. French people have always bought lots of French-made Renault cars, in part because they were better value for money than cars made outside France. Some of that value for money undoubtedly came from the fact that Renault did not have the foreign-exchange costs that Fiat, for example, had in exporting from Italy to France. In addition to whatever commissions and fees Fiat had to pay to sell its cars in France and change the profits back from francs to lire, there were the administrative costs of having people and computers oversee the money changing. With a single currency, those additional costs would disappear. Fiat would be able to sell its cars more cheaply in France. All products in the EC would rise and fall more on their merits — because they offered value for money — than because of built-in domestic pricing advantages due to the costs of foreign exchange. A single currency would be a cornerstone of a truly single EC market and would bring down one of the last major barriers among the countries.

The EC created the precursor to a single currency in 1979 in the form of the Ecu, or European Currency Unit. The Ecu is a common currency, as opposed to a single currency. Instead of replacing the other 11 currencies (Belgium and Luxembourg share their franc), it operates in parallel as a 12th currency. The Ecu, its value based on the relative values of a "basket" of currencies from the EC countries, is typically worth somewhere around a dollar, although fluctuations in the 20 percent range are not unusual. The value of the national currencies making up the Ecu can change against the Ecu—though not much—depending on each nation's respective economic health. The Ecu is used primarily by countries and large companies within Europe to settle their debts with each other, although studies show that fewer than 3 percent of the commercial transactions within the EC are conducted in Ecus. The Ecu is also in wide use as an investment currency in the form of Ecu bonds and short-term securities. Most big European banks will offer accounts in Ecus to their corporate customers, and even some retail firms, notably Club Med, have said they are considering allowing customers to be billed in Ecus. But so far the companies that want to do business in Ecus have encountered considerable reluctance among their corporate customers, and there has been no public clamor among European consumers to use the Ecu, or any other new pan-European currency, for everyday money.

A British journalist recently set off in London trying to spend travelers' checks denominated in Ecus. It wasn't an easy assignment. Few retailers knew what the Ecu is, and even fewer were willing to accept the reporter's Ecu checks. "You must be joking, love. This isn't Europe, remember. This is England," a London taxi driver told her. Another newspaper, not above borrowing a good idea, sent out reporters in Brussels, the home of the Eurocracy, with the first and to this point only Ecu currency, a 50-Ecu coin minted in Gibraltar. One reporter at least got a sales clerk at the bookshop in the basement of the EC headquarters to consider taking the coin, but the manager said no.

Some of the EC countries, led by Britain, have expressed misgivings about a single currency. When Margaret Thatcher was prime minister, she wrapped herself in the Union Jack and declared that replacing the pound sterling with a single currency would be a threat to British sovereignty. Of course it would be. Virtually every significant move toward a single market and European economic and political union represents a loss of a bit more self-rule for EC countries. Watching the EC move step by step toward integration and cooperation is fascinating for an American. The process is not unlike what the United States' founding fathers must have gone through when debating federalism versus states' rights in drafting our Constitution. Federalism won then, and there is no doubt it is winning in Europe, too, even if there is occasional squawking about the dreaded "F-word" and the dangers of a so-called United States of Europe.

Thatcher's main objection to a single European currency was that Britain would no longer be able to decide its own economic policy through control of its domestic money supply and interest rates. Instead of the Bank of England making those decisions, they would be imposed by the central European bank issuing the single currency. Thatcher's argument, part of the anti-European stand that caused her own party to dump her in the autumn of 1990, carried little weight because Britain had already joined the Exchange Rate Mechanism. The ERM, remember, was designed to limit swings among the major EC currencies. Because Germany is the economic powerhouse of the EC, the deutschmark dominates the ERM to the point that if German interest rates rise, other countries have to raise their rates, too, to keep their currencies within the allowed 2.25 percent range (6 percent for poorer countries or those that are new to the ERM and going through an adjustment period). In effect, the ERM forces the pound, and all other participating currencies, to "track" or "shadow" the deutschmark.

Despite Britain's occasional kicking and screaming, there is little doubt that a single currency is coming to the EC, probably by the year 2000 and perhaps as early as 1997. It makes too much sense not to happen. In one survey of several hundred European companies, nine of ten executives said a single currency would help their business. The EC's tentative timetable calls for a process of "hardening" the Ecu, making it more available and easier to use, in the mid-1990s, probably beginning in 1994. The next step will be the formation of a central European bank, which would then begin issuing the single currency (florins, I think; you heard it here first . . .) as the individual countries begin phasing out their respective marks, guilders, pesetas, lire, francs, and yes, even pounds. The strength of the single-currency movement is seen in the fact that even non-EC nations such as Sweden and Finland are tying their currencies to the Ecu, too. This is partly to pave the way for their eventual EC membership and partly because Europe's future is with the single currency, inside or outside the EC.

In general, the single currency would be good for Americans doing business in Europe. At worst, for people doing business in just one European country, it would make no difference, although the elimination of intra-Europe currency swings could mean that the EC florin (or whatever) would be more stable against the dollar than the previous national currencies were. At best, for Americans doing business in more than one European country, the advantages will be the same as for Europeans doing business in more than one neighboring country. Instead of paying fees, commissions, and administrative costs for changing dollars back and forth in 11 currencies, the process would be streamlined to one currency. Some American companies are already doing this by conducting all their intra-European business in Ecus.

"Suppose you are a U.S. multinational firm and you have operations in most of the EC member countries," one American financial advisor in Europe explained. "Those subsidiaries are continually invoicing each other and making payments. One of the ways to reduce costs is to net out in one currency. An increasing number of U.S. companies are setting up centers in Belgium for this." Even with a single European currency, Americans will still be playing the foreign-exchange game as long as they want to bring their profits home in dollars. For monitoring purposes, it's often wise for American businesses to keep accounts on how the European operation is performing in local currency as well as on the dollar bottom line. If money is being made in Europe but being lost on the currency play, then perhaps some banking and accounting strategy such as hedging should be used to protect the European profits.

Another aspect of the single market that should help Americans doing business in Europe is the move toward a more unified, standardized banking system. New technology and regulations should help speed up the most notorious bank delays. Much of European banking is still paper-based rather than electronic. As recently as 1991, one study showed that 99 percent of all banking transactions in Italy involved paper records at some point. The single market should mean not only that more banks are computerized, but that their electronic systems are matched up and can communicate with each other for moving money more quickly than the five to ten days that have been the standard. Another key proposal in the banking package would speed up company-to-company payments. This is particularly important because many European public agencies and big companies apparently follow deliberate policies of making late payments. This is done in the States, too, but seems to be even more prevalent in Europe. There are plenty of small companies eager to do business with such big customers, and the big customers take advantage of it by withholding their payments until they absolutely have to fork over. This puts particular stress on small companies that cannot afford the high cost of short-term loans that are often needed to compensate for cash-flow problems when the big bills are late coming in. Under the EC proposal, companies that pay late would be assessed additional charges.

Despite the general agreement that a single currency and a more unified banking system are coming, there are other money matters on which the EC has been in no apparent hurry to unite. Taxes represent a key area. There is no standard EC corporate tax rate, for example. The range of taxes on business profits is from about 10 percent in Ireland to about 50 percent in Germany. But a myriad of allowances and exemptions from country to country, such as the way depreciation is written off, keep European accountants fully employed. In Belgium, which has a nominal standard business tax of 41 percent, the average firm in one recent year paid only 16 percent. An EC study said that the different tax systems can mean as much as a 3 percent difference on after-tax return on investment. But many experts say it's easy to get around the EC tax structures. If you want to put a factory in Germany but are afraid of the high taxes, go ahead and build in Germany but put the sales and administrative headquarters across the border in Italy, where the taxes are lower.

The EC's lack of single-mindedness on single-market taxes extends to the consumer arena, too. Britain imposes roughly a $9 tax on a bottle of whiskey, while southern European countries such as Italy and Spain tack on only about $4. So when the Eurocrats in Brussels were debating minimum taxes for spirits, Britain argued that the lower rates should be raised – and then abruptly reversed itself when distillers from Scotland complained about how much they would lose in export sales if the taxes went up in Italy and Spain. So Britain ended up arguing that it should be allowed to keep its own high liquor taxes while other countries should not be allowed to raise theirs. Britain also objected to setting standard EC-wide VAT (valued-added tax) rates, in effect sales taxes. After months of haggling, the EC agreed that the minimum VAT rates should be 15 percent, which forced several countries to raise their sales taxes but allowed Britain, with a 17.5 percent VAT, to keep its zero-tax exemptions for certain items such as food, books, and children's clothing.

Americans working in Europe face unique tax problems because the United States remains virtually alone among major Western nations in double-taxing its citizens. In most countries, money earned by expatriates working abroad is not taxed by the home country. You have to pay income taxes in the host country where you are living and working, but not to your native country. The United States, however, requires Americans living and working abroad to pay not only the taxes in their host country, but also to pay income taxes to the Internal Revenue Service on earnings above a certain level. The IRS does provide some relief for taxes paid abroad, but the salary levels of most American managers and professionals working abroad nonetheless means they are often taxed twice on the same earnings. Consequently, a good personal accountant is a must.

Upon arriving in London, I turned my taxes over to Touche Ross, thinking that a big international firm would be best equipped to handle the complications that come from earning money from several countries in several currencies. But I was too small for them. I didn't get much individual attention, and I was paying quite high fees for nicely printed and bound versions of the same scribbled accounts that I sent in. On the advice of a friend who worked for Price Waterhouse, I asked around and found a small British accounting firm that specialized in handling American entrepreneurs and branch representatives of American companies. My accounting and tax preparation fees dropped by two-thirds, and I developed a casual telephone dialogue with an accountant who handled both my U.S. and British returns. After a couple of years, he passed my British accounts over to a junior colleague because it would save me even more money. We discuss everything from how much of my children's babysitting fees I might write off in Britain to whether I should "go off shore" and incorporate in Gibraltar or the Channel Islands. So far that hasn't been right for me, but many other American entrepreneurs, trading companies, and consultancies do go off shore. One attractive option is to incorporate in Ireland, which costs about $300 and provides many of the advantages of an off-shore tax haven while at the same time providing a toehold in the EC. Dual citizenship and becoming a "perpetual traveler" are other tax-dodging structures that accountants are only to happy to erect, but they're not generally worth the trouble unless there is a lot of tax to dodge.

Most Americans approaching Europe are shocked at how much it costs to live and do business on the other side of the Atlantic. A ten-minute phone call between Paris and Phoenix can cost up to twice as much if it's dialed in France rather than in Arizona. Business hotels under $150 a night are rare, and restaurants in many European cities are so expensive that only travelers on expense accounts can afford them. Locals simply don't go out to eat unless they're entertaining visitors on company business. Generally, the farther north in Europe, the more expensive. A beer in Sweden may be $10 even at a neighborhood bar, and people trying to scrimp might find themselves paying $7 for a Big Mac. Many Americans operating on their own or setting up an exploratory operation in Europe find it economical to rent shared offices on a temporary basis. Initially, this can be a good way to get a respectable address, someone to answer the phone, and some clerical support when necessary, without the considerable expense of looking for locations, negotiating a lease that is inevitably too long, interviewing and hiring staff, buying furniture, and so on.

Depending on your perspective, the employee perks in Europe can be good or bad. American companies sending people to Europe or hiring Europeans do not want to appear to have two pay scales, one domestic and one foreign. Yet they also have to provide compensation for the Americans who are uprooted, usually temporarily, and they must match the standard packages that are offered by European companies. As a result, American expatriates typically get additional benefits such as housing allowances, cost of living payments for the most expensive cities, free vacation flights home every year or two, school fees for their children, and help on both taxes and tax preparation. A company car is standard in many European countries. (In Britain one of six new cars is purchased as a company car.)

Time off is often an issue. Europeans are used to six weeks of vacation a year, plus a dozen or more days off for national holidays. In some offices employing both American expatriates and European locals, resentments arise over disparities in pay, benefits, and time off. Some companies allow only American or European holidays, and a few allow employees to take both. Whatever the arrangements, most American companies reckon that sending an employee to Europe will cost two to three times the employee's salary in the States. American expatriates are paid in a variety of ways: sometimes in dollars, sometimes in the local currency based on its exchange value against the dollar, and sometimes in a combination of the two. Whenever the employee's salary fluctuates according to the dollar's strength or weakness, the employee should not hesitate to ask the company to make revisions when there's been a significant strengthening. Otherwise, the employee is losing salary and buying power in Europe.

Living or working abroad often presents investment possibilities that Americans back home never see. Besides my Polish CD, I've made a number of other more conventional, less risky European investments that I probably never would have thought about from the States. British banks and building societies (roughly the equivalent of U.S. savings and loan associations) typically pay higher interest rates than U.S. banks, as much as four to five points more. And there are many ironclad opportunities for savings in British government certificates, the equivalent of U.S. savings bonds. On behalf of my kids, I bought one version in 1987 that had a floating interest rate, but has never paid less than 11 percent a year. During the same period, I never got more than 6.5 percent from any American savings account. The following year I bought an index-linked certificate that guaranteed interest at the official inflation rate, with 4.5 percent a year on top if held for five years. The year after that I bought another five-year bond with a guaranteed 12 percent annual interest rate. In contrast, the best I could do on a CD issued in the States was about 8 percent. In each case, I tried to invest pounds that had been converted from dollars when the dollar was strong. Ideally, I'll be able to wait until the dollar is weak to cash in and convert back to dollars. There are various types of British bonds and savings accounts in which interest is not automatically withheld. These are particularly attractive investments on behalf of children and other nontaxpayers, and can make a nice base for a long-range college savings plan that has the flexibility to wait for a weak dollar and bring the money back to the States at any time over a period of several years.

Convertible bonds also remain appealing in any currency. Elizabeth Anderson, a New York-based investment banker, told me how she happened across–and promptly purchased–a $10,000 bond issued by a big British company. The bond carried an annual interest rate of 9.75 percent, with an option to be converted to pound-denominated from dollar-denominated at any time before maturity. The base was an exchange rate of $1.57 to the pound. As long as the dollar remained stronger than $1.57, Anderson was happy to keep it in dollars. But when the dollar began to weaken, she began to think about converting. Just before the bond matured, the dollar dropped to $1.73, a weakening of about 10 percent. Anderson converted the bond to sterling before cashing it in, and thus got $11,000 when she changed the pounds back into dollars. Plus, of course, she had been pocketing the 9.75 percent annual interest all along. This sort of investment offers two ways to win, along with a built-in hedge. Even if the exchange rate went against her, Anderson was still getting her interest. The only lose-lose scenario would be if the exchange rate went against her and world interest rates rose to the point that she would have been getting more than 9.75 percent by putting her money somewhere else.

The same principles apply in off-shore currency funds. In managed funds, the managers choose how to invest your money in various funds in different currencies. In single-currency funds, you choose which currency you want to be in, and the managers choose the investment vehicle or vehicles for you. Profits can be accumulated or distributed. In either case, there are two ways to win: on the profits paid by the funds and on the currency exchanges. Again, the safest rule is to give yourself enough flexibility that you can go into such funds when the dollar is strong and then wait to bring the money out when the dollar is weaker. Here's a currency investment tip: When the EC begins to harden the Ecu and move toward introduction of a new single currency, there are bound to be some over-the-going-rate investment products – bonds, funds, and the like – to encourage people to convert other currencies into the new money. When it happens, consider jumping on them, especially if the dollar is strong.

Many Americans who play the stock market never look at foreign shares. That is, they ignore two-thirds of the world's equity pool in what is becoming an increasingly global market. Most brokers now recommend that the typical portfolio include anywhere from 10 to 40 percent foreign holdings. When abroad, there are opportunities to become familiar with European companies that are considering expansion into America. If they are good companies with good products that will sell in America, that's the time to get in. A good example is the Body Shop, the British cosmetics-with-conscience chain that entered the U.S. market in the late 1980s and expects to have more than 300 American shops by 1996. Since the Body Shop announced those expansion plans, a number of canny Americans have done very well with its shares on London's International Stock Exchange.

Most Americans, however, don't buy directly on foreign exchanges. Instead they make their foreign equities purchases in American Depositary Receipts (ADRs) issued through banks in the States and quoted on the U.S. exchanges just like the shares of American companies. Many brokers and investors prefer ADRs because they remove the foreign currency play. You buy ADRs in dollars, and when you sell them you get dollars back, no matter what has happened to the company's native currency. Even the ever-growing number of brokers who do invest directly on the London, Milan, Frankfurt, or other European stock exchanges downplay the currency aspects. Like all brokers, they emphasize long-range investing and say the key is to find good companies in countries with expanding economies. They say don't worry about the foreign exchange movements because they will even out over the long run. One of the keys to good investing, naturally, is to find a good broker. After working with a range of brokers in the States and in Europe over the years, I've settled on an American broker who has several years' experience in Europe and is now in charge of a small office on the Continent for a big Wall Street firm. This combination provides what is for me a comfortable range of American and European expertise and good blend of big-firm resources with small-firm attention.

Working in Europe also affords the chance to find and get good prices on quality products. A BMW is cheaper, for instance, if you pick it up at the factory in Germany, drive it to avoid the new-car import duties, and then, when the time comes, ship it back to the States yourself. A friend recently priced Volvos and told me the $23,000 model he was looking at in the States could be picked up in Europe, driven around on vacation, and then shipped home for $19,000 – a savings that would more than make up for his family's air fare. French crystal, Irish linens, Italian shoes, and many other such products are cheaper at the source. There are also some interesting collectibles more widely available in Europe. One acquaintance has been buying up the works of promising young Eastern European artists whose prices are sure to inflate if and when they are discovered. My own collecting in Eastern Europe has been limited to a few chips of the Berlin Wall and a Russian soldier's watch with a Gorbachev face. Instead, I've concentrated on antique maps, which are more widely available in Europe, and particularly in London, than in the States.

A few American niceties and necessities are still harder to find or more expensive in Europe. Betty Crocker cake mixes are either impossible to find or cost several dollars a box, and forget about tortillas and other packaged Mexican-food fixings. Computers and compact disks are much more expensive, but floppy disks are a lot cheaper in Europe. Finally, for some reason, tennis balls are two to three times as expensive in Europe as in the States. I routinely ask visiting relatives to fill up any extra room in their suitcases with good tennis balls. British friends who have country houses with tennis courts are always eager to invite a weekend guest who is sure to contribute a few cans of new balls. It's a no-lose foreign exchange for all parties.

CHAPTER 12

————————————— ♦ ♦ ♦ —————————————

Social Sensibilities

Walter Marlowe, a native New Yorker, is an investment banker who has spent most of his professional career based in Europe for various U.S. and European financial institutions. When he joined a leading Finnish bank's London operation, he began working on a big deal that involved both Scandinavian and Arab interests. At one point, an Arab millionaire considering a major investment announced that he was going to Helsinki and wanted to be briefed. Ordinarily, Marlowe meets clients in Helsinki, shows them around town, has dinner with them, briefs them on the project, and generally acts as the bank's gracious host. Unfortunately, Marlowe had another meeting scheduled in London. So he asked one of the bank's managers in Helsinki to line up a substitute. Unfortunately, the two or three obvious choices – senior, internationally experienced investment bankers who were up to speed on the project – were busy, too.

"Don't worry, we'll get one of the regular Finnish guys from the office to do it," the manager suggested.

Marlowe immediately canceled the London meeting and said he would be able to make the trip to Helsinki after all. "One of the regular Finnish guys would probably want to entertain the Arab the way Finns entertain each other, sauna and all," Marlowe said. "He'd meet the Arab at the airport, start telling him dirty jokes and say, 'Hey, let's get naked and drink 200 beers.' That doesn't go down too well with conservative Arab businessmen, especially if they're devout Muslims. And I found out in Helsinki that this particular Arab was in fact very religious. No dirty jokes, no getting naked, no drinking. It could have been a disaster."

Americans doing business in Europe cannot avoid or ignore the social aspects of everyday life, the confounding and confusing cultural quirks from country to country. Europeans are proud of their respective cultures. And while they are often likely to make concessions to the manners of visiting Americans, they appreciate it when a visitor has taken the trouble to learn some of their ways. In this final chapter, I'll examine some of the cultural peculiarities most common to Europe in general and certain European countries in particular.

When making appointments, it's best to try to arrange things well in advance. In a few countries, notably Britain and the Netherlands, top executives' schedules are often arranged by their secretaries or assistants. It's seen as a matter of efficiency. In other business cultures, particularly southern countries such as Spain and Italy, most top people handle their own diaries, and their assistants may not even know where they are, what they are doing, or when they might be available. It's usually best to make appointments for mornings; in some countries, particularly among bureaucrats and civil servants, afternoons are reserved for lunch, siesta, and recovering from lunch and siesta.

When meeting people, in both social and business settings, Europeans shake hands more than Americans do—even if the person they encounter is someone they saw the night before. In a meeting in Germany and Holland, for example, it's typical to shake hands with everyone in the room, both upon entering and leaving. The Dutch and Germans also like to give and get little nods when meeting someone. In some offices, everyone shakes hands with everyone else first thing in the morning and last thing in the afternoon. Despite all that flesh pressing, Europeans generally take longer to become friendly or familiar. Business is more formal, more reserved. Except in Britain and Ireland, where first names are used almost as quickly as in the States, it's always safest to address someone by his or her last name, with the title Mister, Doctor, or Frau, as appropriate. But even that formal style of address has pitfalls in some countries. In Belgium, for instance, a Flemish northerner will want to be addressed as "Mister," while a southern French Walloon may be offended if not called "Monsieur." Europeans are often more comfortable being introduced by someone else than introducing themselves. On a number of occasions at parties or conferences, I've approached someone, introduced myself, and talked for several minutes before getting the other person's name, usually only after pointedly asking for it.

Northern Europeans are more like Americans in that they look each other straight in the eye when talking. Many southern Europeans, however, are uncomfortable with a direct gaze, and in some countries a man will assume that a woman's unwavering stare at his face is a sign of sexual interest. Similarly, conversation is often more indirect, oblique, or subtle. Except in Scandinavian countries where there is little tradition of small talk, coming to the point too quickly is seen as a typically blunt and distasteful American trait. At the same time, direct confrontation can be extremely useful when trying to embarrass someone into providing assistance. "Look, I need some help, and I'm hoping you'll provide it," is one approach that's often effective, although on several occasions I've pulled out the big guns with, "I'm sorry if I don't know how things are done in your country, and if I've done something to offend you I apologize. I just don't understand why you're being so rude to me." An American, following the "Never apologize, never explain" dictum, might get angry at this sort of comment. But no European wants to be accused of being rude to a foreigner, even a demanding American.

While Americans like to indulge in a minimum of small talk and get right down to the brass tacks of business, initial meetings in countries such as Italy or Spain may be mostly casual, getting-acquainted conversation with little direct mention of the deal. The best advice is to follow the lead of the Europeans. If they bring up business first, go for it. If they don't, an American should probably go no farther than the leading remark – "Yes, this country's climate (history, people, or whatever) is one of the reasons I'm eager to do business with you . . ." – that opens the door, if the Europeans are ready for it to be opened. Typical casual conversation centers on your trip, your initial impressions of the city and the country, other places you have visited or will be visiting, and what sorts of nonbusiness things you would like to see or do during your visit, including restaurants, museums, parks, sports, galleries, shops, and theater. Most Europeans love to talk about their local attractions and are eager to make recommendations, although some may feel pressured if they perceive that an American is putting them on the spot to make guarantees.

In a few countries, such as Italy, small talk quickly gets down to families. Americans who have children may score points by producing cute photos. In most European countries, however, family chatter is considered too personal. In France, it's considered bad form to ask if someone has brothers and sisters, or even what a new acquaintance does for a living. In Britain, asking where a business executive went to school may be perceived as snooping so that you can gauge the person's social class. Also, some Europeans are mildly offended by Americans' casual terms for foods associated with their countries. For example, in Scotland they don't call it "scotch," they call it "whiskey." In London, no one knows what an "English muffin" is. To the British, it's just a muffin. It is the same with

French toast and French fries in France. In a Danish bakery, don't ask for a "cheese Danish" unless you want to be told that this is an American bastardization and that the Danes themselves *never* use cheese in pastry.

Avoid discussions about politics, when possible. Americans pay more attention to European history than Europeans do to ours, but they also pay more attention to U.S. current events than we do to theirs. Americans often find Europeans surprisingly sophisticated about American government and politics, and they are frequently more willing to venture a controversial opinion than an American would be. It's best to remain noncommital where possible, although some Europeans have developed finely honed conversational rapiers that pierce our own national pride and prompt even the most cynical American to a patriotic defense. Remember, much of Europe does not, and never has, shared America's sense of virtue. In terms of morality, many Europeans never viewed the United States as holding higher ground than the Soviet Union during the Cold War. Similarly, many Europeans do not feel that they share in capitalism's victory over communism or that the Gulf War was a particularly glorious triumph from either a military or a moral standpoint. Americans often see Europeans as being jealous of American wealth, influence, and power in the world, and they often are. But we have to be careful not to act as if we know that they are envious or that we think they should be. One of the most fundamental differences between Americans and Europeans is this: Europeans are more likely to accept things as they are, with a resigned shrug; Americans are more likely to insist on change and work to make things better.

Be aware of regional political differences and don't routinely lump all the citizens of a country together as one nationality. Most European countries are actually made up of competing national and ethnic identities, and their bitter rivalries get U.S. attention only when they erupt in bloodshed, as seen in the civil strife in Yugoslavia and elsewhere. There are many similar nationalist identities across Europe, where people may not take to the barricades but do fight to preserve their own language and culture; Galacians, Bretons, Welsh, Basques, Catalans, Frisians, and Flemish are examples. It's instructive to remember that Spanish is actually the second language for one-quarter of the people of Spain. And while Scots are generally among the most friendly and welcoming Europeans to visiting Americans, a sure way to trigger a Scottish temper is to refer to all of Britain as "England."

In any conversation with a political background, Americans should remember that most European countries have an entirely different approach and attitude toward government. Many Europeans, particularly in the Scandinavian countries, see government as their friend or partner. All across Europe, many more industries and companies are owned and operated by the government, and the public sector accounts for far more of the gross national product than it does in the States. Socialism, and communism for that matter, are not regarded as the threats that they were in the States. Many political parties across Europe, including perennial ruling parties, still call themselves socialist.

In some countries, labor unions retain more influence than they ever had in most U.S. states, and now the European labor movement is using the single market to try to build even more power. One of the instruments for this is the EC's controversial Social Charter, a sweeping set of proposals that promise to set EC-wide standards for health and safety and guarantee equal opportunity for workers. Under the Social Charter proposals, workers will be guaranteed 4 weeks annual vacation, 14 weeks of maternity leave at full pay, and more say in management decisions, including layoffs, plant closings, introduction of new technology, and any other changes in working conditions. Larger companies may be required to have workers' representatives on their boards. Americans also often find that Europeans have more liberal or activist attitudes and policies on issues such as women's rights and environmental protection. The EC is moving toward a system of "eco-taxes" on fertilizers, pesticides, lubricant oils, and batteries, along with heavy fines for polluting companies and tough standards for "eco-labels" that would require products to carry what amounts to environmental impact statements on their packaging.

While some Europeans consider questions about their families intrusive, in many countries—with the notable exception of Britain and Ireland—sex and sexual issues may be discussed openly and freely, including in front of children. To much of Europe, the United States is quaintly puritanical, and Europeans are blasé about nudity on their beaches, TV programs, billboards, and print advertising. Many Americans have difficulty getting used to the idea that men and women sometimes share public restrooms in Europe and that there may be a female attendant in men's public toilets. In some countries, particularly in Germany and Scandinavia, it is considered bad form for a man to compliment a woman on what she is wearing or the way she looks, or for a woman to make similar comments to a man. Such compliments are more acceptable in southern countries, although they can be misinterpreted. In the southern countries, foreign women still sometimes draw the leers, whistles, and comments of men on the street. Ignore it if at all possible, and avoid making eye contact. Whatever happens, women should not do what one American woman did in Paris a few years ago. Trying to discourage a whistler by saying *"Cochon! Cochon!"* which is the term for "Filthy swine," she mispronounced it and said *"Couchons! Couchons!"* which means "Let's go to bed."

In some countries, such as the Netherlands, taking off your jacket in the office means you are about to throw yourself into your work. In others, such as neighboring Germany, it means you are going to coast for a while. Body language is also important. Europeans, despite all the hand-pumping and the penchant among young men to walk arm in arm or holding hands, often don't like being touched by relative strangers even in a friendly manner, such as a good old-fashioned American back-slap. In Greece, it's rude to throw back your head, as Americans sometimes do when laughing or showing surprise. The American thumb-and-finger sign for "OK" is obscene in some countries, particularly Spain, and in Britain the equivalent of the American middle finger is two fingers, the index and middle, raised with the back of the hand facing out. So if you go into a British restaurant and gesture "two" to the maitre 'd, make sure you do it like Churchill did, with the palm facing out. When standing or walking while talking to someone, it's considered rude to keep your hands in your pockets in many European countries.

But most casual conversation takes place sitting down, usually over food or drink. For many European executives, lunch and dinner with business associates are an integral part of the working day, even if business is not discussed directly. The table is the arena for practicing the art of conversation—talk purely for the sake of talk—and for getting to know a potential business partner. Too many Americans make the mistake of begging out of evening dinners. It must be said, however, that eating with Europeans can be a trying experience, particularly if they have a big lunch as early as 11 A.M., as the Finns sometimes do, or supper as late as 11 P.M., as Spaniards often do.

Table etiquette is often different, too. When drinks or glasses of wine are poured, always wait until the host or hostess makes a toast, says "Skol" or "Cheers," and takes the first drink. And while northern Europeans, particularly the British and Scandinavians, are known to occasionally get drunk in public, anything more than a little merry tipsiness is frowned upon in the southern wine-drinking countries such as France and Italy. Across Europe, the knife is usually wielded in the right hand and the fork in the left, and that's where they stay. Almost no one does the familiar American transfer—cut with knife in the right hand, put the knife down, shift the fork to the right hand and then take it to the mouth. Unlike the States, where any idle hand is to be parked in the lap, the style in Europe is to keep both hands in sight, wrists resting lightly on the edge of the table. In private homes, small portions are always a good idea, partly because you're expected to take seconds, after politely declining until offered again, and partly because it's considered rude to leave food on a plate. If invited to someone's home for a meal, flowers are generally appreciated, except in Spain where flowers are given only on the most special occasions. In other countries, don't bring red roses because they are associated with romance, or chrysanthemums or white asters because they are usually seen only at funerals.

Business gifts are not as common in Europe as in Asia, but are sometimes appreciated, particularly when a friendly relationship has been established in which discussion of family and children has been a refrain (almost always in southern Europe, particularly Italy). American T-shirts, sports gear, or company pens that can ostensibly be presented for the children often go down well. T-shirts can backfire, however. One U.S. software company that took over a French firm sent a group of American executives over to reassure the French managers about post-merger cooperation. Various company-logo items were on the French managers' beds when they checked into the hotel where the meetings were scheduled, including T-shirts that were supposed to be worn to a get-acquainted cocktail party. All the Americans showed up wearing their company T-shirts. All the French left theirs in their rooms.

Here, in wholly subjective form, are my own sociocultural impressions of some of the European countries where Americans are most likely to do business. France first. One of the most important things for the American business visitor to realize about France is that lunch, three courses plus wine, is almost sacred. Americans often think that all of France is one huge Jerry Lewis cult. Yes, Jerry Lewis has received some awards in France, he sometimes appears on French TV for weighty discussions of the "meaning" of his humor, and there are occasional Jerry Lewis film festivals. But France actually has a relatively small Jerry Lewis cult, which is not particularly evident among business people, and many of them are offended by Americans poking fun at this supposed national fixation. In fact, most French humor is heavy irony that Americans often don't find funny at all. To me, the classic example of French humor is the magazine cartoon printed during a school strike. Two *gendarmes* are looking at an illegally parked bicycle, and one of them says, "It must belong to a teacher." The joke, as it was explained to me, was that teachers cannot afford cars. Right.

The French are renowned for their immovable civil service and government bureaucracy—centralized, legalistic, and generally not helpful if there is any rule, either real or made up on the spot, that can get into the way. Besides the usual Saturday afternoon and all-day Sunday closings common throughout much of Europe, some French shops are closed all day on Monday, too. The French do not put as much weight on materialist accumulation as Americans; they don't care as much about living in a bigger, better place, having a nicer car, or moving up to a better sound system. They do care much more about personal style, particularly in their appearance (which is one reason the French managers taken over by a U.S. company refused to put on the American corporate T-shirts).

To many French, it is more important to perform with flair as an individual than to be a good team player. French managers working with Americans are known for being creative, but not especially cooperative. The French are said to be good at the stuff of dreams—Arianespace, Concorde, the TGV bullet train, the Channel Tunnel—but bored by the trivia of everyday chores. French workers want answers from the boss. Unions are strong. Finally, the French can indeed be rude, imperious, and unhelpful. But most are not that way. Most French people are just like people everywhere else—welcoming and accommodating, particularly for foreign visitors—especially in central Paris.

In many ways, much of Germany looks like any prosperous section of Middle America, with offices, highways, malls, and sleek suburbs. People even dress like well-off Midwesterners, inoffensively and for comfort, but always clean and tidy. Germany is sharply split between north and south, however, and people from Hamburg think those from Munich are stuck up, and vice versa. Weekends and working hours are inviolable, and many Americans are puzzled as to how Germany managed to become an industrial powerhouse when every office is deserted by 5 P.M. Shopping hours are among the most restrictive in the world, with many stores closing by 6:30 P.M., all day Sundays and most Saturday afternoons. How legalistic is Germany? Put it this way: More than 2 million cars, many of them perfectly serviceable BMWs, Mercedes, and Volkswagens, are junked in Germany each year because of a law that says the seller of a used car is liable for the new owner's repair bills for a certain amount of time after the sale. As a result, people junk their used cars rather than selling them to someone who might come back months later with a repair bill.

German banks dominate business, and German businesses are most likely to go to their banks for straight loans when they need money rather than looking for some more creative, and less expensive, means of corporate finance. Germans like rules and don't like uncertainty. Underlings are less likely than in other countries, such as France, to expect two-way communication with the boss. Meetings are formal and are less often for discussion and decision-making than for handing down decisions that have already been made. Germans are punctual and don't like to take work home. The trappings of wealth are important. Possessions, including the type of car one drives, are seen as symbols of success. Within companies, status is often measured in part not by the fact that a worker drives a Mercedes, but what kind of Mercedes and how expensive it is.

Office doors in Germany are often kept closed, and no one should enter without knocking. Sometimes an appointment should be made, even with a colleague down the hall. Co-workers and business associates are usually known as *Herr* Such-and-such or *Frau* So-and-so. It takes a long time to get friendly enough with someone to use first names or the familiar *Du* as opposed to the formal *Sie* form of address, and no American should try this until the German suggests it, which may occur over a ritual drink. I know one American who, whenever he is frustrated by German arrogance or rigidity over some small matter, hangs an arm around the German's shoulder and says, "Listen, Fritz. . . ." The German is horrified at this familiarity and will usually do anything to get away from the American and out of such an uncomfortable predicament. Women, except those under age 20 or so, are generally called *Frau* rather than *Fraulein,* even if they are not married. The *autobahn* is every bit as terrifying as it sounds, and only good, confident American drivers, people who are not afraid of driving 90 mph in the slow lane, should attempt it. In Munich, people really do wear *lederhosen* on the street. The beer halls and sausages are every bit as good as they're cracked up to be, and Oktoberfest, which is really in September, draws huge crowds to the beer gardens to eat, drink, and sing.

Italy is a wonderful country. All Italians seem to have figured out how to live, even if some of them haven't figured out how to work. In business, their habits and attitudes are sometimes maddening to foreign visitors. One common joke is that the Italians, unlike some other European Commission members, are in favor of giving more authority to the EC because they have never been able to govern themselves and want someone else to do it for them. We in the States have the idea that Italy is unstable because governments seem to fall every few months or so. In truth, the same conservative-leaning political grouping has run Italy pretty much since World War II. Though prime ministers come and go, Italy has remained one of the most stable democracies in the world over the past half-century.

In dealing with Italians, it's important to remember that trust, loyalty, and personal relations are important, and they won't be rushed into anything without satisfying themselves as to the quality of the people they are dealing with. Also, while career achievement is probably the driving force in countries such as the United States, and to a similar extent in Britain, nothing is more important in Italy than family. Larry Sullivan, a British-based American who has been dealing with major Italian companies for years, spent a lot of time building up a business friendship with one young Italian executive who was obviously on the fast track. On one trip, the young Italian told Sullivan they wouldn't be working together anymore. He was giving up his job and abandoning his promising career to return with his wife and their small children to the tiny village where she was raised. The man explained that his wife missed her family, and they both agreed that it would be better for their children to grow up in a village environment. The increase in long hours and business trips as he moved up the ladder were interfering with enjoyment of his family, so he removed the obstacle. In America, we work hard and devote ourselves to our careers in order to be better providers for our families. In Italy, people are more likely to work less hard in order to devote themselves to their families. Yet, I doubt any Italian on his death bed ever said, "Gee, I wish I'd devoted more time to my career and less to my family."

Italians are proud, particularly of their heritage. Tuscans are more reserved than southern Italians, and Florentines in particular have a near-arrogance about their city's contributions to world culture since it was the cradle of the Renaissance. Florentines will be quick to tell you that their city originated everything from eyeglasses and paved sidewalks to capitalism and architecture. But Florence is not immune from classic Italian bureaucratic dithering; it took over ten years for the city council to decide whether and how to replace some paving stones in the main city square. Italian bureaucrats, civil servants, and many office workers typically come home for two to three hours in the afternoon for noisy pasta feasts with their families. Many are not available to visitors in the afternoons when they return to their offices to concentrate on "paperwork."

There are no easy Italian translations for "understatement" or "privacy." Italians are capable of transforming the most minor problem into high drama. As someone once said, a red light in Italy is a matter of opinion. But even more than waving arms and arguing, perhaps the Italians' greatest delight is in subverting the rigid authority that confronts them at nearly every turn. A good example was reported recently from Rome. It seems that a group of early-evening passengers on a city bus came to realize that their driver was a rookie who was not sure of the route. The passengers quickly entered an impromptu, unspoken conspiracy to send the befuddled driver on a roundabout tour of the town. They were delighted at the chance to create a little ripple of anarchism in the system, even if they were late getting home for *antipasto*. One man, with tears of laughter rolling down his cheeks, directed the driver down a series of side streets and almost got dropped off at his front door.

Italians are creative and like new ideas and new ways of doing things. They dress stylishly, though often more formally than the French, and never drink without eating, too. They may want to have dinner with business associates, but don't necessarily want to talk business. Many people, especially those who are middle-aged and older, like to be addressed formally as *signore* or *signora* or, if they have a college degree, *dottore* or *dottoressa.* An American man meeting an Italian woman, either socially or professionally, may be called upon to do some quick and shrewd interpreting of her body language. When she offers her hand, she may merely want to shake. Or she may expect the back of her hand to be kissed. Or she may be about to pull the man in for a kiss, or possibly two, on the cheek. It may seem daunting, and it's rare that any foreigner can get it right – hand kiss? the cheek? the other cheek, too? – but it doesn't matter. Little social fumblings typically make the Italians laugh and serve to break down social barriers rather than offend anyone.

My admiration for the Netherlands is summed up by the fact that almost every Dutch woman seems to know how to roll a cigarette, even if she herself doesn't smoke. More than perhaps any other nationality, the Dutch are practical-minded people who have liberated themselves from many of the rest of the world's conventional attitudes. Living in the most crowded European country, they prize their privacy, yet keep their window shades open – part of a historical concern that neighbors will think some misbehavior is going on, wryly adapted by the prostitutes sitting behind lacy curtains under red lights. The Dutch are extraordinarily tolerant, open-minded, and willing to undertake social experiments large and small. While they have been hard-headed traders for centuries, they also have gone farther than any other country in allowing use of marijuana and registering legal heroin addicts, permitting doctors to help the aged and infirm commit painless suicide, providing health and welfare for the poor and disabled, and setting up strict anti-pollution programs.

Of course, sometimes these well-intentioned programs backfire. My favorite was Amsterdam's "white bike" program in the 1970s. The city bought dozens of white bicycles and scattered them about downtown. The idea was that anyone could take a white bike and ride it anywhere in the central city and just leave it. Then someone else would come along and ride it to another downtown destination. Unfortunately, it took about two days for junkies to repaint all the white bikes and sell them to buy dope. Minor failures such as this do not discourage the Dutch, however; they merely go on to the next social experiment. The Dutch are frugal and have little verbal humor; they rarely tell jokes. Most babies are born at home, with midwives handling the deliveries. Early the next morning, and every morning for the next few days, a young woman shows up at the home. Sent by the government, she spends all day cleaning house, shopping, greeting visitors, making meals, and generally looking after the household so the mother can concentrate on the baby. Extremely civilized.

The Dutch pride themselves on being rational and logical, and most offices operate informally. A team approach is common. The Dutch like meetings, but they are often run like discussion groups where an issue is chewed over a few times before a consensus is reached. The Dutch are outspoken, opinionated, and difficult to embarrass. They scorn anyone who appears to be pretentious, ostentatious, or in any way full of himself or herself. Someone who is very late for a meeting or postpones at the last minute may not get another chance; to the Dutch, that's a sign of being unreliable. The Dutch don't ordinarily like to do business over a meal, but do like to talk seriously over drinks, either after office hours or late in the evening, after dinner. The little "brown cafes" of Amsterdam, dating back to the 17th century, are a favorite watering spot. Finally, a 1991 survey indicated that the Dutch are more knowledgeable about sex than the people of any other European country, and that Americans are less knowledgeable than any of the Europeans. But the kicker was this: Among Europeans, most respondents to the survey said they would be much more interested in having sex with an American than with a Dutch person.

In Spain, men who do business together often kiss each other in greeting. But American men needn't worry; Spaniards don't ordinarily try to kiss foreigners and would probably be quite taken aback if an American visitor walked into the office and started planting sloppy ones. Most modern Spaniards, many of them educated in American universities and having served apprenticeships in American business and industry before coming home, stridently object to the *mañana* stereotype of laziness and inefficiency. One young banker told me vehemently how this had all changed, and that Madrid and Barcelona had effectively adopted New York-style working hours. I happened to spend most of the day in an adjacent office. This fellow came in at about 9:30 A.M., read the papers, and looked at his mail until taking a half-hour break for coffee at 11:00. Lunch in a nice restaurant took almost three hours, and then he repaired to the local *tapas* bar with some friends shortly after 6 P.M. When I pointed out that this was a relatively leisurely schedule by many Americans' standards, he pointed out that it was positively grueling by Spanish standards and said that many workers still go home for lunch and a *siesta* in front of the TV. At least his long lunch had been for business, he argued. And the reason he comes in so late in the morning is that he often has business dinners. Most good Madrid restaurants do not even open until 9 or 9:30 P.M., he said, and it may be 11 P.M. before the food arrives.

Spaniards often interrupt each other in conversation, which is seen as a sign of interest rather than rudeness. To them, it is rude for an American to keep bringing a discussion back to business before they're ready. They remain reserved in many ways, with an air of cosmopolitan sophistication that sometimes borders on conceit. Bankers are the business elite, and the country is just emerging from years of a stodgy, old financial aristocracy. Accounting, records, and statistics are often woefully inadequate by American standards, but the Spanish know that they have one of Europe's "go-go" industrial and agricultural economies to complement a tourism boom fueled by cheap labor and the best climate this side of Hawaii. Meetings are less for discussions than for managers to issue instructions. But Americans who have done business in Spain sometimes complain about the lack of urgency in many offices, and how even apparently strong managers have difficulty making decisions and then getting underlings to implement them. There is little formal forecasting or planning, but a great deal of pride in somehow making things come out right in the end after all. "Spaniards have a habit of waiting until the last minute and then coming through. Improvisation is a Spanish virtue," one American said.

Praise and criticism are rare because they make Spaniards feel patronized. It's more important to be a good person, honest, honorable, and generally nice, than to be known for being intelligent, shrewd, or a professional success. But these old attitudes, including the *mañana* inefficiency, are changing rapidly because of the many Spanish young people who are determined to be, for the lack of a better term, raging yuppies. Going to bullfights and *flamenco* nightclubs, driving BMWs with mobile phones, taking vacations in London and New York, they seem determined to make up for the fun their parents and grandparents missed during the long reign of Generalissimo Francisco Franco. All in all, Spain has made remarkable progress, and shows remarkable promise, in the less than two decades since it was transformed from fascist dictatorship to free-market democracy.

Americans know a lot—or rather, think they know a lot—about Britain and Ireland. But that doesn't keep dozens of American business visitors and tourists from being hurt every year by stepping off the curb in London, Glasgow, or Dublin into the path of vehicles driving on the left-hand side of the road. Since Sweden switched to right-hand driving in 1967, Britain and Ireland are the only two countries left in Europe that use the "wrong" side of the road. Given its history—dating back to the Age of Chivalry when passing knights steered their horses to the left so their sword arms would be in position to draw and strike if necessary—it's unlikely that either Britain or Ireland will change to the "right" side of the road in the near future.

It's important to remember that England, Scotland, and Wales are all individual countries that make up Great Britain. The United Kingdom includes the province of Northern Ireland, which should not be discussed casually unless you are willing to get into an argument that you cannot finish—or that anyone has been able to finish for the past 300 or 400 years. Britain still has vestiges of its class system, particularly in the financial services industry where people are classified as "gentlemen" or "players." Perhaps more significant these days is the north-south divide: London and the southeast are wealthy, but northern England and Scotland are wracked by poverty and unemployment that have spawned an economic underclass.

The British conduct virtually every aspect of business in much the same way as Americans, except that their loathing of confrontation and conflict often leads to awkward but expedient solutions to problems. "Illogical compromise tends to be a British socioeconomic cultural characteristic. . . ," one commentator noted recently. Britons—most don't particularly like being called Brits, but few will make a point of objecting—are skeptical, pragmatic, and cynical, and their verbal humor, full of clever plays on language, is a delight to Americans. The tough unions lost much of their power during the Thatcher years, but the decline in many public services also made Britain a less kind and gentle place for its working classes. Like New York, London is becoming a city with sharper and sharper divisions between rich and poor.

Unlike the States, accountants are usually more important to a company or to a deal in Britain than lawyers are. Accounting is critical to budgeting and dominates overall planning. When dealing with the British, remember that what seems like a polite request or a mild suggestion may really be a demand or a set of instructions. Someone who says "Sorry!" may actually be apologizing or expressing anger or indignation. And the British laugh at the American search for perfection and "having it all." While Americans snatch up books on how to be better parents and raise smarter children, two British best-sellers are *How Not to Be a Perfect Mother* and *How Not to Raise a Perfect Child.* The author said she couldn't find an American publisher who would put the titles out in the States. Although their television and advertising is more risqué than ours, British attitudes toward sex are much closer to conservative American than libertine continental European. The Irish are among the most devout Roman Catholics and most sexually conservative people in Europe; contraceptives were illegal until 1985, and divorce remains unconstitutional. And whatever you do, never suggest to an Irish person that you "get a ride" with them. It's a vulgarity.

Many American businesses have discovered Ireland in recent years. One high-tech company built a plant there because of the availability of so many educated, able 18-year-olds. And an American insurance company has moved its entire claims division to Ireland; Americans telephoning a nationwide toll-free number from their homes in Dubuque or Paducah are connected with the lilting voice of an Irish clerk who takes the information to process the claim. Even Northern Ireland, with its reputation for sectarian violence, is undergoing an economic resurgence, much of it funded by U.S. companies taking advantage of British government assurances that all losses from terrorism will be compensated in full. Ireland boasts the highest literacy rate in the world, and perhaps the highest verbal rate, too. It is all but impossible to meet any Irish person without getting into a good "crack" or talk. In County Cork, I once got a salmon off a fishing boat and made my way to the home of a local woman who reputedly would smoke it. She agreed to do the fish, but not before having me and my family in, showing us around her house, fixing tea, introducing us to her shed full of rabbits and hamsters, and then taking the better part of an hour to demonstrate her smoking operation. We finally tore ourselves away, and an hour later looked out the window of our rented seaside cottage to see her leaning on the stone fence, waiting for us to come out and chat some more. So we did.

All in all, the personal aspects of doing business in Europe can be very appealing, especially for Americans who live in Europe, too. Tom Callahan, the accountant based in Frankfurt for TRW (Chapter 10), often shows up at work in a golf shirt and sweater, unless he's got a big meeting. He's married, with two young kids, and saw no reason not to seize the opportunity to further his career and broaden his personal horizons by taking the three-year overseas posting. "My wife and I always liked to travel," the Chicago native said. "We thought it would be interesting to live in another culture, and I thought it might help my career. Certainly this job offers more responsibility than I'd have back in the States. There's a longer leash."

He was surprised that the transition to living in Germany was not more difficult. For instance, not speaking German has been only a small obstacle. Callahan bought a book on German at the airport on his way to Frankfurt, but has rarely looked at it since. "And it only took a month or two to get used to things like smaller refrigerators, different shopping hours, and different choices available in the stores. It's really helped that there are so many other expatriates around, especially the Americans. You automatically have something in common with them. We all have similar backgrounds. But we have friends from other countries, too—English, Pakistani, Japanese people. They're all in business here in Germany, and they all speak English. For us, the toughest adjustment was leaving our families back in the States. Also, the dark, short days in winter, when it's so rainy and cloudy, are kind of a drag." Callahan and his wife took it upon themselves to meet their new German neighbors. "We went knocking on doors. Some of them didn't speak English, so we had pretty short conversations. But they all love babies.

Now we give our neighbors apples from the trees in our back yard, and some of them brought candy and stuffed toys over for the kids at Easter. Overall, it's been a great experience. After Germany, we've decided we'd like to live somewhere else in Europe for another two or three years before going home."

Few Americans who live and work in Europe regret it. Most say it is one of the most rewarding experiences of their lives. But it is never a decision to be taken lightly. Certainly going abroad is a risk, in that it usually means more responsibility and more chances for a high-profile failure. But a European posting also typically offers more rewards, and many companies now put a premium on international experience.

People with families have special problems. What if the family doesn't want to go? What if one or more family members are miserable in the new country? How much long-term resentment will come from spouses or children who are forced to give up their own work or school, even temporarily? Anyone considering a job in Europe should anticipate and discuss the possibility of such problems, not only with the family but also with the employers or partners who are supporting the move. Before moving, both sides – the executive going to Europe and the U.S. managers sending him or her – should know what is expected in terms of the length of the posting. Furthermore, there should be an understanding that the family can come home earlier if things go sour for any reason or no reason at all. For parents, schools are a major concern, but most European capitals have good international or American schools. One Indiana professor who has spent two sabbaticals in Europe said his children moved back and forth smoothly. "The last time, we left the States on a Friday and my son started the new school on Monday. He found that most of his classes were studying the exact same things. They were even using some of the same books." The big advantage of the American schools in Europe, the professor said, is the mix of students: "My son's classroom discussions of the problems in the Middle East included the comments from kids from Israel, Iran, Iraq, Kuwait, and Saudi Arabia. Their debates really brought it to life for him."

Not everything about living in Europe is positive, of course. Shops are often closed when you need them. Locals ask you to repeat everything, no matter what language you're speaking, even in England, because all they hear the first time is your American accent. People who would never want to explain or apologize for their own countries automatically want you to do both for the United States. Pizza isn't usually as good, and it's harder to find familiar consumer items such as chocolate chips, maple syrup, and cake mixes. Paying taxes and voting can be complicated, and there's always the big decision about whether to renew your U.S. driver's license and hope you don't get stopped, or go to the considerable time, trouble, and expense required to pass a European driving test.

But there are many compensations, professionally and otherwise. Weekends in Paris. Christmas in London. Sailing antique schooners on the Wadenzee, soaking up the sun on the Mediterranean, or island-hopping in the Aegean. Skiing on the same Alpine slopes used for past and future Olympics. Train rides through the highlands of Scotland or the lush fields of Poland. The restaurants in Budapest, the medieval-costumed *palio* horse races around the square in Siena, the country churchyards and castles in almost every country. Even more rewarding than the places of Europe, however, are the people. The more time Americans spend in Europe, whether working, living, or both, the more they find their American edges rubbed off—the more international or global they become. The more they understand other people and cultures, the more they understand America and Americans.

Like Tom Callahan, many Americans living and working abroad almost inevitably find themselves socializing with other expatriate Americans, but most also try to cultivate other friends as well, particularly natives of the country where they are living. I've found that the most common denominator

260

among my foreign friends is that they, too, have traveled, lived, and worked abroad. A few expat Americans, the ones who are constantly complaining about the inadequacies of their host country or comparing it unfavorably with "back home," should be avoided because they are boring. And if there is one thing that doing business in Europe is not, it's boring.

——————————— ♦ ♦ ♦ ———————————

Appendix

American Chambers of Commerce in Europe

European Council of American Chambers of Commerce
21 Avenue George V
75008 Paris
France
Telephone 33-1-47-23-70-28
Fax 33-1-47-20-18-62

American Chamber of Commerce in Austria
Porzellangasse 35
A - 1090 Vienna
Austria
Telephone 43-222-31-57-51
Fax 43-222-315-151

American Chamber of Commerce in Belgium
Avenue des Arts 50, Bte. 5
B - 1040 Brussels
Belgium
Telephone 32-2-513-79-28
Fax 32-2-513-79-28

American Chamber of Commerce in France
21 Avenue George V
F - 75008 Paris
France
Telephone 33-1-47-23-70-28
Fax 33-1-47-20-18-62

The American Chamber of Commerce in Germany
Rossmarkt 2
D - 6000 Frankfurt/M.1
Germany
Telephone 49-69-28-34-01
Fax 49-69-28-56-32

The American-Hellenic Chamber of Commerce
16, Kanari Street, 3rd Floor
GR - 106 74 Athens
Greece
Telephone 30-1-36-36-407
Fax 30-1-36-10-170

The U.S. Chamber of Commerce in Ireland
20, College Green
EI - Dublin 2
Ireland
Telephone 353-1-679-37-33
Fax 353-1-67-93-402

Israel-American Chamber of Commerce
35, Shaul Hamelech Boulevard
Tel Aviv 64927
Israel
Telephone 972-3-25-23-41
Fax 972-3-25-12-72

American Chamber of Commerce in Italy
1, Via Cantu
I - 20123 Milan
Italy

Telephone 39–2–86–90–661
Fax 39–2–80–57–737

American Chamber of Commerce in the Netherlands
Carnegieplein 5
NL – 2517 KJ The Hague
The Netherlands
Telephone 31–70–365–98–08
Fax 31–70–364–69–92

American Chamber of Commerce in Portugal
Rua D. Estefania 155, 5 ESQ
P – 1000 Lisbon
Portugal
Telephone 351–1–57–25–61

American Chamber of Commerce in Spain
Avenida Diagonal 477
E – 08036 Barcelona
Spain
Telephone 34–3–321–81–95
Fax 34–3–321–81–97

Swiss-American Chamber of Commerce
Talacker 41
CH – 8001 Zurich
Switzerland
Telephone 41–1–211–24–54
Fax 41–1–211–95–72

Turkish-American Businessmen's Association
Rumeli Cad. No. 63/7
Rumeli Palas
T – 80200 Sisli
Istanbul
Turkey
Telephone 90–1–130–30–81
Fax 90–1–130–47–34

American Chamber of Commerce (UK)
75 Brook Street

London W1Y 2EB
England
Telephone 44-71-493-03-81
Fax 44-71-493-23-94

Associations for Americans Abroad

The Association of Americans Resident Overseas
49 Rue Pierre Charron
75015 Paris
France
Telephone 33-1-42-56-10-22
Fax 33-1-43-59-77-03

American Citizens Abroad
157 Route du Grand Lancy
1213 Onex
Geneva
Switzerland
Telephone 41-22-792-16-59
Fax 41-22-793-39-15

Federation of American Women's Clubs Overseas
Wanbachergasse 1
1130 Vienna
Austria

Index

273